101 961 711 X

D0303552

0 JUL 2010
combk

War Stories

SHEFFIELD HALLAM UNIVERSITY
LEARNING CENTRE
WITHDRAWN FROM STOCK

REFERENCE

The Culture
of Foreign
Correspondents

Mark Pedelty

Routledge ■ New York & London

Published in 1995 by
Routledge
29 West 35th Street
New York, NY 10001

SHEFFIELD HALLAM UNIVERSITY
RS
070.4333
PE
ADSETTS LEARNING CENTRE

Published in Great Britain in 1995 by
Routledge
11 New Fetter Lane
London EC4P 4EE

Copyright © 1995 by Routledge

Printed in the United States of America.

All rights reserved. No part of this book may be reprinted or reproduced
or utilized in any form or by any electronic, mechanical or other means,
now known or hereafter invented, including photocopying and recording, or in any information storage or retrieval system, without permission in writing from the publishers.

Library of Congress Cataloging-in-Publication Data

Pedelty, Mark.
War stories: the culture of foreign correspondents / Mark pedelty
    p. cm.
    Includes bibliographical references and index.
    ISBN 0-415-91123-0 (cloth) — ISBN 0-415-91124-9 (pbk.)
    1. War correspondents.   2. Journalism—Objectivity.   I. Title.

PN 4823.P43   1995   94-23388
070.4'332—dc20   CIP

British Library Cataloging-in-Publication Data also available.

To Karen

I am aware that this discussion is unconventional anthropology; but these are unconventional times. We are all involved in unconventional and portentous military and political events in this country, perhaps more directly than many of us have realized until recently. These events have world-wide consequences. It is time that we accepted some unconventional responsibility for our acts, be they acts of commission or of omission.

—from Gerald Berreman's 1967 article "Is Anthropology Alive?" *Current Anthropology* 9(5): 391–96.

CONTENTS

Why an Anthropologist Studied a Press Corps. Discipline, Power, and Ideology. An Example of Institutional Influence. Framing the Violence. History and Structure of the Salvadoran War. A Structural History of SPECA. The *Salvador* Reporters.

PART ONE: WAR AND IDENTITY

Running with the Pack. Guerrilla Safari. Las Vueltas. Myth and Practice.

The Effects of the "Safe Conduct" System. Accepting the Silence. Terror as a Means of Press Control. Threats. The Question of Spies in the Press Corps. The Textual Effects of Terror. "Boredom Punctuated by Terror."

Rosa's Stories.

PART TWO: STRUCTURE AND PRACTICE

The Embassy and the Press. *A Team*. *B Team*. The Language of Team Competition. Interdependence and Ideological Control. The Political Control of SPECA.

According to a "Western Diplomat." Brenda. "Editors Suck." The Ray Bonner Effect.

Her, Rigoberta Menchu. "The Blood Has to be Purged."

The Problem with Parachuting. Hard Work, Routine, Disease, and Insanity. The Second Floor. The Psuedo-Event as Press Ritual. The Press Conference as Drama. Manufacturing Consensus.

The Opinion and Storytelling Ritual. War as "Fun." Ritualized Sexual Practices. Drugs and Alcohol. Burn-out.

Images of Comandante Carmelo. Joe in El Mozote. Dancing in Perquin.

ACKNOWLEDGMENTS

I thank the Regents of the University of California for providing the necessary funds for my research in the form of a William Harrison Mills Traveling fellowship, Graduate Humanities Research Grant, and Lowie Funds for Anthropological Research. I am indebted to the Center for Latin American Studies and Tinker Foundation for providing additional research funds.

I am also indebted to Nancy Scheper-Hughes, Jack Potter, James Anderson, Margaret Conkey, Beatriz Manz and other members of the Berkeley faculty who have encouraged, inspired, and aided in my work on this project. I also thank the members of the Center for Latin America Studies workshop on political violence and terror: James Quesada, Margarita Melville, Liegh Carol, and especially, Sheila Tulley. Thanks to Tim Strawn, Rod Benson, Peter Redfield, and Rebecca Chiao for their useful comments. It has also been my privilege to work with Todd Gitlin. This project would neither have been born nor completed were it not for the considerable contribution he has made to my educational development, in general, and this ethnography, in particular. I would also like to express my gratitude to Thomas Long for the photograph which appears on the cover and for his exemplary visual and print news coverage of Central America as a whole. Finally, special thanks to Gerald Berreman, adviser to this project. He has struggled to make the discipline, the department, and the university a more humane place. His scholarship and example have been, and will continue to be, an aid and inspiration.

I especially thank my parents and family for their support. Above all, I acknowledge the contributions of Karen Miksch. I would not have been able to complete this, nor had the desire to, without her aid and companionship.

A special thanks to Elba, Calixto, Blanca Rosa and other Salvadoran friends who taught me about El Salvador, got me through the periods of illness, and made my time there a pleasure. A special thanks to Carmelo, who lived and died to improve the world.

Finally, I thank all the journalists and others who participated in this study. I wish I could list all of you here. You have shown incredible kindness letting me into your lives and work. I am extremely grateful and hope this book will in some small way aid you in your struggle against violence and censorship.

A LIST OF ACRONYMS

ACEM	Foreign Correspondents Association of Mexico
AID	U.S. Agency for International Development
AFP	Agence France Press
AP	Associated Press
ARENA	Nationalist Republican Alliance
CDHES	Human Rights Commission of El Salvador (non-governmental)
CISPES	Committee in Solidarity with the People of El Salvador
COPREFA	Armed Forces Press Committee
ERP	People's Revolutionary Army
FDR	Revolutionary Democratic Front
FENASTRAS	National Federation of Salvadoran Workers
FMLN	Farabundo Marti National Liberation Front
OAS	Organization of American States
ORDEN	Democratic Nationalist Organization
PCN	National Conciliation Party
PDC	Christian Democratic Party
RN	National Resistance
SALPRESS	Salvadoran Press Association
SPECA	Salvadoran Foreign Press Corps Association
UCA	Jose Simon Canas Central American University
UDN	National Democratic Union
UES	University of El Salvador
UPI	United Press International

REPORTING
SALVADOR

"Within the logic of capitalism
the free press is simply another market
and in its totality
every person it touches must pay for it:
for the people, freedom of the press costs twenty cents per head."

—from the poem "Statistics Concerning Liberty"
by Salvadoran poet Roque Dalton (1987:16)

I was visiting a member of the Salvadoran Foreign Press Corps Association (SPECA) when suddenly the shout "Un muerto! Un muerto!" ("a corpse") rang out in the halls of the Camino Real Hotel.[1] The reporters spent most of their time at the Camino—writing, talking, playing, but most of all, waiting in their rented offices. They waited for interviews, press conferences, and if really lucky, a corpse. It was the fall of 1991 and the war in El Salvador was coming to an end, but the battlefield death toll remained as high as ever as both sides fought for territory and increased leverage at the negotiating table. The number of "political" killings had been steadily decreasing, however, so this corpse excited the journalists.

"Un Muerto!" The members of the corps poured into the hall, smiling and laughing, hoping this one would be news. Like disciplined firemen they jammed into the elevators, ran through the lobby, jumped into their vehicles and were off. They would not have to go far. The body had been dumped just blocks away.

The photographers took the lead, moving towards the body *en masse* while searching for the most dramatic angle.

They began shooting immediately. Rather than anarchic competition, the photographers performed a disciplined dance they had developed and perfected during countless other encounters with the dead. They moved slowly around the body, synchronizing their movements in silence. Alonzo, a Salvadoran journalist, explained: "You look at things with the view of the press, not that of a man. To see the dead, you look at the corpse from different angles and then do interviews of the survivors. 'How did it happen? Who was killed?' This is not normal." Not normal for them, but necessary.

The young, tired looking Green Cross worker standing near the body had taken part in this performance just as often. He had already done his initial body work, measuring the man's corpse as well as his relative location to the curb and corner—a forensic archaeologist conducting a surface survey. He held a blanket, but dared not cover the body until the photographers' dance ended. He stared at the photographers with contempt while other journalists approached to interview him.

A small crowd gathered on each side of the street. They stared at the dead man, comparing his corpse with others they had witnessed first-hand or in the daily paper. I looked for some emotion in their eyes. There was none. The adults and even the children had that stone-faced stare so common among Salvadorans. Emotion, passion, allegiance are too dangerous to exhibit in public.

I too was dancing with the photographers, so as not to get in their way or in their photographs. As they continued their "soft murder" (Sontag 1977:15) of the corpse, I scribbled meaningless notes, anything to avoid looking at the dead man. "You know how it is," wrote Vietnam correspondent Michael Herr, "you want to look and you don't want to look" (1968:18). This is a common attitude among reporters, a near-addiction to violence. Participant observation, the great lie of Anthropology, betrayed me in this regard. Unlike my research subjects, I could not get over my initial feeling of basic revulsion, disbelief, and incomprehension looking at these macabre images. It takes much more practice.

Everyone has some relationship with terror. For many it is anesthetized distance, violence via remote control, voyeurism. Others are more directly involved in the sort of violence that characterizes contemporary El Salvador, unwilling participants in a culture of unarticulable fear and terror. War correspondents have a unique relationship to terror, however, a hybrid condition that combines both voyeurism and direct participation. For these "participant observers" violence is not a matter of "values" in the moral sense of the term, but instead "value" in the economic. They need terror to realize themselves in both a professional and spiritual sense, to achieve and maintain their culture identity as "war correspondents."

"He is laid out like Jesus," I wrote in my note pad, "his arms outstretched, legs crossed at the ankles, a bullet hole in the open palm resembling a nail wound." I wrote that and other senseless words; anything to keep busy, anything to keep from thinking about the cooling flesh in front of me as human, as a person who minutes before got shot while attempting to steal a woman's purse. That was, in fact, the story. The corpse was the culmination of a failed robbery attempt on a bus, an ex-combatant trying to steal food money from others who also barely had enough to eat. A vigilante foiled the thief's attempt, killing him with a shot to the head, and somehow, one through the hand. The driver stopped the bus long enough to open the door and shove the man's body out on the street before continuing his route. It is a common saying among Salvadorans that "through ten years of war, El Salvador has not stopped working."

As the formal conflict came to an end, the fundamental structures of social injustice and daily violence, which first gave rise to the war, continued without interruption. As the combatants began returning to civilian life, the violence simply became more dispersed and less organized. Therefore, this corpse represented a typical Salvadoran story. Too typical, too confused, and ultimately, too complicated for news.

"Cultural constructions of and about the body," explains Nancy Scheper-Hughes, "are useful in sustaining particular views of society and social relations" (1987:19). Dead bodies have served the metaphorical purpose of sustaining the first world view of third world society as conflicted, tortured, and perhaps, barbaric. "No body, no story" has become the foreign correspondents' most basic rule (Massing 1989:43).

Likewise, dead bodies have been a primary phenomenological and metaphorical site of political contestation. Salvadoran opposition groups and international solidarity organizations use images of corporeal violation as a means to sensitize the world to terror and violence, perhaps having the reverse affect of "making the horrible seem more ordinary" (Sontag 1977:21).

Part of the reason corpses have been an integral part of this discourse is that they have no power to speak for themselves. "When the camera is focused on those who have been literally reduced to bodies, dead bodies," writes Max Kozloff, "the photograph's exploitation is shameless. The dead are recommended as subjects because they lack any defense against the camera and because they have top political value" (1987:210). That is what brought the press running from the Camino in this case. As they sped by the barefoot kids begging for change at the corner, over the ravine-sewer *barrancas* where many Salvadorans live, past a fortified car dealership, to their destination in a middle class neighborhood, they hoped to find such a commodity, a body with "top political value," a fetish to embody the more mundane and constant violence all around them.

Yet, this body, the corpse of a Salvadoran thief-ex-soldier, would not become currency in the aforementioned battle. It lacked sufficient "political value." It would neither be highlighted on a government billboard condemning FMLN (Farabundo Marti National Liberation Front) "terrorism," advertised in the "urgent action" alerts of the left, nor splashed across the front page of the world's newspapers. The messy nature of the incident would provide political capital to no one, because it would not fit easily into the two dimensional discourse of terrorism and human rights. Wrong body, wrong story. This corpse served no journalistic purpose and was soon forgotten.

As the journalists moved back toward their vehicles, they spoke of an upcoming party and made jokes at each others' expense. This was a normal scene for them. Respect for the dead is not a cultural universal, at least not during war and not for journalists. But, reporters are a community in and of themselves. They work together, play together, and often, live together. They share an integrated set of myths, rituals, and behavioral norms. They are, in short, a culture—as coherent as any in the postmodern world. This work is an ethnography about this seemingly familiar, yet oddly alien and exotic culture.

Why an Anthropologist Studied a Press Corps

Like Hortense Powdermaker (1950), the first anthropologist to do research among media professionals, I have had to convince many people (from friends to immigration officials) of the legitimacy of my research. "Is that anthropology?" asked several. As Powdermaker argued in the first chapter of *Hollywood: the Dream Factory*, "Why an Anthropologist Studied Hollywood," anthropologists bring important theoretical tools and methodological skills to the study of popular culture, mass media, and professional groups (Henry 1963:45–99). My choice to focus upon the practices and beliefs of the people who report news is representative of this anthropological emphasis. I spent over a year observing and interviewing journalists, sitting in on SPECA meetings, eating with journalists, spending time at their houses, watching sporting events, interviewing their sources, lounging in their offices, reading their work, attending press conferences, and traveling to the countryside with them. I was involved in a continual dialogue with the corps.

"Ethnography is hybrid textual activity," writes James Clifford, "it traverses genres and disciplines" (1986:26). That is certainly true here. I have borrowed theory and insight from Communications research, Journalism, Literary Criticism, Sociology, and of course, Anthropology, and hope this work may serve as a bridge between those fields. In that interest, I will avoid the standard theoretical polemic and will refer to theoretical issues only as needed to explicate the culture in question. As an interdisciplinary text, there is precious little space to be given over to the internecine quarrels that currently dominate and often paralyze the social sciences. To borrow a phrase from my journalist-subjects, much of the current debate is simply too "inside baseball"—that is, too self-referential—for the purposes of interdisciplinary research, ethnographic inquiry and public scholarship.

The levels of surveillance and representation involved in media ethnography are daunting. It feels odd observing those in the act of observing others, writing about their writings about others, and so on. The object of study becomes increasingly difficult to locate.

Ronald, a young U.S. reporter, joked about hiring someone to study my behavior as well. Although a Salvadoran man occasionally followed me during my research (probably dying of boredom), I don't believe Ronald ever followed through with his threat. Nevertheless, his comments demonstrate the ambivalence many of my subjects felt being studied by an anthropologist. Making jokes about kinship charts and "life among the primitives," the subject-reporters often did not know if they should feel flattered, insulted, or threatened by my panoptic presence: flattered, because finally somebody wanted to interview *them*; insulted, because they—established professionals and Pulitzer prize winners—were being subjected to scrutiny by a mere anthropologist; and finally, threatened by the self-reflection social research inevitably engenders. The interviews seemed both cathartic and painful as the journalist-subjects tried to make sense of their lives. Given the stressful conditions, I am doubly grateful every SPECA journalists agreed to participate in the study.

Discipline, Power, and Ideology

Ward Goodenough argues that a good test of an ethnography is whether it explains to the outsider how one should act in the primary scenes of a given society (1957). I hope this work lives up to that standard. I will attempt to explain why journalists behave as they do, explaining their work within the "disciplinary apparatuses" that pattern many of their actions. I have chosen that hybrid term—a merging of Michel Foucault's "discipline" with Louis Althusser's "industrial state apparatuses"—in order to avoid the theoretical limitations represented in simpler notions of power, such as repression and censorship. As Michel Foucault explains, power "doesn't simply weigh on us as a force that says no," but instead "traverses and produces things, it induces pleasure, forms knowledge, produces discourse. It needs to be considered as a productive network which runs through the whole social body, much more than as a negative instance whose function is repression" (Foucault 1984:60–61). Although there are repressive factors in reporting, the more powerful influences are disciplinary. Certain forms of knowledge are favored and certain discourses privileged.

A number of "pleasures"—pay, promotion, notoriety, identity, fantasy—compel correspondents to take part in the production of these institutionally-favored discourses. News production, therefore, is more than a question of "censorship," a form of repression easily identified and relatively simple to resist. Whereas, regimes of censorship attempt to silence dissent (and usually fail), disciplinary regimes overwhelm, co-opt, incorporate, and transform it. Censorship is a simple, negative state—a significant silence. Discipline is an active, productive, and creative form of power, a more subtle, sophisticated, penetrant, and effective means of control than that which is implied by the term "repression."

By attaching the term "apparatuses," I seek to salvage a sense of organizational efficacy and political economy, concerns which are mostly missing or subordinated in the dispersed narratives of poststructuralism. The latter have focused almost exclusively upon the discursive "network which runs through the whole social body" (Foucault 1984:60–61), ignoring differentiated arrangements therein. Like all complex organisms, the "social body" contains nodal centers, hierarchies of control and specialization. Press power, for example, is coalesced into hierarchical regimes of production and distribution that must be carefully outlined. To ignore these is to fall prey to a sort of vulgar idealism whose generalizations obfuscate, rather than define the complexities of contemporary social power.

The following disciplinary apparatuses most heavily influenced reporting of the Salvadoran war: military press controls and targeted violence (chapters 1, 2 and 3), the hierarchical structure of the corps (chapter 4, 12 and 13), elite sources (chapters 5 and 6), reporting conventions, myths, and rituals (chapters 7, 8 and 9), the standard news narrative (chapters 10), and news organizations (throughout). While each of these is interrelated, the final has the most fundamental and immediate effect on the work of journalists.

Most U.S. media organizations are large corporations or subsidiaries thereof. As Ben Bagdikian explains in *The Media Monopoly* (1990:4):

> Today fifty corporations own most of the output of daily newspapers and most of the sales and audience in magazines, broadcasting, books, and movies. The fifty men and women who head these corporations would fit in a large room. They constitute a new Private Ministry of Information and Culture.

To a significant degree, the ideological content of news texts is representative of the world view of the stockholders, executives, owners, and especially, advertisers who produce, manage and profit from news production (Herman and Chomsky 1988).[2] To contend otherwise is both politically naive and contrary to the basic anthropological premise that a culture's "utterances" (Malinowski 1922:24–25) or "ensemble of texts" (Geertz 1973:193–233) are interpretable components of their symbolically structured world view. If such a reading is appropriate for Balinese cock fights, Tlingit potlatch, or Trobriand Kula, why not corporate news?

News organizations do not function alone in the productive role, however. Sources are also extremely influential (Herman and Chomsky 1988:18–26). Foreign correspondents routinely rely upon elite authorities and powerful institutions as news sources (Sigal 1986:18, Tuchman 1978:15–38). The most important of these in El Salvador include (in declining order of importance): the U.S. Embassy, the Salvadoran government press office (SENCO), both FMLN radio stations (*Radio Venceremos* and *Radio Farabundo Marti*), The Armed Forces Press Service (COPREFA), and finally, the University of Central America (UCA). This is not to say that SPECA journalists are more sympathetic to the U.S. Embassy than the UCA. In fact, the reverse is usually true. However, the selective pressures of editors and the weight of traditional press practices prompt them to privilege the voices of U.S. and allied elites.

In addition to institutional influences, there is the more inclusive question of ideology. Ideology is often defined as an explicit sociopolitical program, propaganda aimed at legitimating a clearly defined system of domination (McLellan 1986:50–63). This definition of ideology is most appropriately applied to totalitarian states such as the former U.S.S.R., where both the means of coercion and the rationalizations thereof lay on the surface. The citizens of the U.S.S.R. consciously recognized the products of PRAVDA and other state organs as propaganda. PRAVDA never claimed otherwise. The situation is considerably different in advanced capitalist-democracies, especially the U.S., where the dominant means of communication are rationalized in an obfuscational idiom of neutrality, independence, and objectivity.

The journalistic ideal of objectivity began developing in the last century. Objective journalism did not become the dominant mode, however, until well into this century (Smith 1980:61). In addition to providing a hedge against tendentious reporting, the objective code also guided the incipient mass media in their production of news sufficiently "acceptable to all of its members and clients" (Schudson 1978:4). Objectivity was partially a marketing tool.

The positivistic pretenses of U.S. news media have created a set of irresolvable contradictions for working journalists. While the rules of objective journalism prohibit reporters from making subjective interpretations, their task *demands* it. A "fact," itself a cultural construct, can only be communicated through placement in a system of meaning shared by reporter and reader.

Journalists cannot resolve this contradiction between professional myth and practice, only manage it through judicious use of news *frames*. Frames are "persistent patterns of cognition, interpretation, and presentation, of selection, emphasis and exclusion by which symbol-handlers routinely organize discourse, whether verbal or visual" (Gitlin 1980:6–7, Goffman 1974). Mainstream journalists tend to adopt frames whose logic is drawn from the most penetrant and unquestioned cultural values, myths, and ideologies—perspectives least likely to be challenged, or perhaps even identified, by audience and journalist (Hallin 1983:22–25). News frames that contain our most deeply held cultural subjectivities will therefore appear as "natural" expositions of reality (Gitlin 1980:6), common sense portrayals rather than constructed, interpretive frameworks. In other words, the objective reality of news is formed of our most fundamental and intractable subjectivities, what Herbert Gans calls "enduring values" (1980:41–52). Taking a critical view of these values, or at least the media manipulation thereof, Michael Parenti writes, "The worst forms of tyranny—or certainly the most successful ones—are not those we rail against but those that so insinuate themselves into the imagery or our consciousness and the fabric of our lives as not to be perceived as tyranny" (1986:7).

In the North American vernacular, "ideology" is considered the antithesis of "objectivity" (McLellan 1986:50–63, Gans 1979:29–30, 183–86). The belief in objectivity has itself become an ideology, however, not in the simpler sense of the term, but as a system that both legitimates and *obfuscates* relations of domination. In claiming to be objective, media organizations shield their close affinity for and incorporation within dominant institutions and ruling class structures. Objectivity asks us to accept the world "as it is" (or how it has been constructed for us) rather than take a more active part in the creative process of discovery (Thompson 1990). The ideology of objectivity "serves to inhibit imagination" (Rachlin 1988:134). Incorporated into this network of knowledge production, we cede much of our creative social power to those with the greatest means to produce "objective" truths and the greatest interest in maintaining them (Gitlin 1980:6–7).

Because I am challenging the basic premises of positivism, however, I will never resort to the banal claim that journalists and their texts are "biased." We all are, regardless of our stake in power. Instead, I will attempt to demonstrate how the particular biases of news are connected to structures of domination, and how they are operationalized in the practices of journalists. Todd Gitlin argues (1980:10):

> I retain Gramsci's core conception: those who rule the dominant institutions secure their power in large measure *directly and indirectly*, by impressing their definitions of the situation upon those they rule and, if not usurping the whole of ideological space, still significantly limiting what is thought throughout the society. The notion of hegemony that I am working with is an active one: hegemony operating through a complex web of social activities and institutional procedures.

That is the general theory of ideology I use here. I will examine the "social activities and institutional procedures" of SPECA journalists themselves to delimit the ways in which they are, and are not, patterned by the needs of power.

An Example of Institutional Influence

During the early period of my fieldwork, I was speaking with an experienced European reporter about the issue of institutional influence.[3] As another journalist entered the room and began asking me questions, my informant suddenly disappeared. Rejoining us minutes later, she was holding computer print-outs of two reports she had recently written about the same event. One report was produced for a European news institution, the other submitted to a U.S. newspaper. As the author herself pointed out, the difference between the two news articles was quite striking. They are as follows:

The U.S. Report

Leftists rebels in El Salvador have admitted that one of their units may have executed two U.S. servicemen after their helicopter was shot down last Wednesday.

An official FMLN rebel statement issued yesterday said two rebel combatants had been detained, "under the charge of suspicion of assassinating wounded prisoners of war."

The U.S. helicopter was downed in the conflictive eastern province of San Miguel as it was flying back to its base in Honduras. One pilot was killed in the crash, but a Pentagon autopsy team concluded that the other two servicemen in the helicopter were killed execution-style afterwards.

Civilians confirmed that the two servicemen had survived the crash, although no-one actually saw the actual execution.

"The FMLN has concluded that there are sufficient elements to presume that some of the three, in the condition of wounded prisoners, could have been assassinated by one or various members of our military unit," said the rebel statement. It also said that their investigations had determined that their initial information from units on the ground was false.

At first the guerrillas said the bodies of the Americans had been found in the helicopter. Then they said that two of the three had survived the crash but later died of wounds.

Salvadoran officials have said that if the Americans were executed the guerrillas should hand over those responsible. The call was echoed by Rep. Joe Moakley (D-Mass), the Chairman of a congressional special task force on El Salvador.

"We would expect and we would demand that the FMLN turn over to the judicial authorities those responsible, if not this lack of action will have serious consequences," he said.

But the rebel statement made no promise to do that. "If responsibility for the crime is proved, the FMLN will act with all rigor, in conformity with our normal war justice," read the statement. The rebels said that because of the nationality of the victims, the investigations would be carried out publicly.

The rebels also defended shooting down the helicopter which they said was flying in "attack position" in a conflicted zone. The UH1H Huey helicopter is the same model as those used by the Salvadoran army and was flying very low to evade anti-aircraft missiles.

The rebel statement did not say whether those detained were in charge of the guerrilla unit which shot down the helicopter. Western diplomats believe it unlikely the unit would have time to radio for orders. The hilly terrain also makes radio communication over any distance difficult.

A U.S. embassy spokesman in San Salvador said State Department and embassy officials are studying the rebel statement.

In the last few days the rebels have privately sounded out United Nations officials about the possibility of setting up an independent commission made up of U.S. and U.N. investigators as well as the FMLN, according to a senior rebel source. However, no public proposal has been made.

The killings have opened up a debate in Washington as to whether $42.5 million in military aid to El Salvador, frozen by congress last October, should be released. The money was withheld in protest at the lack of progress in investigating the murders of six Jesuit priests by elite army soldiers a year ago. (the final four paragraphs concern the Jesuit murder case)

The European Report

Nestled amid the steep mountains of Northern Chalatenango province, a simple wooden cross on a small hill marks the grave of a teenage guerrilla fighter. There is no name on the grave. None of the villagers from the nearby settlement of San Jose Las Flores who buried his body two years ago knew what he was called.

In life the young guerrilla had little in common with three North American servicemen who were killed last month after the rebels shot down their helicopter. They were enemies on opposite sides of a bitter war. But they shared a common death. They were all killed in cold blood after being captured.

When the young rebel was killed two years ago, I remember taking cover behind the wall of a church of San Jose Las Flores. One moment I was watching two adolescent guerrilla fighters sipping from Coke bottles and playing with a yo-yo. Then I remember seeing soldiers running, crouching, and shooting across the square. The crack of automatic rifle fire and the explosion of grenades was deafening in the confined space.

The whole incident lasted about twenty minutes. As soon as the soldiers left, whooping and yelling victory cries, we ran across the square to find the body of one of the teenage guerrillas still twitching. The villagers said that he had been wounded and surrendered. The soldiers had questioned him—and then finished him off at close range in the head. The bullet had blown off the top of his skull.

I remember clearly the reaction of the then U.S. ambassador when asked about the incident. "That kind of incident cannot be condoned," he said, "but I was a soldier, I can understand — it happens in a war." In a country where tens of thousands have been killed, many of them civilians murdered by the U.S. backed military or by right wing death squads, there was no suggestion of any investigation for the execution of a prisoner.

At the beginning of January this year a U.S. army helicopter was shot down by rebel ground fire in Eastern El Salvador. The pilot died in the crash. But two other U.S. servicemen were dragged badly wounded from the wreckage by the rebels. Before the guerrillas left they finished off the two wounded Americans execution style with a bullet in the head.

The present U.S. ambassador referred to the guerrillas in this incident as "animals."

The killings made front page news internationally and provided the climate needed by President Bush to release forty-two and a half million dollars of military aid, which was frozen last October by Congress. U.S. lawmakers wanted to force the Salvadoran army to make concessions in peace talks and clean up its human rights record.

The two incidents highlight a fact of political life in El Salvador, recognized by all, that it is not worth killing Americans. Until the helicopter incident, in more than a decade of civil war the rebels have only killed six U.S. personnel. They have a deliberate policy of not targeting Americans, despite the fact that most guerrillas have a deep hatred of the U.S. government. As many have been killed by the U.S.' own allies. Extreme groups in the military, who resent U.S. interference, murdered four U.S. church workers and two government land reform advisers in the early 1980s.

In fact the rebels, because of the outcry and the policy implications in Washington have had to admit guilt in the helicopter incident. They have arrested two of their combatants and say they will hold a trial. They have clearly got the message.

Up until the Gulf War El Salvador has easily seen the most

prolonged and deepest U.S. military commitment since Vietnam. However, it is a commitment for which few Americans have felt the consequences.

The first is a rather typical U.S. news report, a set of basic facts and elite source quotes strung together in a dispassionate and "balanced" narrative. The second is typically European (with the caveat that there are significant differences among various European news media). As opposed to her U.S.-bound writing, the author presents her own voice in the European report. The frame is mostly of her own making. Featuring just two quotes, both from like-minded sources, the European report is not "balanced" like its American twin. Furthermore, the reporter offers critical comment in her European article, signaling the reader that her sources' statements are disingenuous. Authorial intervention of that sort is generally considered taboo in U.S. journalism, a fact that led another European "stringer" (reporters who write for several client institutions or "strings") to complain that the American system "goes against the whole point of having a correspondent in the first place."

As for news frames, the American report validates the anger of U.S. officials and legitimates the predicted release of aid. As the European report ironically concludes: "The killings made front page news internationally and provided the climate needed by President Bush to release forty-two and a half million dollars of military aid." That critique applies frighteningly well to the author's other article. The editors of the U.S. newspaper in which her article appeared wrote an editorial supporting the administration's subsequent release of military aid.

There are, however, subversive aspects to the U.S. report. The author's clever quote of the ubiquitous "Western diplomat" makes it clear the FMLN high command was probably not involved in the killing ("Western diplomats believe it unlikely the unit would have time to radio for orders"). Likewise, her addition of information concerning the Jesuit murders calls the potential release of aid into question. In other words, underneath the objective text and the source-dominated frame, lies the author's critical voice, subsumed but not completely silenced.

The author has a very good reputation among the corps. One colleague referred to her as "the reporter of record." Indeed, her work is often exceptional. Why then did this reporter write two very different, even contradictory reports? The answer is simple: she had to. Every journalist must conform to the criteria of her clients. A system of sanctions and rewards—employment policies, prestige endowments, and monetary compensation—facilitate this disciplinary training process.

Framing the Violence

War and related political issues have dominated international coverage of

Central America (Soderland 1985). Press critics and academic analysts have faulted journalists for applying the following frames in their coverage of the Salvadoran war: successive U.S.-supported Salvadoran governments described as "moderate," ignoring "the regime's responsibility for the excesses being committed by security and paramilitary forces" (Anderson 1988a:239, Herman 1990:5–6, McCoy 1992), the FMLN represented as aggressive, extremist, "Marxist," and "out of touch" (Cockburn 1989, Hallin 1986b, McAnany 1983:207,209–10, McCoy 1992:68), the civilian population portrayed as a mute mass of "innocent-victims-caught-in-the-cross-fire" (Anderson 1988a:247, 1990), nonviolent grassroots Salvadoran and U.S. solidarity protest movements ignored (McAnany 1983:204, Thompson 1992:28), U.S. orchestrated elections presented as free and fair (Herman and Brodhead 1984:93–152, Spence 1983, 1984), and U.S. foreign policy framed as neutral, benevolent or, on occasion, merely "mistaken" (Saunders 1991, Sumser 1987).

Near the end of the war, most of the aforementioned frames were still in use, though modified to incorporate new developments.[4] The news image of FMLN guerrillas softened considerably with the end of the cold war and its concomitant rhetoric. Likewise, stronger criticism of the U.S. role emerged as congressional opposition increased during the final years of the war. News of El Salvador was shoved to the back pages during this period, however, as the region dropped out of the administration's public agenda.

This is not to say news audiences have acritically adopted the aforementioned news frames. As communication researchers have demonstrated in recent years, audiences have the power to "negotiate" texts, to "read" media products in discordant, sometimes subversive ways, applying their own cultural values and phenomenological experience to form new, critical conceptions of media texts (Morley 1980, Radway 1984). A major proponent of this perspective, John Fiske, believes this media-consumer dialectic may even form a threat to the "dominant classes" via its unintended encouragement of "cultural difference" (Fiske 1987:326). Fiske goes so far as to claim "the cultural economy drives the financial in a dialectic force that counters the power of capital" (1987:326).

I do not share Fiske's optimism. The fact that different groups interpret media texts in different ways, is not so much a sign of resistance to consumer capitalism, but instead evidence of its continued health. Consumer capitalism is a system of cultural, economic, and textual production that "proceeds by differentiation" (Jameson 1984:75), one that encourages the development of variegated "lifestyles": cultural subgroups largely defined by consumption practices (yuppies, generation "X," sports fans, heavy metal youth, etc.) (Leiss et al. 1985). These consumer cliques develop and differentiate in dialectical relation to their associated product ensembles. For every fashion a following, not to mention a channel, mag-

azine, and product assemblage. Genre has joined race, gender, and class—
the traditional axes of social control—as a primary mode of social
distinction. While I agree there are dialectical tensions in the media-consumer relationship, I do not believe the empirical evidence warrants
Fiske's far-reaching claims.

Like James Curran and Colin Sparks, I prefer "a middle path"
(1991:216) (Morris 1988). Social subgroups certainly have the capacity
to interpret and redefine media texts. Nevertheless, as long as people are
functioning primarily as "consumers," critical or otherwise, they are still
lending their support and social power to the dominant system, consumer
capitalism. The "resistance-through-reading" critics (Tetzlaff 1991:10)
have mistakenly posited conspicuous consumption—the ironic "I watch
it, but don't believe it" mode—as a means of rebellion against a system
predicated upon that very activity.[5] As evidenced in everything from the
cocky posturing of Joe Isuzu and the supercilious grin of Peter Jennings,
to the looking-back-at-you barbs of Beavis and Butthead, the consumer-
citizen is *encouraged* to take this ironic (thus banal) "critical" stance, a
paradoxical position whereby the consumer-citizen "mocks the game by
playing it or plays it by mocking it" (Gitlin 1989:353). News consumers
spend hours watching news of Tonya, Nancy, and O.J., and then several
more providing "critical" analyses thereof. Meanwhile, they (we) have
consumed the product and played the game (Tetzlaff 1991). This "mental habit of dismantling images," warns Elaine Scarry, "can lead to an
ironic stance" which does little but "let us dwell in the comfort of our own
'knowingness'" (1993:69).

As consumers, citizens and critics alike, we turn to orient ourselves "in
relation to the theatrical spectacle rather than the reality of events themselves" (Scarry 1993:59). Meanwhile, we are increasingly "infantilized
and marginalized" from the real means of political and economic power
(63). Our most fundamental human problems are mediated, trivialized,
and distanced as a result. In exchange, the "ideology of freedom" has
come "to mean the freedom to consume images rather than freedom to
shape the reality behind the images" (Anderson 1988a:245). Granted,
there are many signs of pop culture's potential. Thus far, however, there
is little evidence of its political efficacy. The viewer-citizens' active imagination has not been matched with imaginative action.

While all media, both factual and fictional, "seek to reduce and fix"
their audiences' interpretation of texts (Curran and Sparks 1991:222),
active reinterpretations of news are particularly discouraged. Unlike other
mimetic objects—art and fiction—news is promoted as a direct, objective
translation of reality.[6] Art and fiction present a much more open invita-
tion to critical interpretation, because they make no such claim to reality,
fact, or even truth.

Furthermore, the news media "transmit the only nonfiction that most

Americans see, hear, or read" (Gans 1979:298). The audience's dominant frames of interpretation are themselves mostly drawn from this monopolized domain. This lack of "an oppositional ideological tradition" in the U.S. further inhibits news consumers' ability to critically dissect news (Curran and Sparks 1991:227, Iyengarand and Kinder 1987).

Likewise, the lack of alternative knowledge about, or experience of, the world outside the U.S. makes it extremely difficult for news consumers to read "foreign" news in a critical manner. If the news does not present information concerning the actual role of U.S. operatives, weapons, and capital in Central America, for example, it is hard to believe casual readers will somehow themselves come to an accurate understanding of these issues.

Finally, it would appear the U.S. people are not doing a great deal of news "reading" anyway, in either the interpretive or literal senses of the term. In May, 1981, during the height of coverage, 40% of the respondents in a Gallup poll admitted they were "too poorly informed to hold an opinion about El Salvador" (McAnany 1983:200) (Turk 1986). In 1983, President Ronald Reagan lamented, "the great majority of Americans don't know which side we are on."[7] Informal encounters with various news audiences have lead me to believe Reagan was correct. Upon returning to the U.S., I was often asked if the Contras are still active in El Salvador (admittedly, my own understanding of recent crises in Europe and Africa is hardly any clearer). While this structured ignorance goes well beyond news, part of the blame must be ascribed to the corporate media. The news presentation is often too superficial to give readers a clear understanding of an issue or event—critical or otherwise (Iyengarand and Kinder 1987:127–29, Day 1987:306). While making claims like "All The News That's Fit To Print" and "That's the way it is," the news often fails to tell us much of anything at all.

Nevertheless, in producing cryptic texts the news media continues to fulfill an ideological role by obfuscating important realities of power. This was particularly clear in my dealings with SPECA. I asked each reporter to explain the causes of the Salvadoran war. The following factors were cited by almost every one: plutocratic rule enforced by military means, social inequality, and U.S. intervention. Yet, aside from occasional human rights pieces dealing with isolated abuses by the military and death squads, these fundamental issues were rarely mentioned in mainstream U.S. news reports. The most fundamental causes and contexts of the war, as defined by the correspondents themselves, were mostly ignored. The dominant means of power were mystified and legitimated in the process (McCoy 1992 and Anderson 1988a).

History and Structure of the Salvadoran War
The war in El Salvador is a continuation of the process of colonialism, state-building, and feudal antagonism that started with the Spanish con-

quest (Montgomery 1982:33, Schmidt 1983:43, Wolf 1969:3). The most brutal modern manifestation was *La Matanza* (the massacre) of 1932. That year, Farabundo Marti led coffee workers in an uprising against the wealthy landowners of proto-industrial El Salvador, a landed elite known as "The Fourteen Families" (North 1985:29–42, Anderson 1981). Using the failed uprising as an excuse, the military, under the guidance of General Maximiliano Hernandez Martinez, slaughtered as many as 30,000 peasants, most of them members of El Salvador's indigenous population (Parkman 1988). As a result, most remaining *indigenas* abandoned the cultural practices that once distinguished them from the *Ladino* majority (Chapin 1990:21–27).

In the four decades following *La Matanza*, the oligarchy-military alliance blocked any attempts at reform, often resorting to violence to control their political opposition. In that same period, El Salvador, a country the size of Massachusetts, became one of the world's largest coffee exporters.

In 1972 the military stole a presidential election from Jose Napoleon Duarte and the Christian Democratic Party (PDC). As economic injustice and repression intensified over the following seven years, a number of church, student, and union groups began to coalesce into an effective opposition movement. Hoping to avoid a revolution, a group of reformist military officers, backed by the U.S., staged a coup in 1979 and established a civilian-military junta.

In January of 1980 the junta collapsed when most of the civilian members resigned in protest of the army's continued repression. By March, another junta had been formed which included Duarte. The new junta began to push reform programs, including land redistribution and nationalization of financial institutions. These reforms were met with a wave of military and paramilitary terror, including a number of political assassinations. The oligarchy clearly and brutally demonstrated their unwillingness to tolerate even minor challenges to their extreme privilege. The most publicized assassination was that of Monsignor Oscar Arnulfo Romero, whose murder was linked to Major Roberto D'Aubuisson, founder of the Nationalist Republican Alliance (ARENA) (Montgomery 1982:212).

In November of 1980 five rebel factions formed an umbrella organization called the Farabundo Marti National Liberation Front (FMLN). Also in that year, the Salvadoran military and closely affiliated death squads further intensified their murderous activities. Victims in 1980 included six opposition political leaders, three U.S. nuns, a U.S. church worker, and thousands of lesser-known civilians.

In 1981 the FMLN launched their first of many "final" offensives. Failing to ignite a popular insurrection, they instituted a long term plan which sustained the movement for another decade despite large deficits in armaments and troops (10,000 guerrillas vs. 56,000 Salvadoran soldiers). U.S. aid escalated as Ronald Reagan vowed to block the development of "hostile, communist colonies" in the Americas (Reagan in Gettleman et al 1986:14). Death squad activity continued apace. Their victims in 1981 included a government land reform official, two U.S. representatives of the AFL-CIO, and thousands more Salvadoran civilians (North 1985:Appendix I, xv).

In 1982, ARENA gained control of the National Assembly and suspended land reform. The war continued, and by 1984 Duarte won the presidency in an election boycotted by the left. The U.S. increased military aid to El Salvador and initial talks between the FMLN and Duarte government failed. By this time, 50,000 Salvadorans had been killed, the majority of them noncombatants murdered by the military and death squads. Almost one million Salvadorans fled the country, one fifth of the nation's total population. Duarte was largely a figurehead, unable or unwilling to reign in the military (McClintock 1985).

In 1988, following a period of slow and punctuated improvement in the Army's human rights record and the return of exiled opposition leaders Ruben Zamora and Guillermo Ungo, the situation regressed. ARENA gained majority control of the National Assembly and the number of political killings increased dramatically. In response to the Army's renewed terror campaign against unionists, church workers, and members of the *popular organizations* (grass-roots opposition movements), the FMLN assassinated eight mayors. The executions and a highly effective governmental propaganda campaign eroded the FMLN's popular support.

Nineteen-eighty-nine brought several turning points in the war. First, the FMLN proposed to join the electoral process, which the government rejected. Nevertheless, both sides began formal negotiations to end the war. In March of that year, Alfredo Christiani, a member of the oligarchy hand-picked by D'Aubuisson, was elected president. He promised to negotiate with the FMLN and curb death squad activity. On October 19 a bomb exploded in the home of Ruben Zamora, who escaped unharmed. In response, the FMLN attacked the military high command ten days later. The next day, October 30, a large bomb destroyed the headquarters of FENASTRAS (National Federation of Salvadoran Workers). Ten unionists were killed and thirty-three others were wounded.

Those events lead to the most important moment of 1989, the November FMLN offensive. The guerrillas took the battle to the streets of several major cities, including San Salvador. The nationwide offensive took most U.S. correspondents by surprise. Many had been signaling the rebels' presumed weakness and imminent collapse in their reports leading up to the "November surprise."

Three thousand three hundred Salvadorans were killed in the first thirteen days of the offensive, many of them civilians killed in the government's air campaign. It was not until the fighting reached the affluent neighborhood of *Escalon*, however, that the government agreed to a temporary cease fire to evacuate the wounded.

The offensive failed to incite a popular rebellion, either due to lack of popular support for the FMLN, the military's superior fire power, or a combination thereof. Many SPECA journalists believe the FMLN offensive would have succeeded were it not for the government's successful use of air power against the guerrillas and their supporters. The guerrillas were gaining territory at an astonishing pace before the air force began its fairly indiscriminate bombing and strafing of FMLN-occupied neighborhoods.

On the fifth day of the offensive, six Jesuit priests, their cook and her daughter were executed by the Salvadoran military. The Jesuit massacre renewed debate in Congress over U.S. aid policy, leading to its eventual suspension. The offensive demonstrated the FMLN's inability to spark a popular insurrection and take power through military means. Yet, the offensive also showed the rebels could not be defeated militarily. Tired of the stalemate, the Salvadoran government began to negotiate in earnest. On New Years Day, 1992, the final peace accords were signed and the eleven year old war came to an end.

When I first visited San Salvador in June of 1990, the situation was still far from settled. In the two year period between the November 1989 offensive and the final cease fire, thousands more died in order for their respective sides to gain advantage in the negotiation process. My research took place during this final stage of the war and the initial phase of "peace."

Much more important than the events, personalities, and organizations in the preceding chronology, however, are the social structures underlying them. The most fundamental social reality in El Salvador is the economic and cultural gulf separating the oligarchy and the majority of Salvadorans (Alegria 1986). In a primarily agricultural country, only 5.6% of the farmers owned ten hectares (just under twenty-five acres) or more arable land in 1971, an amount "generally taken as the minimum amount of land required to support an average peasant family" (Jung 1987:67). Ray Bonner explains (1984:16–17):

> In the late 1970's the wealthiest 5 percent of the country's families cornered 38 percent of the national income; the poorest 40 percent fought over 7.5 percent. It was the most unequal distribution of income in all Latin America. As recently as 1983 only 6 percent of the population earned more than $240 a month. A market basket of basic needs cost $344 per month.

In the 1970s, the decade preceding the war, over 70% of the rural population was considered malnourished (Chapin 1990:7). According to Salvadoran government statistics, 60% of Salvadorans still live in poverty, 33% in extreme poverty.

In the impoverished barrios of San Salvador, especially those in the steep ravines or *barrancas* that run throughout the city, hundreds of thousands live in make-shift shacks of tin, scrap wood, and other scavenged materials. In a rare and moving exposition, a U.S. correspondent wrote of one dump-site squatters colony:

> This is a site of retching foulness where cows, children and vultures stand side by side, wrenching survival from a mountain of rotting animal corpses and human waste. Where flowering trees once sheltered flocks of fabulously colored birds that drank from clear, flowing rivers, a seemingly endless stream of trucks now disgorges cargoes of poisonous trash.
>
> No trees grow here. Streams are clogged with garbage and the eroded silt of barren, chemical-ridden soil. In this circle, shrouded by smoke from perpetual fire, humans also are not spared: fifty-year-old men look seventy; teenagers are physically the size of six-year-olds; a cut on the arm can lead to amputation.

The correspondent received a great deal of flak for having submitted this report. His editor called it an "angry editorial" and cut out the most graphic passages.

In the wealthy areas of the city, such as the *Escalon*, fortress-houses of the rich overlook the squalor of the ravines below. A U.S.-style shopping center rises above one of these slums along Calle Escalon. While the oligarchy shop for luxury furniture items, high priced art, compact discs, surf boards, and imported food from the Middle East and Europe, the slum dwellers below wash their clothes and cook their food in bacterial waters.

Young girls growing up in the barranca hope to land servants' jobs in middle class homes or wealthy estates. They are paid less than $50 a month, with only one weekend off. Many members of the oligarchy (or "garchs" as the journalists call them) brag about how roughly they treat their *chicas* (maid-girls). The local elite get angry when foreign residents attempt to pay their servants more, fearing this will "spoil" them.

The antagonisms engendered by this system of privilege and inequality have fueled the latest Salvadoran war, as well as the violence that preceded it and followed. Throughout, the United States has consistently backed the privileged classes and the closely allied Salvadoran military, blaming external forces for fomenting disorder (Gettleman et al. 1986:7–39). Successive U.S. administrations have accused Cuba and the Soviet Union of exporting communism to the region, a convenient means of legitimating U.S. counter-insurgency campaigns (Klare and Kornbluh 1988). In the 1980s the United States continued its tradition of using Central America "as a stage on which to act out a fantasy role of international toughness and resolution" (Sundaram 1991:160), pouring $4 billion of aid into El Salvador during the 1980s, most of it going directly towards the procurement of weapons and training for the Salvadoran military, the rest supporting counter-insurgency through the United States Agency for International Development (AID) and related programs (Fried 1987).

A Structural History of SPECA

When the war began, only a handful of stringers from Europe, Latin America, and the United States were reporting El Salvador. Journalists flocked to the country soon thereafter, however, when President Ronald Reagan proclaimed "America's economy and well being are at stake" in the war (Reagan in Gettleman et al 1986:11–14, Heertsgard 1988: 109–115, Herman and Chomsky 32–33, 107–109). The permanently stationed press corps increased to over 200 journalists. The presence of "parachuters" (journalists who fly in for short periods to cover major events and crises) swelled their ranks to include more than 700 reporters during the 1982, 1984, and 1989 elections, and once again during the FMLN November offensive of 1989 (Massing 1982:49, 1989).

Long before the war was over, however, the administration's public discourse shifted to other parts of the world, and the media began to abandon El Salvador. The *New York Times* in 1985 published 360 news reports and editorials, 239 fewer than 1984. The decline was even more dramatic in the following years. There were fewer stories written during the next three years, 1986–1988 (121,134, and 107 respectively), than in 1985 alone (see chapter 10). What one journalist referred to as "the third generation of Salvador journalists" came to the country during this period of declining interest. This change-over caused a major disjuncture in corps consciousness. Those who witnessed the overt public terror of the early 1980s were replaced by newcomers who would experience a period of more discreet and carefully targeted violence. Greater restrictions were placed on press movement during the latter period, further removing the correspondents from the worst effects of the war. One of the few to have reported the entire war, stated: "They don't know what it was like."

The Offensive of 1989 provided a "book-end," in the words of one reporter, to both the war and the news coverage thereof. Recognizing the war might soon be over, the press corps began its rapid withdrawal from the region. Like most other third world nations, El Salvador is now rarely covered at all. Even the landmark presidential elections of 1994 received scant news attention.

The withdrawal has not been a completely uniform process. The corps underwent qualitative as well as quantitative changes as it became smaller. News organizations began to rely much more heavily on stringers for daily coverage of El Salvador as the major news agenda, and many staff correspondents shifted to Eastern Europe, Russia, and the Middle East. Into the vacuum swept a number of new SPECA stringers joining those already in San Salvador, forming a news bridge between occasional staff visits (Horton 1978:vi). I arrived seven months after the 1989 offensive and witnessed most of this transition. The transformation of the corps has still not reached its final destination, however, which will involve an almost complete replacement of international journalists by Salvadoran stringers, responsible for covering the same sort of "earthquake-and-bus-plunge" stories (Maslow and Arana 1981:52) which dominated prewar coverage.

At the mid-point of my research there were eighty members of SPECA (forty-eight men, thirty-two women): thirteen U.S. and British staff correspondents (sometimes called the "A Team"), twelve U.S. and British stringers filing reports solely or primarily to U.S. institutions, seven U.S. photographers employed by U.S. and European photo agencies, thirty-four Salvadorans working for U.S. and other international media, and fourteen other journalists, mainly Latin Americans and Europeans, writing for international media (I will call this residual group "internationals").

I have emphasized those journalists who work for the U.S. press thus far, and will continue to do so. There are three reasons for this. First, the largest bloc represented in the foreign press corps is comprised of journalists working for U.S. news institutions. Most SPECA Salvadorans, for example, are employed by U.S. organs. Second, the U.S. news media has an inordinate influence both within the corps and internationally (Betran and Fox de Cardona 1980, Rota and Rota 1987). Three of the last four SPECA Presidents were U.S. citizens. Finally, I and most of my readers are residents of the U.S. and, therefore, most directly effected by "American" media. Nevertheless, the voices and practices of journalists who do not work for U.S. media will play an important role in this ethnography as well, providing a rich comparative sample and much of the critical commentary.[8]

The *Salvador* Reporters

It is the story—a sense of narrative place and time—that separates ethnography from other forms of sociological exposition. This story will occasionally involve outrageous examples of press misconduct, but will more often illustrate the honest attempts of earnest and intelligent journalists whose work is influenced by a mass of traditions, rules, and institutions whose purposes are often antithetical to their own. People like Joe, a young Texas expatriate who loves to play war; Paul, a giant with the strength to focus through tears; Harold, "an old curmudgeon" whose truthful fictions have long graced the front pages; Pedro, a Salvadoran photographer who lost his hand, but not his camera; Katherine, a prize-winning journalist who cannot be bothered with the little details or big truths; George, the romantic; Shawn, who refuses to let a little thing like shrapnel get in his way; Maria, the Italian humanist; and Alonzo, who sees the soul in the corpse. Those and other journalists breath life into this ethnography, as do the central characters of the war itself: guerrillas, politicians, and soldiers, not to mention the ever-deafening discourse of "Western diplomats" (U.S. embassy officials).

Finally, this ethnography is a story about a place where some 80,000 people have been murdered in the last twelve years while a million more have been displaced from their homes and families. It is a place which so fascinates and horrifies these reporters that many have lingered long beyond "the story." It is a space within which they have developed their identities as *Salvador* reporters.

For many Americans, the very word *Salvador* invokes a nebulous sense of terror. They may not know who fought the war, what is was fought for, nor the extent to which their own tax dollars fueled the conflagration, but they are usually aware something horrific and bloody has happened there. "Salvador," the sloppy and jingoistic shorthand for El Salvador has become synonymous with death squads, guerrillas, and counter-insurgency, just as "Nam" became shorthand for the terrors of that war.

Perhaps the main difference is that the U.S. audience was made to feel as if "we" were directly participating in the Vietnam war, or more recently, "Operation Desert Storm." The news media invited the American audience to view those wars through the eyes of United States soldiers. Not so in the case of El Salvador. The U.S. provided training, weapons, and most of the strategy, but practically none of the flesh. As a result, U.S. viewers might have been moved to pity the Salvadorans' tragic situation, but they were never invited to empathize with "our boys." Of course, the war was still represented through American experience, with American characters and symbols. However, the nature of the experience was much different, much more distant. "We" were invited to watch this war as cold voyeurs rather than invested participants.

Both Oliver Stone's semi-fictitious film *Salvador* and Joan Didion's nonfiction text by the same name (Didion 1983) illustrate this sense of ambivalence. The main characters in each—Didion herself in the book and "real" reporter "Richard Boyle" in Stone's film—represent the contradictions of geographic proximity and social distance. Although both characters express outrage at the acts of the U.S. government and great sympathy for the Salvadoran masses, one gets the sense neither finds a group of direct participants with whom they can truly empathize. Conversely, the Vietnam correspondents, even those who were critical of the U.S. effort, tended to use American grunts as their empathetic vehicle when writing about the horrors of that war.

Didion leaves the country "without looking back," sitting alone and frightened on a passenger jet, surrounded by American missionaries, people much like herself whom she loathes nonetheless (Didion 1983:106–107). What could be more "American"? Boyle finds himself back in the United States as well, equally frightened and alone after attempting, and failing, to help just one Salvadoran (his lover) escape the war. Both Didion and Boyle remain orphaned, no one to share their experience or to assuage their lingering feelings of guilt, anger, and impotence in the face of atrocities caused, in large part, by their own government.

The *Salvador* ethos provides a collective sense of identity to the corps. It is one of their "favorite clichés," to borrow a phrase from Pierre Bourdieu, something to be "slipped into, like a theatrical costume, to awaken, by the evocative power of bodily mimesis, a universe of ready-made feelings and experiences" (1984:474). Just as "I've been to Nam" imbues the speaker with an aura of greatness, having survived hell, the reporters throw around symbols of "Salvadorness," mutually reaffirming their unique status as war correspondents. They know that "Central America stands a better chance...of getting you killed" than any other part of the world (Lord 1984:14). They let everyone else know that as well. "We aren't just covering the weekly Junior League meeting in Des Moines," says Joe, a hyperkinetic young man who wears his "war photographer" identity like a name tag. They are the least domesticated of journalists—wild men in a wild situation, having a great time. In the words of Marla, another young North American reporter: "There is an attitude among a good amount of men that this war is their personal form of entertainment."

So, if you are a parachuter or other outsider, you say *Chalatenango* when referring to the rebel province. If you are a *Salvador* reporter you say *Chalate,* casually, as if you spend weeks there soaking up the *onda* (*caliche*/slang for "the situation") or *coyuntura* (moment) for your eventual book; a book that will be the final word on war, reporting, and humanity. Like Conrad's Marlow, you will one day give your readers a glimpse into the very *Heart of Darkness,* the most recent sighting thereof having been *Chalate.* Your job with the *Minneapolis Tribune* is just a side-gig to pay the bills while laying the foundation for your eventual masterpiece.

Some SPECA reporters draw upon the lore of Vietnam in order to construct their *Salvador* identity. They quote lines from Herr's *Dispatches* (1968)and the fictional forms he inspired, including *Apocalypse Now.* They exhibit a keen sense of nostalgia for Vietnam—a war they never experienced—drawing constant comparisons between the two conflicts, only half of which truly apply. Herr describes this journalistic predilection for mythical wars and reconstructed pasts (1968:225):

> [A]ll you ever talked about anyway was the war, and they could come to seem like two very different wars after a while. Because who but another correspondent could talk the kind of mythical war that you wanted to hear described?

The *Salvador* reporters had El Salvador, but would have preferred Vietnam.

Like most of the reporters in Herr's book, the majority of *Salvador* reporters rarely went near the actual battle sights. If they did, perhaps more would have developed the sense of sadness, moral outrage, and ambivalence presented in Herr's work. Instead, this type of reporter, the *war correspondent*, is like the accountant who rides a Harley. He projects a renegade identity to himself and the world in a desperate attempt to live up to the American myth of the independent man. Instead of simply accepting the routines and his status as a paid professional, always at the beck and call of his employer, the *Salvador* reporter casts the image of a maverick investigator, poised to uncover the hidden truths of corruption and conspiracy.

In reality, most war correspondents are no more independent or free from discipline and censure than their domestic colleagues. Therefore, I will challenge the view that news is reported by independent, tenacious, and objective journalists who function as watchdogs against the abuses of power. To presage the punch-line to this study, I have concluded that reporters play a relatively small role in the creative process of discovery, analysis, and representation involved in news production. Instead, they are mainly conduits for a system of institutions, authoritative sources, practices, and ideologies that frame the events and issues well before they, the mythical watchdogs, have a chance to do anything resembling independent analysis or representation.

Daniel Hallin argues that the "ideology of the journalist" is, among other things, "myth" (1986:23). He explains: "It is, in short, a 'myth'—but in a particular sense of that word. Far from being a mere lie or illusion, it is a deeply held system of consciousness that profoundly affects both the structure of the news organization and the day-to-day practice of journalism." The "Salvador" identity is a social manifestation of the myth to which Hallin refers, a claim to independence and neutrality, a wondrous creation that imbues the rather mundane practice of objective journalism with a sense of adventure, poetry, and romance.

Journalists are not the first North Americans to bring these notions to El Salvador. Before the war, thousands of *gringo* surfers came to pay homage to El Salvador's famed Pacific surf. They too found El Salvador an excellent medium for their foreign fantasies. The war correspondents came seeking more than mere adventure, however. They sought truth. Yet, like the weekend warriors who preceded them, most SPECA journalists barely skimmed El Salvador's surface. Their institutions, professional conventions, and other disciplinary structures encouraged them to produce surface texts, to describe violence, politics, and society as if such things are caused by the same seemingly random forces as earthquakes, floods, and hurricanes. We, the news audience, are caught up in this whirlwind adventure as well; places, images and events flash by in rapid succession, an unintelligible pastiche of terror whose effect is to unsettle rather than enlighten.

Eric Wolf argues the goal of anthropology should be "the creation of an image of [humanity] that is adequate to the experience of our time" (1964:94). Surely, the goal of journalists should be similar—to provide an adequate definition of events, the context in which they take place, their underlying causes, and most importantly, our connection to them—to engender what sociologist C. Wright Mills calls "The Sociological Imagination," a sense of knowledge and interconnectedness linking individuals to the larger world in which they live (1959). Unfortunately, the international news system is currently inadequate to the task. In the following pages, I will demonstrate a few reasons why this is so. My purpose is not to create a paralyzing sense of outrage or despair, however, but to suggest positive alternatives, many of which already exist, if only in the cracks and margins of the current system.

War

and

Identity

WAR
GAMES

Delighting in their distinction as "Those Crazy Guys Who Cover The War" (Herr 1968:188), war correspondents often publish their exploits in boldly entitled autobiographies like *War Reporter* (Harris 1979), *War News* (Anson 1989), *Means of Escape* (Caputo 1991), *Trial by Fire* (Barnes 1990), and *Dangerous Company: Inside the World's Hottest Trouble Spots with a Pulitzer Prize-Winning War Correspondent* (Tuohy 1987). They name their autobiographical essays with equal subtlety, crafting titles like "Hell Sucks" (Herr 1968:70–85) or "News From Hell," Anna Husarska's recent *New Yorker* essay (1992). The back cover blurb on Harris' *War Reporter* exemplifies the live-for-the-adventure and die-for-the-truth theme running through each of the aforementioned works (1979):

> Looking for the action, he found it. The jungles of Vietnam, the streets of Northern Ireland, the deserts of the Middle East, the Hills of Cyprus.... For the past fifteen years crack Hearst foreign correspondent J.D. Harris has risked his life to bring the news of war to the American People.

The autobiographical texts portray war correspondents' work as frenetic, occasionally insensate, yet ultimately heroic.

Once past the obligatory self-deprecating statements of the introduction, the focus turns to the reporter's courage, cunning, and professional conviction. Husarska brags (1992:99):

> All those who have reported from here, even the seasoned war
> correspondents, agree that Sarajevo is the most dangerous assignment
> they've ever had. So it is only natural that nearly every journalist who comes
> to the former Yugoslavia makes it a point of honor to 'do' Sarajevo.

The subtext of Husarska's essay is that the war correspondent, given her intimate association with the dangerous and important moment, is herself courageous and consequential. Beneath the surface message "War is Hell" lies a claim to cultural status and professional identity, what Herr calls the "haunted, haunting romance" that accompanies the title "war correspondent" (Herr 1968:188). War correspondents live (and sometimes die) to be distinguished from *plain* correspondents.

The practice of war reporting seems an endless dance with death in the autobiographical texts, a life of close and constant contact with extreme violence. War correspondents live in the trenches, their perilous routine broken only by an occasional late night bar session or red eye flight. There is scant mention of the countless hours spent sitting in press conferences, interviews, taxis, and offices waiting for something "big" to happen. The time consuming act of writing is also ignored.

Popular films like *Salvador, Under Fire, The Killing Fields*, and *The Year of Living Dangerously* similarly represent the war correspondent as courageous, fiercely independent, and intensely committed to truth—the classic "lone rebel motif" (Tetzlaff 1991:28). While such films also contain implicit critiques of journalism, the protagonists fit squarely within the rugged individualist model of the aforementioned autobiographies. As in the autobiographies, film reporters are unencumbered by editorial censorship and other institutional constraints. The pop culture protagonists ply their trade with near lunatic courage.

That self-promoted image is contested, however, by critical voices both within and outside the world of journalism. Many members of the international solidarity movement, for example, promote a very different view of the foreign correspondent.[1] Before beginning my research, I was often told by solidarity workers that SPECA reporters did little more than attend U.S. embassy functions and get drunk in the bar of the Camino Real Hotel. While war correspondents present themselves as rugged individualists, these critics envision them as mindless agents of U.S. foreign policy.

While both positions contain certain truths, neither provides an adequate description of war reporting. Most reporters are neither the die-for-the-truth adventurists they would have us believe, nor the lobotomized barflies of solidarity discourse. The truth is much more complex, and in certain ways, more disturbing. Starting with a description of a typical field excursion, I will offer a third and, I hope, more accurate picture of the war correspondents' difficult work.

Running with the Pack

On Thursday, April 11 a regional commander of the FMLN, Antonio Cardenal, was ambushed and killed along with thirteen guerrilla soldiers. Cardenal, *nom de guerre* Jesus Rojas, was the nephew of Nicaragua's President Violeta Chamorro. Although much is known about the life of this seminarian-turned-guerrilla, the facts surrounding his death remain clouded. The FMLN claimed Cardenal was executed after capture, a standard *tiro de gracia* ("shot of grace": bullet in the head). Such executions, although common, violate the Geneva Conventions. Salvadoran Army officials flatly denied the FMLN's accusation. They claimed Cardenal and his troops were killed in an ambush. We may never know which of the two versions, if either, represents the truth. However, we may have once had the chance.

On Saturday night, April 13, 1991 a group of reporters gathered at the Camino Real Hotel. At first, only I and a stringer named Shawn were present. Shawn was telling me about his latest adventures when Joe, a photographer, walked in, having heard us chatting as he walked by. Joe was trying to drum up support for a trip to Chalatenango, the site of Cardenal's death. Shawn wanted to go as well. After a few other journalists entered, the group reached critical mass and a consensus was reached: the story merited attention. We would be going to *Chalate* early the next morning.

As mentioned in the introduction, an FMLN execution of two U.S. advisors made international headlines just a few months before. Most SPECA reporters believed the ambushed guerrillas had received similar treatment, the tiro de gracia. Of the eighteen guerrillas attacked in Chalatenango, thirteen were killed. Not a single Salvadoran Army soldier died in the attack. As one reporter explained, "That just doesn't happen." There is rarely such an imbalance in casualties, even after a successful ambush.

According to the FMLN high command, the attack broke a "gentleman's agreement" between the warring parties. Neither side was to kill the other's leaders within their respective "retroguard" (controlled territories) during the negotiations. Therefore, the April ambush threatened to destablize the continuing peace negotiations and marked an escalation in the war. Further adding to the potential newsworthiness of the story, the local alternative press reported that two U.S. military advisers had taken part in the ambush.[2] (It was later confirmed by a SPECA reporter that American advisers were, at the very least, involved in planning the attack. That fact was never reported in the U.S. press, however.)

The event interested the reporters, although most doubted their editors would find similar news appeal in a story merely involving Salvadoran deaths. The doubters fell in line, however, once a few colleagues decided to make the trip. They could not risk getting scooped. As a result, the story was covered by committee, a common practice known as "pack journalism."

On the positive side, packs function to provide greater protection and allow for more efficient resource sharing (vehicles, fuel, communications equipment). Many stringers would have difficulty affording those expenses if they were not able to share them with others. Several journalists were critical of the pack practice, however, calling the *ad hoc* coalitions "rat packs," "gang bangs," and even, "goat fucks." Paul compared the pack outings to "camping trips." (I once accidentally referred to a pack outing as a "picnic," momentarily upsetting those with me on the excursion.) The critics' antipathy towards the "pack mentality," however, did not keep them from participating in pack outings themselves. The risk of getting scooped was too great, even for the most independent-minded journalists.[3]

Guerrilla Safari

At six o'clock Sunday morning about twenty journalists and I piled into a caravan of four-wheel drive vehicles, heading north. SPECA reporters jokingly referred to these excursions to the conflicted zones as "guerrilla safaris." We made a brief stop in the town of Guazapa for sweet breads, coffee and the latest word on local military actions around Volcan de Guazapa, a volcano fifteen kilometers north of San Salvador. The volcano was controlled by the FMLN throughout most of the war.

After driving another hour we reached the capital of Chalatenango province, a town by the same name. The ritualized bartering for access began there. The army controlled the town and access to the main roads leading into the mountains. To get to the guerrillas, we had to receive permission from the local military commander. Often, the frustrated young journalists would haggle with the media-savvy Army officers for hours before being allowed to pass or, quite often, forced to turn back.

Such negotiations involved a ritualized exchange of lies. First, the journalists misrepresented their true goals, claiming to be in the area for general reporting purposes. Rarely did they openly state what all parties concerned already understood: that they were there to talk to FMLN leaders. Of course, the military officers knew the reporters' true destination and purpose. Rather then challenge the imputed goal, however, military officials usually played along, adding their own fictions to the fray with lines like: "I'm sorry, terrorist actions have been very heavy in the area." Next, reporters would be asked to wait a short period while the guards spoke to their commanding officer via walkie-talkie. The reporters would be sent to town in order to gain permission from the regional commander, even when carrying valid passes signed by the high command in San Salvador. The local commander had only the limits of his imagination to consider when inventing reasons why the reporters could not pass into "his" territory; ad hoc obstructions presented with a smile. The military seemed to genuinely enjoy this aspect of their work.

If the game went well for reporters, they would be detained for hours and later allowed to pass. Factors that influenced the outcome of the ritual included: disposition of the local commander, the ability of the journalist to perform the ritual with competence and confidence, the nature of recent events in the area, and the institutional status of the reporter(s). A *New York Times* staff correspondent was much more likely to gain access than a *Fresno Bee* stringer or reporter for *The Nation*. The staff correspondent, however, was much less likely to make the trip in the first place.

Jerry, a stringer who rode next to me during the Chalatenango "safari," summarized the press access ritual:

> You know that they are lying and they know that you are lying. They know that you know that they are lying. It is a game. The only problem is that it is a game that they can decide to take seriously at any moment.

Jerry became visibly shaken as we drew near the *reten* (road block).

Even though journalists were, according to law, allowed full access to the countryside at the time, the army collected our press credentials upon arrival in Chalatenango and asked us to wait in a back room of the local barracks. We were served coffee and pastries while a pleasant, corpulent Army Officer arrived to baby-sit our group.

Joe and Michele, photographers for competing wire services, immediately began asking the well-nourished official what he thought about the recent ambush. After receiving vague, off-the-topic responses, the pair started pressing for access to the conflicted zones, using kind and measured tones. "It is too dangerous there today," said the officer, "It is for your own protection." "That is part of our work," explained Joe, "We are paid to take risks." "Is it the excitement of the work that you like?" asked the military man. He seemed to be genuinely interested in the response, though there was a sense of anger and derision in his voice. Joe did not respond. The truthful answer, however, is an unqualified "yes."

Trying to recoup lost propaganda points, Joe asked the official about the ambush, "If you can kill so many of the guerrillas this easily, doesn't that mean that you are really in control of all this territory?" Michele chimed in: "Yes, that was a big blow to the FMLN, right?" The officer grinned, refusing to be baited or swayed by their rather obvious attempts to gain favor. Adriana, another photographer, commented on such tactics: "I have heard journalists say very right-wing things thinking that is what they [the military] want to hear. Such deception is not good."

Whether "good" or not, "such deception" takes place relatively often.

On one occasion, Joe tried to get by a hospital guard by posing as a U.S. official, hoping to gain access to a U.S. citizen being guarded there by the National Police. The tourist had entered El Salvador without a valid visa or the ability to speak Spanish. He was being detained for deportation and panicked. Attempting to escape, he climbed up through a ceiling panel and then came crashing back down on a desk, injuring himself.

Joe was hoping to get an exclusive photo and interview the young man in his hospital room, as were other SPECA reporters. As the first journalist to arrive on the scene, Joe issued the following command to the sentries: "Please inform the Embassy staff that I will be waiting in his room." Joe was hoping they would assume from his tone and appearance that he actually worked for The Embassy. Neither Joe nor the others' attempts were successful, however, including a U.S. TV network film crew which tried to sneak in under the guise of a "police video" squad. It was quite an intense game for such a non-issue.

Deceptive press tactics rarely worked during the war. The journalists in question had only been in the country for a few years, whereas the military had been dealing with international press throughout twelve years of war. As usual, the Chalatenango officer baby-sitting our unhappy crew saw through Joe and Michele's transparent attempts to win his confidence and quickly changed the subject to soccer. It would take more than a few feigned pleasantries for the *prensa enemiga* (enemy press) to win him over.

The journalists sat there impatiently, drinking their coffee, eating military-issue donuts, and waiting for permission that would never come. We looked like a bunch of school kids waiting in the antechamber of the principal's office, left with nothing to do but ponder our transgressions. Any second I expected Joe to throw a spit ball at the officer-in-charge. Feeling a little claustrophobic and embarrassed, I left the office. Surprisingly, I was allowed to wander freely around the inside of the *cuartel* (barracks).

Near the front entrance a poster instructed soldiers on proper methods for dealing with the locals. The commandments included: "Number 3. Offer fair payment for acquired goods," and "Number 10. Show respect for young women." This was the new Salvadoran Army. Power with a smiling face. George, a staff correspondent, called it the "love bomb" strategy. The same army units that had wiped out tens of thousands in the first half of the decade had been instructed by their U.S. *patrones* to win the people's hearts and minds in the second. The corrupt and brutal fighting force had added public relations to its arsenal, a weapon that proved more powerful than all the helicopters, jets, and 500 pound bombs combined. In fact, the U.S.-designed "hearts and minds" strategy became the perfect complement to the Salvadoran military's program of selective murder and torture. One military man explained the program to me using a garden analogy: one must not only remove the weeds, but cultivate the desired plants as well. The military did a fairly effective job of weeding out dissent from the general population, while at the same time spreading enough fertilizer to stave off what once appeared an inevitable revolution.

After reviewing other posters, the billiards room, and various other compartments of the cuartel, I walked back to find Joe and Shawn arguing outside the office where the reporters were sequestered. Shawn was criticizing Joe for having made his disingenuous comments to the army officer. Joe defended himself, claiming he was speaking in earnest, that the ambush really did demonstrate the army's control of the area. "Nobody controls it!" Shawn responded, a little too loud. After a dead pause, Shawn made a conciliatory gesture to his younger colleague, stating "All I know is that *we* aren't in control here." They were certainly not in control. Journalists rarely are. In this case, the Salvadoran military had the upper hand, just as it was, and still is, in control of the Salvadoran state. And so, after a long wait, we were denied permission to go beyond the reten. The officials in charge politely requested we return the next day and try again. The reporters tried again two days later, and were stopped well before they made it to Chalatenango (see chapter 13).

The journalists gathered on the square outside the cuartel to discuss the issue. Shawn pointed out that the Archbishop had mentioned the ambush in his homily that morning. "That is a story," said Shawn optimistically. In other words, Shawn and the others were suddenly discounting the importance of going into the countryside to cover the issue first-hand. The group as a whole began to follow Shawn's logic. They proceeded to convince themselves the story was not really newsworthy in the first place and that access to the FMLN-controlled territories was, therefore, non-essential. They were trying to recoup a sense of power and autonomy in a situation almost completely out of their control. This was one of hundreds of incidents where I witnessed the members of the corps making a virtue of necessity.

While the journalists were talking, a small, nervous man approached me. He said he was a reporter for a Chalatenango radio station and asked for a ride to the conflicted zone. He assumed we would to try to gain access to the FMLN-held areas by extra-legal means. Explaining that I was merely an anthropologist (always good for a quizzical stare), I told him to ask one of the journalists for permission. Instead, he stood next to me and listened carefully to the ongoing discussion. I pointed him out to a reporter, who claimed the man was probably a spy for the military. Instead of asking the others for a ride, he simply walked off as the discussion ended. Although I had no way of assessing the spying charge, I was certain that if he were spy he was scouting the wrong crowd. This band was no more attuned to happenings in the FMLN-controlled territories than anyone else with access to a short wave radio and spare time to listen to rebel broadcasts.

Not all of the journalists were willing to give up so easily. Joe offered us the option of taking a back route. Most of his colleagues had already made up their minds to call it a day, however. They headed back to San Salvador, either fearful of breaching army orders, missing their daily deadlines, or wasting time on a story that was probably dead already. They knew their editors would not be interested in the deaths of Salvadoran combatants, even if they had been executed after capture. Whereas, the executions of two U.S. advisers had become the biggest news event of the year, the potential post-capture executions of thirteen FMLN soldiers was not worth a single paragraph to most editors. The U.S. advisers' executions garnered 41% of total television network news coverage of El Salvador in the United States in 1991. Most initial reports relied solely on U.S. State Department claims made before independent verification by journalists. Conversely, Cardenal's death was never mentioned on U.S. TV, and barely at all in U.S. newspapers (conversely, Spain's *El Pais* published two stories and mentioned the incident elsewhere).

The reporters were aware of their employer's ethnocentric judgments concerning the value of Salvadoran lives. In this case, it was certainly not worth the risk of disobeying the Salvadoran military, wasting an afternoon running around the countryside, and spending hours writing a story which would, no doubt, be filed in the editor's trash bin. "It could be sent," explained Shawn, "But, if it isn't published, you've gone to work for nothing." The journalists are cognizant of their institutions' conventions, having internalized the basic rules through training and practice.

Las Vueltas

Joe was not to be deterred, however. While most of the pack made its way back to San Salvador, Joe decided to drive into the FMLN-controlled zone via an unguarded passage. Those of us who had been riding with him continued on with him as well. In addition to Joe, our group was composed of Jerry, Maria (an International), and Michele. A Salvadoran crew working for an international Spanish language television news service followed as well. Their troupe was led by Angelica, a young, energetic, and well respected television correspondent.

The roads in northern Chalatenango are little more than wide trails, more potholes than smooth surface. The going was slow, but the scenery beautiful as we climbed up and around the steep green mountains, gazing down narrow river valleys angling toward the Rio Sumpul. The mountains' curve paralleled the winding path of the river. It was here on May 14, 1980 that Salvadoran and Honduran troops massacred 600 peasants as they attempted to flee across the Rio Sumpul to Honduras. Striking beauty and abject horror, the story of El Salvador.

Children stared and waved as we passed small villages tucked into the mountainside. Included among them were the famous blonde haired *Cheles* (Salvadoran slang for light skinned people) of Chalatenango. At each small hamlet, Joe would ask a local villager: "Have you seen any of the *muchachos* " ("boys": a euphemism for FMLN soldiers). Not sure how they should answer, each chose "no," the safest reply.

After driving an hour and a half, we made our first guerrilla sighting as two young combatants darted across the road and disappeared into the high grass along the embankment. A bit further, we found another young rebel walking by the road. He said we would find more *compas* (slang for guerrilla soldiers) in Las Vueltas, a small village just ahead. Indeed, we found several young FMLN men and women gathered at a small store there. They had just returned from a fire fight in Las Minas, a tiny village 2 kilometers away. After sending word to their comandante and receiving his permission, they walked us up a hill to meet with their battalion. About a dozen compas were resting there at a spot overlooking the deceptively peaceful village.

Rudi, their comandante, was a very young man. He was visibly shaken by the deaths of his ambushed (and executed?) comrades. Jerry and Maria began interviewing Rudi as the TV crew finished lugging their heavy and unwieldy equipment up the hill. After the crew set up their camera and sound equipment, Angelica interjected a few questions of her own. She asked the commander a couple of general questions and then, just moments later, the crew started disassembling and repacking their equipment. The TV interview lasted less than five minutes. Once a sufficient video image of the commander had been acquired, their work was finished. The cameramen wandered over to join several compas relaxing on top of a large, smooth boulder.

Meanwhile, Jerry and Maria continued their interview with Rudi, asking questions about Cardenal's death, the FMLN's control of territory, the ongoing negotiations, potential cease-fire arrangements, and Rudi's place in future postwar politics. Rudi spoke of Cardenal in loving terms. As tears came to his eyes, he described how Comandante Rojas treated all his troops as friends and equals. "In the FMLN there is no rigid hierarchy," he explained, drawing a distinction between the rebels and their enemies.

While Jerry and Maria continued the interview, I joined a group of compas, mainly boys in their early teens. In the course of our conversation, I learned that the bodies of the ambushed rebels were resting in Arcatao, fifteen kilometers to the east. They offered to take the journalists and me up in a truck to examine the corpses first hand. I told the reporters about the offer. Joe, as always, seemed ready to go. The others were not so willing, however, because it would involve a journey to Arcatao over some very rough roads and an overnight stay in the area. After a short discussion, the journalists declined the offer. We loaded back into Joe's Toyota Land Cruiser and began the journey home.

We had been following a circuitous path. Therefore, we had the choice of either heading back the way we came or exiting through the backside of the Chalatenango reten, just eight kilometers away. Fatigue overcame fear. We decided to complete our circuit. Minutes later, we waved nervously to the confused soldiers at the reten as we drove by. They let us pass through, probably afraid their superiors would find out about our unsanctioned excursion if they detained us, blaming them for our unauthorized entry.

The ambush and alleged executions went almost completely unreported. Although the FMLN accusation of a post-capture execution did receive brief mention in the *New York Times*, no other major U.S. daily covered the event. Institutionalized ethnocentrism and military obstructionism combined to kill a story many SPECA reporters had originally considered newsworthy.

Myth and Practice

Obviously, the Chalatenango field trip differed greatly from those found in typical war correspondent autobiographies. In fact, very little of what I observed during my research meshed with the autobiographical and popular culture images described at the beginning of this chapter. Whereas, in reality, very little war reporting is conducted at actual battle sites (during any war), war correspondents' published memoirs and pop culture texts are constructed almost entirely of combat narratives.

For SPECA reporters of the early 1990s, the necessary vignettes were derived almost entirely from the FMLN offensive of 1989. That was an event during which the war came directly to them, having taken place in San Salvador itself. Thrust into a very newsworthy situation, they were often conducting their coverage from locations near or within the actual battle sites. The offensive provided many of the young SPECA journalists with the stories they needed in order to begin creating their professional identities as war correspondents. (Even the offensive was covered in packs, however. Paul enjoyed showing off his photos of a particularly large pack of reporters hiding behind a brick wall during the offensive while a Green Cross volunteer stands out on the street shielding them, waving a large white flag.)

Yet, the offensive, and the coverage thereof, was an aberration. Under normal conditions, most of the war correspondents' time was spent in the city attending press conferences, conducting interviews with official sources, reading press handouts, and listening to local news reports on the radio. Most war reporters reconstruct battle scenes from these and other second hand sources. During the entire period of my research, only a few correspondents visited the countryside to observe combat, despite the fact such battles took place almost every day. The excursion described in this chapter is, therefore, fairly representative of the SPECA journalists' collective practice.

In fact, for many SPECA reporters the April 14 pack outing was their first such excursion in months. While a few photographers ventured out at least once a week, most of the reporters did so only on rare occasions. Some had only visited the FMLN-held territories a couple of times during their entire tenure in El Salvador. (At first, I kept asking reporters to take me "to the field" with them, thinking I was missing the most important part of their work. I soon realized, however, that their "field" was the capital itself). Because of editorial mandates and the narrative structure of news writing—particularly the emphasis on elites—journalists conduct most of their business in press offices, conference rooms, and local restaurants. Therefore, the autobiographical discourse of war correspondence is not, for the most part, a representation of normal routine, but instead an aggregate of exceptional moments. These works offer a glimpse into the relatively rare, but memorable moments when reporters find themselves in the center of explosive violence.

As highly edited and personal texts, however, the autobiographies also offer a glimpse into the typical war correspondent's desired projection of themselves, their preferred sense of identity. The autobiographies, and the fictional accounts they parallel, form a body of myth that other journalists draw upon in constructing their own professional identities. The mythological corpus of press corps culture contains a shared narrative of adventure, independence, and truth that imbues the correspondents' heavily controlled practice with a sense of magic and purpose. The myths become anodynes, narcotic fantasies (and "phallusies") which assuage the pangs of mundane, difficult, and disciplined labor.

TERROR
AND CONTROL

"A further paradox inheres in a drive for knowledge that is dictated by fear; for in the long run, the product of fear is a certain vital ignorance."

—Jules Henry, in *Culture Against Man*

The Salvadoran military placed restrictions on the movement of journalists throughout much of the war. During the latter half of the conflict, these restrictions were codified into law as the *salvoconducto* (safe conduct) system. Reporters wishing to cover events in the FMLN-held territories, which the Salvadoran military called "conflicted zones," were obligated to obtain a "safe conduct" pass.

The territorial definition of the conflicted zone was constantly changing, depending on recent events, current military strategy, the applicant's status, and the disposition of the military officer in charge. A conflicted zone could be as large as two-thirds of the country or as small as a single house. For example, one afternoon Shawn received word his house was being vandalized. He rushed home to find soldiers blocking the door. They told Shawn to apply for a salvoconducto pass at the Estado Mayor (Salvadoran military headquarters). "I needed a salvoconducto just to get into my fucking house!?" screamed the agitated correspondent.

Similarly, the military barred Paul from entering a church one day, asking that he obtain a salvoconducto pass first. Hoping to photograph a group of wounded FMLN soldiers who were seeking sanctuary inside the church, Paul visited the *Estado Mayor* to obtain requisite documentation. "That is crazy," said a military press official, "You don't need a pass to go into a church. We don't give passes for something like that." Paul reiterated the demand of the sanctuary guards. "Then I guess you can't enter the church," replied the grinning bureaucrat. Kafka, Catch 22, 1984—correspondents working in El Salvador have the privilege of experiencing the plagues of modernity alongside the terrors of feudalism while working their way through multiple, arbitrary layers of military bureaucracy. The correspondent must constantly navigate a system whose primary function is not to function. The bureaucratized military, in close association with the militarized government, continued to invent bigger and better obstacles to press coverage as the war developed.

The processing of a salvoconducto pass application would usually take one to three days. Once a pass was obtained, it was usually only good for another day or two. Even with the pass in hand, journalists were usually held for hours at regional military installations before being sent on or denied access anyway. After one or two days spent applying for the pass and haggling over access at the local cuartel, correspondents were left with very little time to cover events. Furthermore, there were often periods during which the military simply refused to offer passes to any journalists. These unofficial moratoriums occurred twice during the period of my research, each black out lasting for several months.

Likewise, official declarations heralding the lifting of press restrictions (usually for elections) offered no guarantee of free access. Such was the case during the Chalatenango excursion described in the preceding chapter and an earlier incident involving the detention of eighteen journalists. Among the detainees in the latter case were six foreign correspondents, including the President of SPECA, held and threatened by army Colonel Leon Linares. "If this happens again," Linares told one, "you could all be dead." The military confiscated the journalists' film and equipment before sending them off sufficiently frightened.

The Effects of the "Safe Conduct" System

The effects of the salvoconducto system were wide-ranging. First, it was nearly impossible to cover breaking news in the FMLN-held territories. Events are rarely considered news if over a day old.[1] Second, reporters were greatly distanced from events, participants, and first-hand witnesses. While almost all reporting involves a secondary or even tertiary chain of communication, SPECA journalists became even more spatially and temporally removed under the salvoconducto system.

Due to the restrictions, reporters became almost exclusively reliant upon COPREFA and rebel radio broadcasts for information regarding combat. Ignacio Ellacuria, one of six Jesuits massacred in November, 1989, correctly stated: "I don't know, with the possible exception of some incidental radio or TV reporter, who could be considered a war correspondent in El Salvador. We are at the mercy of what COPREFA and Radio Venceremos tell us" (APES 1990:62). Unfortunately, the information and casualty figures provided by these oppositional sources were usually irreconcilable. Therefore, many reporters simply averaged the discordant statistics. Accuracy became a moot question as the apparent "winner" would be whichever side most greatly exaggerated their battlefield successes. Accuracy was the first casualty of the salvoconducto system. Juaquin, a Salvadoran journalist working for a European wire service, lamented, "With the salvoconducto system, you cannot report the news with proximity." That, quite obviously, was the purpose of the system.

The salvoconducto system also created problems for journalists writing feature stories. It was impossible to do a careful job of researching a feature piece in the limited amount of time a pass allowed. "It makes it harder to do feature pieces about the guerrillas," explained Cary, a stringer, "and it makes it harder to do pieces about civilians in certain areas."

A freelance photographer described the impact of the salvoconducto system on her work [note: she is not a *Newsweek* staff journalist]:

> It has a very negative effect, especially for the way that I approach things. It hampers my ability to cover a story.... The pass only gives you three days, half spent getting through. So, you can't live with the peasants. *Newsweek* zips up and zips back and doesn't have time to understand the process of what is happening in that place. People don't spend enough time covering rural areas and land tenure, which make life move in the *third world*. They spend too much time in the City with elites. That [covering the rural area] is what we should be doing, but you can't.

The stated purpose of the system was the safety of the reporters, but as Harold explained: "They use it to control the news. They will tell you it's for safety, but most reporters can take care of themselves. Most only take reasonable risks."

A few SPECA journalists had been working in El Salvador before the salvoconducto restrictions were instituted in the mid eighties. Although their vision of pre-pass days may be clouded by nostalgia, these veterans claimed it was much easier working before the pass system was developed. "Now if you have two interviews in the city," lamented Othello, a stringer who covered the entire war, "you're not going to bother going out to the countryside, because you just get fucked with and sent back."

A couple of journalists who left their postings before the pass system even began, remembered the early days differently. "People didn't go out because either they'd been there for two years and were burned out," explained Rosa, an ex-SPECA journalist I interviewed in Guatemala, "or they didn't want to get screwed by The Embassy" (close press scrutiny of Salvadoran military activities angered Embassy officials). She explained the stakes of alienating The Embassy:

> Being screwed by The Embassy there is a big deal, because then you don't really get into the press conferences; you don't get the access; you don't get the confirmations; you can't get "The Embassy spokesman said such and such."

For these and other reasons reporters were city-bound in the pre-pass period as well, even without official restrictions on their movement.

In addition to Embassy sanctions, pre-pass journalists also had to deal with selective pressure from the military. "As far as the army was concerned," said Rosa, "if you could get away with it, you could do it. The thing was, though, that they would shoot at you if they found you." Once, after Rosa survived a hail of bullets, the local commander offered this lukewarm apology: "You shouldn't have been there and we shouldn't have shot at you."

Once in operation, however, the salvoconducto system became a much more effective means of press management than random gunfire. It could be used in a safer, more selective manner and would do less damage to the military's international image. The system enabled the army to have a significant effect over international news coverage. The military manipulated the system not only to hide what they wished to keep secret, but to provide greater public exposure to certain other events as well. For example, after staging special missions to force the FMLN from their normal zones of occupation, the army would offer journalists free movement to cover the "liberated" area. The subsequent news reports made it appear the military had greater control than was really the case. Once the journalists were gone, the FMLN would retake the area in question with relatively little effort. Few international reporters, however, took part in the army's obvious propaganda ploy, although it was a staple of local coverage. A notable exception during the period of my research was a report written in the *New York Times* about the rebel-stronghold town of Perquin. The parachuting reporter filed the story during a rare and brief take-over of the town by the Salvadoran military, a well coordinated piece of coverage that made it appear the FMLN did not control the general area.

Most permanently based SPECA reporters, however, refused to go along with the special mission ploy. In broader context, however, they were all manipulated by the salvoconducto system. "Sometimes if they feel in control," explained Marla, a stringer, "they will let you through to get their point of view." Jerry put it more bluntly: "The army opens up the gates and we go." They would open the gates particularly wide around election time in order to legitimate what the FMLN, grass roots organizations, and many opposition parties saw as illegitimate, war-time polls or *Demonstration Elections* (Herman and Brodhead 1984:93–152). In accordance with this strategy, the salvoconducto system was suspended in

March, 1991 for the National Assembly elections.

The staff correspondent or *A Team* leadership of SPECA took credit for the 1991 election suspension, unaware or unwilling to admit that it was the government's propaganda strategy, not their limited protests, which was responsible for the temporary removal of restrictions. "SPECA had no success negotiating with us," the Colonel in charge of COPREFA bragged, "We suspended the system when we were ready to" (interview). The Salvadoran government wanted international journalists to go out and cover the elections, to legitimate them.

They also reinstituted the system when they "were ready to." Soon after the elections, the system was back in place and reporters were forced to agitate for access once again. Like mice in a maze, the journalists were guided around a physical and ideological plane largely controlled by those conducting the war.

Accepting the Silence

Despite the considerable effects of the salvoconducto system, the pass system received almost no mention in the journalists' news writings. Only a few vague references were provided in the hundreds of articles I have examined. Even alternative media were mostly mute on this significant issue. Although most SPECA stringers wanted to mention the press restrictions in their news stories, the majority of SPECA members voted against it. The staff correspondents who controlled SPECA, and the Salvadoran journalists who were working for them, comprised a bare-majority bloc that argued forcefully against such action.

Despite their stonewalling, however, the high status staff disliked the restrictions almost as much as the rest of SPECA. "It is more difficult to work in El Salvador than most other Latin American countries," said the SPECA president, "There are restrictions placed on almost everyone's movement, especially our movement." Yet, he was the lead proponent of the conservative coalition who consistently voted against publishing articles about the salvoconducto system. The president and his colleagues believed it would neither be efficacious nor proper for SPECA to aggressively protest the press restrictions. They repeatedly mouthed the phrase, "We are not a union." Furthermore, the conservative coalition feared alienating the military and government officials if they pushed too hard for an easing of restrictions.

The stringers angrily rejected the staff position as disingenuous. They complained that the *A Team* simply did not care about freedom of press movement, because they rarely visited the countryside anyway. The permanently employed staff correspondents could file from the capital without risking loss of income. Conversely, the stringers needed to have access to the conflicted zones in order to write interesting and marketable stories about the war.

However, because the *A Team* refused to write about the restrictions, the *B Team* had little choice but to follow suit. While reporters, including stringers, are ostensibly free to write whatever they choose, in truth the staff correspondents and their institutions set the news agenda. It would have been professional suicide for the stringers to greatly deviate from the *A Team* agenda when providing copy to mainstream news media, whose editors would be hesitant to purchase the deviant reports anyway.

Furthermore, in publicizing the limitations placed upon their movement, SPECA journalists would have been subverting their claim to objectivity and independence. Among themselves, they admitted "the system affects your ability to report what is going on in the country in an impartial, even handed, and fair manner." To say so in their news reports, however, would have greatly undermined their authority and contradicted the professional codes that rationalize their labor.

Finally, to report the salvoconducto system would not only have subverted their professional legitimacy, but also a dominant news frame—that successive U.S.-allied Salvadoran regimes were "moderate," democratic entities caught between the violence of left and right wing extremists (Anderson 1988a:239, Herman 1990:5–6, McCoy 1992). As Othello argued, the pass system was "absurd and flies in the face of so much of the rhetoric of democracy." That rhetoric formed a nearly inviolate frame, however, which realities like press censorship and control were not allowed to penetrate. As a result, press restrictions provided a double benefit to the U.S. and allied Salvadoran regime. The salvoconducto system not only controlled journalists' movements, but did so without public notice, an "invisible hand" made all the more powerful in its textual transparency. The reporters' discussion of the salvoconducto system, like many fundamental truths of the war, remained safely backstage.

The significant silence surrounding the pass system betrays a common double standard in U.S. reporting. Press restrictions are often highlighted in the coverage of regimes antagonistic to the goals of U.S. business and governance (Sigal 1986:26). Coverage of Nicaragua, for example, often included descriptions of the Sandinistas' press censorship. Ironically, *A Team* journalists spearheaded that attack. From 1982 to 1992 there were fifty stories from Nicaragua listed under the heading "censorship" in the *New York Times* index, yet not a single story similarly listed about El Salvador.[2] Yet, according to every journalist I spoke with who worked in both countries, the Salvadoran controls were far more rigid and effective.

In many ways, the restrictions were simply taken for granted by the corps. They started to deal with the salvoconducto system as an environmental reality. Deadlines, inefficient phone service, military restrictions and other seemingly immutable contingencies formed a set of intractable disciplines. As a result, SPECA members demonstrated greater anger at journalists who violated the salvoconducto rules than at their military handlers who invented those rules. One such incident involved Adriana, a photographer. Following standard practice, she and a fellow reporter fabricated a story at a reten in order to gain access to a conflicted zone. Unfortunately, their lie was poorly crafted. Adriana told the officers that they "were going to visit the [Salvadoran military] brigade" further down the road. Adriana's fib had the flaw of being demonstrably false once they failed to show at the brigade. Their cover was blown almost immediately. Meanwhile, they had been allowed to pass through the reten and were buried deep in forbidden territory.

Adriana felt they should sneak out of the area at night so as not to be seen by the soldiers whom they duped. Her colleague disagreed, so they came back through the reten in broad daylight. Naturally, they were searched and detained, about six hours in all. "I was terrified," Adriana said, "because the *campesinos* in my photos would be dead if the military found my film." Fortunately, Adriana hid her film in a travel bag amidst her "dirty underwear," where it remained safe. Nevertheless, Adriana's initial carelessness was professionally unethical. She had seriously endangered her photo subjects.

It was not on ethical grounds that SPECA criticized Adriana, however, since most reporters endanger their subjects on a fairly routine basis. Instead, it was her provocation of the military which made them react. Journalists who were refused salvoconducto passes soon after the incident blamed Adriana for having precipitated a tightening of military restrictions. Soon thereafter the entire corps was kept from attending the exhumation of an FMLN doctor raped and killed by the military. The corps seemed to blame Adriana's recklessness more than those who created and enforced the restrictions.

Adriana provides her interpretation:

> In the press corps there is a sense that these are the rules and you shouldn't break them. This was an important enough story that I thought we should. My colleagues may not have done the same thing.... It is an example of how the [salvoconducto] rules hamper work and divide the press corps when the real issue is that we don't have free access.

Unfortunately, the journalists felt powerless to effect the "real issue" of access, and indeed, probably were. As a result, Adriana provided an unwitting yet safe outlet for the corps' collective sense of powerlessness and frustration.

Terror as a Means of Press Control

The salvoconducto system was only one of several anti-press weapons in the military's arsenal. Two others, expulsion and terror, were also quite effective. While few U.S. reporters were thrown out, several Europeans and Russians were shown the door, or barred from entering in the first place. Paul complained that "there have been a lot of people who have come here from Europe, as journalists, and been thrown out of the country and they can't come back ever again." Many Salvadoran reporters, including several working for international media, were forced to flee the country as well (Vernau 1989:95–102).

As was true in the case of the salvoconducto system, U.S. reporters were rather silent on the issue of expulsion and exile. Paul complained:

> When Jason Blackchild was thrown out [of Nicaragua], the *New York Times* made a huge deal out of it. All these U.S. press organizations were up in arms. But here, it's not ten or twenty, it's more like fifty! And nothing has been done about it. It's bullshit, ya know.

Salvadoran military terror worked equally well. Nearly forty reporters—mainly Salvadorans, Europeans, and photographers—were killed covering the conflict in El Salvador. Numerous other Salvadoran and foreign journalists were forced to flee under threat of death. Furthermore, several alternative press institutions were destroyed at the start of the war, their personnel killed or exiled.[3]

According to A. J. Liebling, "Freedom of the press is guaranteed only to those who own one" (Bates 1989:194). In the case of Salvadoran local press, such freedom has only been available to a handful of conservative owners and publishers. As a result, the typical Salvadoran news consumer is only exposed to a narrow band of extreme right wing perspectives. The national press has been closely aligned with the government and military, effectively distributing their propaganda throughout most of El Salvador's history (Sol 1984). Most moderate and left press institutions have been destroyed through arson, intimidation, and/or murder. In 1980, *La Cronica del Pueblo*'s facilities were burned. The newspaper's editor and a photographer were kidnapped, tortured, and murdered. A year later, *El Independiente* was bombed. *El Independiente*'s editor was forced into exile after a failed attempt on his life. "My crime was to run a newspaper," he complained, "the only remaining independent voice in El Salvador" (Pinto 1981).

There was not a single alternative newspaper paper in El Salvador during the war until employees took over the operations of a failing organ, *Diario Latino*, in 1989. *Diario Latino* was fire bombed just over a year later, on February 9, 1991 (Huff 1994:13). I interviewed the *Diario Latino* staff a few days after the attack. As I looked around their destroyed facility, I was particularly struck by the dead silence of their giant printing press, its huge metal skeleton symbolizing the right's antipathy for press dissent. They managed to destroy almost all of the newspaper's antiquated equipment and work facilities. Only murder could be a more effective deterrent.[4]

One afternoon at a surfing contest near La Libertad, I met the son of a journalist who had been slain during the early part of the war. He provided a rather startling demonstration of the effects of terror on the Salvadoran population. Like his father, he too hoped to become a member of the press. Despite his grandmother's wishes he intended to become a photo journalist. His interest was not generated out of family tradition or politics, however. "It would be a lot of fun to take photos of all the demonstrations and stuff," explained the young man. The photographer-to-be knew practically nothing about the circumstances surrounding his father's death, having been too young to understand the nature of the assassination when it took place. He still was not clear on the reasons behind the killing and considers himself apolitical, more committed to beach parties than politics. The history of his family represents the recent history of the nation itself. The will to revolution has been successfully expunged through the most simple, violent, and effective means available. Much as torture involves "the making and unmaking" of the victim's world (Scarry 1985), political terror radically reforms the social body. Terror atomizes the community through the production of fear and pain, then unites its weakened and individuated members in a web of mutual fear and distrust, reducing each person's life project to the primordial purpose of subsistence and survival. The victims are drawn inward, cut off from others, both living and dead.

While the military and death squads' threat to local alternative institutions has been much more intense and sustained, international journalists (including Salvadorans working for the international press) have been occasional targets as well. On March 19, 1989, for example, three journalists were shot and killed by the military while covering the presidential elections and related violence. Two of them, both Salvadorans, were "specifically targeted by government troops" (Krauss 1991:104). The other, Cornel Lagrouw, was one of five Dutch journalists killed covering the war (Massing 1987:44). Lagrouw was with other journalists filming combat when gunned down. His colleagues loaded him into their car and rushed back to the city while a helicopter made chase, firing at the fleeing vehicle. Fortunately, they escaped down a dusty, tree lined road. While journalists were targeted less often in the latter half of the war, such incidents were still common enough to make SPECA members act with a good deal more caution than might otherwise be the case.

Terrence, a staff correspondent considered to be one of the few true conservatives in the corps, complained that too much was made of assassinations of foreign reporters.[5] He cited the fact that many more local journalists had been killed before and during the war. According to Terrence, there was an element of "arrogant" racism represented in SPECA's overemphasis upon murdered foreign journalists, but added that it is "a very understandable projection of your own fears about the situation, that you could get killed. You think, why isn't someone protecting us, God damn it! It's like a gut reaction." Whether an intellectual or "gut reaction," the murders of past colleagues weighed heavily in the minds of SPECA reporters.

Threats

Threats against SPECA journalists were relatively common, especially during the early 1980's. Ray Bonner of the *New York Times* received over eighty. Another *Times* correspondent left the country twice due to threats. A *Newsweek* reporter received a death threat his first night in El Salvador, one week after a photographer for the same magazine was assassinated. Two men cornered the reporter in the public bathroom of the Camino Real Hotel, calling *Newsweek* a "communist" magazine and suggesting he leave the country immediately. With a chair propped against the door, the neophyte war reporter laid awake all night rethinking his decision to work in El Salvador. He was "scared fuckin' to death" by that and later threats. Nevertheless, he managed to work for several years in El Salvador.

It is common knowledge among SPECA and Salvadoran society as a whole that the foreign press is disliked by the Salvadoran right and military. Whereas, war reporters' myths promote their independence, tenacity, and bravery, the right's mythology represents them as pariahs. They are lumped together with the FMLN, grass roots opposition movements, local alternative press, church workers, and the international solidarity movement as "communist subversives." "To the military, we are the enemy," explained Jorge, a SPECA Salvadoran, "If not the principal enemy, then as imputed friends of the guerrillas."

Military officers and right wing leaders refer to the international press corps as *prensa enemiga* (enemy press).[6] "It is part of the psychological war," asserts Alonzo, another Salvadoran member of SPECA, "They say we are friends of the terrorists." Alonzo was once threatened, his film confiscated after photographing a naked FMLN prisoner being held by the military. "I told them that it is just my job," he explained, "They told me to get a new job." From the military's perspective, the journalists aided the enemy. "You get it off the record," stated Loren, another SPECA Salvadoran, "They say, 'Why do you only report the bad things?' They feel we are causing harm."

During the FMLN offensive of November, 1989, the government dropped leaflets informing the "Salvadoran patriot" he had a "legitimate right to defend [his] life and property." The message continued: "If in order to do that you must kill the FMLN terrorists as well as their internationalist allies, do it!" Many journalists took that to mean that they, the prensa enemiga, had become fair game. While some reporters spent considerable time on the streets during the offensive, others stuck relatively close to the Camino Real, fearful their detractors would use the event as a pretext for acting out their often stated desire to kill them. "We know the guys with the guns want to kill us," said Victor, a SPECA Salvadoran, "and, if they are willing to kill the Jesuits, they are willing to kill anyone."

The U.S. Embassy, rather than protecting reporters, tended to ignore the military's campaign of threats and violence. At times, U.S. officials have even taken part in the campaign to discredit and endanger international correspondents who violate the official line. For example, they published an article by a U.S. journalist in an embassy newsletter under the heading: "Leftist Propaganda in the United States." "They are putting my life in danger," the targeted reporter complained, "They say they are teaching pluralism. How can they say that while, at the same time, they are attacking members of the U.S. press?"

An expatriate American, Gerardo, has also taken part in the campaign to discredit the foreign press. Gerardo publishes a right wing weekly in San Salvador. He has printed numerous articles claiming that members of the "communist" foreign press work for the FMLN, and has published the names of suspected offenders. In fact, Gerardo claims El Salvador's worst enemy is the international press corps. The SPECA president and others telephoned him on numerous occasions to request he stop endangering journalists' lives in that manner. Gerardo only intensified his campaign, considering himself and his publication a bulwark against the communist lies of the international press. During a marathon interview in Gerardo's office, he angrily denounced the SPECA journalists, calling them "Russian plants."

I was reminded of the hatred the Salvadoran elite holds for the foreign press when I gave a lecture at the American school, a private educational system for children of foreign officials, the Salvadoran oligarchy, and the military. After finishing my lecture to a class of high school kids, mainly Salvadorans, I was asked questions like: "Aren't most of the foreign press corps communists?" and "Why don't they write the truth about El Salvador?"

In El Salvador, socialization into militarized society begins very early in a child's life. One morning I watched a grammar school parade pass by my apartment. Little boys followed closely behind Salvadoran army troops leading the procession, trying hard to emulate the soldiers' goose step.[7] The military front was followed by a parade of shiny cars, each with a grade school princess on the hood, immobilized in cumbersome lace and satin dress. The children were placed into hierarchical, engendered configurations, a ritual reenactment of the military's utopian model of Salvadoran society. In these and other daily routines, they learn the lessons one needs to function in a highly bureaucratic and militarized culture. One of the first lessons learned in late and postwar El Salvador is that the communist foreign press kept the patriots from winning the war and wiping out their Marxist opposition (notice the parallel with the U.S. right wing's revisionist history of Vietnam).

The reporters were well aware of the right's paranoia. Lest they forget, occasional threats and public accusations would remind them to proceed with caution. Whereas, in the U.S., most "flak" comes "in the form of letters, telegrams, phone calls, petitions, lawsuits, speeches, and bills before congress" (Herman and Chomsky 1988:26), Salvadoran flak is unmistakably direct. As in the United States, however, the most effective flak in El Salvador "is produced by individuals or groups with substantial resources," with results even more "uncomfortable and costly" (1988:26).

SPECA "discomfort" was fostered by a careful campaign of surveillance and intimidation. The government, military, and right wing political leaders kept careful records of the actions of foreign journalists and were not afraid to make them aware of it. Norma, a SPECA Salvadoran, described how she was treated when asking for a salvoconducto pass:

> The guy taking down all the information says, "We have all of you here in our computer." He starts asking questions and making threats and saying, "Many of you journalists are selling terrorism, especially the Salvadorans."

Many spoke of the military's not-so-secret "list." Carlos, a Salvadoran television crew member called it "a list of those journalists which the government and military consider *personas no gratas*."

Rachel, another SPECA Salvadoran, mentioned similar acts of intimidation. "They would ask questions about my family," she explained, an edge of fear still clinging to her voice. Such intimidation often took place on a petty, interpersonal level. For example, days after Paul visited a brothel on a photo shoot, Roberto D'Aubuisson asked him if the pictures had turned out. D'Aubuisson evidently had informants in the establishment who kept him appraised of visitors' views and movements. In another incident, after a woman delivered a basket of eggs to D'Aubuisson at an ARENA rally, the death squad commander turned to Paul and tossed him one. Later, at an ARENA march, D'Aubuisson asked Paul if he had enjoyed the egg. Naturally, these odd attentions unnerved the photographer. The message was made all the more frightening in its unsettling ambiguity. The only clear message was that Paul's movements were under constant surveillance and review by D'Aubuisson.

In addition to a surveillance and filing system designed by the U.S. Central Intelligence Agency (CIA), D'Aubuisson had a photographic memory (Krauss 1991:72). On the two occasions I was near the man before his death on February 20, 1992, I was impressed by his intelligence, as were thousands who fell victim to his "organizational and operational guidelines for assassinations, kidnappings, and military assault teams" (Pyes 1986).

D'Aubuisson's "guidelines," outlined in a document seized during his temporary arrest in May 7, 1980, also included plans for organizing a political party (ARENA) and engaging in "international diplomacy and public relations." Part of that plan was to watch over, influence, and discredit the foreign press. Symbolic of the program's success, many Salvadorans view the international press as an enemy, though few have ever read a foreign press report.

Salvadoran journalists working in the international press are particularly aware of their compatriots' views and the serious threat from the right, having suffered many more casualties and personal losses than their visiting colleagues (see chapter 14). As one U.S. reporter explained, the military looks at the SPECA Salvadorans as "just locals working for the communist foreign press." As a result, during the war most SPECA Salvadorans refrained from visiting the countryside with their international colleagues.

Threats from the FMLN, having occasionally occurred, were much less of a concern to SPECA journalists. Joe was somewhat frightened when Comandante Juaquin Villalobos took issue with a right wing institution's fraudulent use of one of his photographs. Fortunately, Villalobos' anger was never transferred to Joe himself, who had no control over clients' use of his photos. The FMLN understood they had relatively little power to effect coverage of the war beyond facilitating journalistic access to their "liberated zones," carefully constructing statements to the press, providing propaganda to allied Solidarity organizations, and conducting their side of the war with the press factor in mind. As opposed to the *Sendero Luminoso* (Shining Path) of Peru and other guerrilla movements, intimidation of the press was never part of the FMLN strategy.

Conversely, surveillance, intimidation, and selective murder were an essential element in the military's war strategy, especially during the early years of the conflict. In 1982, for example, four Dutch journalists were killed by the army. One of them, Jacobus Koster, worked for a company that produced *Revolution or Death*, a film about the early days of the war. Salvadoran officials detained and interrogated Koster soon after he arrived in El Salvador. After expressing their loathing for the Dutch journalist's employer, the military let him go with a warning to get out of El Salvador immediately. Undaunted, he and his companions stayed on. Soon thereafter, they were ambushed and killed while reporting in the countryside. This is one of the reasons European journalists largely avoided El Salvador by war's end. They had been killed and exiled at a staggering rate relative to their colleagues from the United States and other regions represented in the corps.

The Question of Spies in the Press Corps

Generally, the members of SPECA trust each other more than those outside their ranks. Yet, fear and distrust also existed within the press corps, especially between the various subgroups (staff correspondents, stringers, photographers, Salvadorans, internationals). Some were even suspected of using their position for spying. Bob, a correspondent who covered the final six years of the war, stated, "I have no proof, but I believe the army has spies in the press corps." "The second floor [of the Camino Real Hotel]," agreed Rosa, "was infiltrated by both the left and the right, the guerrillas and the military."

As evidence, several mentioned the "revolving door" which links NBC News, the U.S. embassy, and the Salvadoran government. An office manager for NBC News in San Salvador later landed a job at the U.S. Embassy, raising doubts among the corps as to his prior activities as a journalist. Another ex-NBC News employee later became an assistant to the Salvadoran Ambassador in Washington.

During the period of my research, two U.S. television network office managers, both Salvadorans, were similar targets of suspicion. Both had worked at the U.S. Embassy before obtaining employment in the international press. The father of one was "best pals with D'Aubuisson," according to a stringer. The other was involved in a relationship with a military official. As if to confirm the suspicions, the latter was welcomed back to The Embassy and given a relatively prominent position when her television bureau closed. It must be remembered, however, that both of the aforementioned journalists were bilingual, unlike most other SPECA Salvadorans. Therefore, they were in great demand for the U.S. Embassy and television network jobs. Therefore, the coincidence of governmental and journalistic employment is not an automatic indication of conspiracy.

Another rather plausible and often repeated charge was that certain reporters, especially parachuting staff correspondents, provided inside information in exchange for privileged access. TV crews were witnessed by other journalists giving away guerrilla positions during the 1989 offensive. Similarly, photographers and "fixers" (logistical aides) complained that parachuting correspondents they had guided to the FMLN-controlled territories occasionally provided information about the rebels' positions in order to obtain inside information from the U.S. Embassy and Salvadoran military.

The press also provided a convenient cover for non-journalists. Solidarity workers would often acquire press credentials as a means to work and remain in the country. They were not members of the corps and very few of them actually wrote news stories. These "lefty tourists" as Ronald called them, often assumed press roles to protect themselves from the government and military. In several cases, North American solidarity workers used the cover of press credentials to smuggle illegal documents through customs, a practice that both endangered and infuriated legitimate journalists. As a result, the military came to associate the press corps with local and international opposition groups. Harold was one of many to complain, arguing that such adventurism greatly endangered the "small and vulnerable" international press corps.

The military also used the press corps as cover, both in the literal and metaphoric senses of the term. During the 1989 FMLN offensive, for example, a group of U.S. Green Berets forced several journalists to exit the Sheraton Hotel, walking among the reporters as protection against potential FMLN snipers (*FYI Media Alert* 1990:2, The Reporters Committee for Freedom of the Press). In a similar incident, the Salvadoran army forced Paul to stop his vehicle in the middle of a fire fight. The soldiers used Paul and his car as a shield against guerrillas shooting at them from a hill overlooking the road. Later that day a guerrilla sniper told Paul he recognized the photographer by the pattern of his shirt, which had been clearly recognizable through his gun sight. Fortunately, the FMLN refrained from firing in both cases.

In another incident, Colonel Rene Emilio Ponce (later to become top commander of the military), drove around the countryside in a vehicle marked "prensa" (press) in an attempt to collect information about guerrilla sympathizers. In short, solidarity workers used press cover as protection against the military, while the military used it to gain access to the thoughts of unsuspecting civilians. These abuses, in combination with military threats and intimidation, served to heighten the general sense of fear and mistrust within the corps.

Because of the distrust that pervades Salvadoran culture in general, and the press corps in particular, reporters have formed very tightly knit subgroups comprised of trusted friends and colleagues. As one moves away from these inner circles, relations become increasingly complex and dangerous. Therefore, when newcomers enter the corps there are numerous discussions concerning their authenticity. Having known one of the stringers from an earlier encounter, and having had mutual friends with others, I had few difficulties in this regard. After a couple of months in San Salvador, I was told that "everyone thinks that you are legitimate except for Ronald, but then again, he thinks every academic but himself is a spook (slang for spy)."

Politico-organizational allegiance is one of the central ordering principles of Salvadoran culture, as essential as ethnicity is to other cultures. There is great danger, however, in exhibiting political affinities in public. Public performance must be strictly noncommittal. Thus, Salvadoran society is a patch work of covert coalitions, ideological and otherwise. This was equally true for SPECA. The journalists who had the greatest tendency toward public display often found themselves under severe scrutiny from colleagues.

In addition to being one of the most well-liked characters in the corps, Paul was also one of the most open about his political views. As a consequence of his ideological transparency, Paul was often suspected by others of harboring "unprofessional" links to the FMLN. For example, he was once falsely accused of assasinating of a Salvadoran politician. Interestingly enough, the accusation was not launched by a political leader or party ideologue, but instead by his ex-lover, a Salvadoran press colleague. Even though Paul was out of the country at the time, she felt he had somehow participated in the hit, later ascribed to the National Resistance. While extreme, this incident demonstrates the level of paranoia in SPECA.

Likewise, SPECA journalists often criticized colleagues' real or imputed links with political and military organizations. The stringers faulted staff correspondents for maintaining close, personal relationships with U.S. Embassy staff and members of the Salvadoran oligarchy. Conversely, staff correspondents complained many of the stringers were too closely involved with the FMLN, "popular organizations" and the international solidarity community (see chapter 5).

Harold, a staffer, complained that Shawn, a stringer, "walked a thin line" in his dealings with the FMLN. Harold and other *A Team* journalists mistakenly saw Shawn's political verbosity as evidence of actual affiliation with the guerrillas. Other journalists, such as Shari, understood the meaning of Shawn's blustery comments differently. She suspected Shawn of working for the U.S. government or military. She argued that authentic FMLN affiliates do not go around bragging about their close ties with the guerrillas. In a world where no one is above suspicion (yes, even Shari had her doubters), those who make political ideology a part of their public performance are particularly mistrusted by their peers.

Accurate or otherwise, these accusations illustrate the high level of insecurity and mistrust that pervades Salvadoran society; a level of doubt that also infects the fairly cohesive and insular world of the press corps. Each reporter has her most trusted friends and colleagues, mostly drawn from the same team. As she moves out from that entrusted grouping, professional and physical safety become less and less secure. Trust resides in the center of concentric categories, dissipating quickly in the contentious outer regions. Spies? Maybe. Fear of spies? Naturally. The corps is embedded in a culture of suspicion and fear.

The Textual Effects of Terror

It is hard to gauge the effects of threats and violence in the reporters' news coverage. In cases involving murder, expulsion, or "facilitated" exit, the effect is obvious; the reporter is completely silenced. Less clear are the wider repercussions of such events, the hypothetical "chilling effect"—a generalized sense of uncertainty and fear that pervades, represses, silences, and atomizes entire communities. Such an effect is hard to measure, however. It is difficult to determine if the significant silences in news of El Salvador result from fear or other factors.

The only means through which I could measure the textual effects of terror were by asking reporters directly. Some, especially the SPECA Salvadorans, admitted they often hold back for fear of military retribution. Emilio, a Salvadoran member of SPECA, warned "you have to think before you print anything here." Most foreign reporters were also forthcoming concerning their fear-induced self-censorship. Terilyn, a newcomer to the corps, was warned away from several stories by her colleagues, including the illegal baby trade (babies are reportedly "produced" and sold to adoptive parents in the U.S.). Such stories are simply too risky.

One bureau chief said he felt comfortable doing investigative work "no more than every six months or so" for fear of military retribution. Months after he made that statement, he was sent packing under serious threats to his life. Partly for this reason, few SPECA members have done in-depth investigations of the Salvadoran military. "The military is a tough nut to crack," explained a frustrated staffer. It is both dangerous and difficult to report on issues closely involving Salvadoran military officials.

One of the few exceptions was Joel Millman, a journalist working under the auspices of a grant. Free from deadlines and other major limiting factors, Millman researched the military's financial interests and investments.[8] Millman's report, "A Force Unto Itself," is an unusually detailed description of the military's institutionalized corruption and economic power (*New York Times Magazine*, December 10, 1990). After his report was published in the *New York Times Magazine*, Millman was told by military officials not to return to El Salvador. A close friend was also harassed by military officials after "A Force Unto Itself" was published.

As in Millman's case, most noteworthy investigative work during the war was conducted by exceptionally prepared journalists visiting El Salvador to complete specialized research pieces (See also Pyes 1983). Unlike the members of SPECA, they did not have to face the potentially violent repercussions of their work. For the same reason, the most critical writings of SPECA journalists were generally completed just before each correspondent permanently left her post. John Carlin's classic article "Just Little Brown Men" is an excellent example (The *Independent*, December 29, 1988).

I asked each SPECA journalist to list the best articles produced during the war. The articles by Millman and Carlin led a fairly short list. Ironically, few of the reports mentioned were produced by permanently stationed SPECA members. Relative freedom from fear may be one of the necessary preconditions for producing critical work. This makes the few permanently stationed journalists who do critical and "dangerous" work that much more impressive.

The pressures of fear and flak are occasionally contested. Some of the most heavily pressured journalists reacted to threats by becoming even more critical of the Salvadoran power elite. Janice, an astute and intractable Australian stringer, is an example. Janice has continued to work in a critical mode despite constant harassment by Salvadoran officials. "If you say that you can't investigate the story or you would be killed," argues Janice, "you aren't doing your job." Bob is also among the select few who refused to acquiesce in the face of danger.

Reporters were willing to admit their fears in private interviews. They were not so willing to do so in public gatherings, however. For example, after a SPECA journalist disappeared in Iraq, some of his closest friends in El Salvador acted unfazed, as if their colleagues disappeared daily. One night, in front of several other reporters, I asked Shawn about his missing friend. Shawn joked in reply, "You already interviewed him didn't you?" In private, however, Shawn spoke in much more measured tones about his friend's disappearance. Despite his public posturing, Shawn was quite fearful for his friend's life. Fortunately, the journalist turned up eighteen days later, having been captured and released by the Iraqi army.

As in the autobiographical discourse, SPECA reporters would publicly deny the affects of fear, laughing off their profound sense of terror with false bravado. In other words, fear itself was subject to the rules of taboo, ceded all the more power through the public silences it produced. As Linda Green explains, fear functions as "the arbiter of power—invisible, indeterminate, and silent" (1994:227). Its enveloping, private presence may have had a profound influence on the journalists' coverage. Its exact role is difficult, however, if not impossible to determine in the case of SPECA coverage. It is hard to interpret silence.

"Boredom Punctuated by Terror"

There is a difference between the issue of *fear*, as detailed here, and the representation of *danger* found in the war correspondents' autobiographical discourse. Whereas, the war journalists' accounts speak much of danger and little of fear, the reverse condition is more common. The members of the corps were only rarely involved in violent and dangerous situations, yet felt a constant sense of fear. This is not because they are cowards, but simply because they are human.

Rather than living lives of constant danger, the journalists' experience is fairly routinized and relatively safe. As Joe was constantly complaining, a lot of the SPECA reporters spend the majority of their time at home or in the office, listening to local news reports on the radio or conducting business by phone. The SPECA journalist's typical routine involves attending press conferences in San Salvador, conducting interviews, writing news reports, and waiting in the office for something "big" to happen. In fact, even Joe spent most of his time doing those things. Excursions to the countryside were, at best, monthly affairs.

Though the moments of danger are fairly infrequent, however, they have a considerable impact. It only takes a limited number of threats and encounters with violence to generate a sustained sense of fear (I certainly felt a great deal of fear, despite my relatively safe ethnographic practice). The violent acts and aftermaths journalists cover add to their sense of danger and insecurity. The reporters' vicarious, yet constant involvement with violence leads to a decentered sense of terror. "Long periods of boredom punctuated by terror," that is how a friend described life in El Salvador. That is how I would describe SPECA life as well. Most SPECA reporters live a fairly predictable, routinized existence. Their relatively safe lives are, nevertheless, under constant threat of rupture.

ON A
WHITE HORSE

Rosa's Stories

I have chosen the career of one war correspondent, a photographer and occasional writer named Rosa, to illustrate several of the aforementioned themes. I first met Rosa in a bar in Quetzaltenango ("Xela"), Guatemala, where she and several colleagues were covering a "Continental Encounter" of indigenous peoples (see Pedelty 1993). She was regaling several young, male correspondents with stories of adventure in El Salvador. Her smoky voice, commanding presence, and exceptional story-telling skill had the audience of foreign reporters wholly absorbed in her performance. These British, Argentinean, and North American men gladly forfeited hours of precious time to Rosa's intoxicating tales. In fact, they paid more attention to Rosa that single night than to future Nobel prize winner Rigoberta Menchu the entire weekend. Shari and I sat down to join them, quickly becoming part of the rapt audience as the beguiling, if slightly intoxicated war photographer held court. Months later I returned to Guatemala to interview Rosa under more sedate circumstances.

Although she was no longer working in El Salvador, Rosa's best stories and most vivid memories were still from what she called "the Salvador years." Her first "Salvador" experience came in the early 1980s, after she had finished seven months of traveling throughout Central America. Tired of touring, she settled down and became a freelance photographer, publishing photo essays of refugee camps and related human rights issues.

Rosa soon interrupted her budding career as a war photographer, however, in order to do solidarity work. She was selected to guide Salvadoran refugees back into El Salvador from Honduras, offering her presence as a protective shield. Like a blonde pied piper astride a beautiful white horse, her job was to lead Salvadoran refugees across the Sumpul River.

If I had not heard it directly from the source, I would have assumed Rosa's story had been taken from a Latin American *telenovela*, billboard, or magazine ad, many of which feature tall, white, blonde women in any number of absurd poses and activities: laying half undressed on a diving board, lip-synching rock songs on popular TV programs like *Sabado Gigante* and *Llevatelo*, or, perhaps, riding a white horse. Perhaps these virgin-siren-saviors represent a desire for escape, for the modernity of North America. The Latin Americans' longing is matched by North American solidarity workers' (and anthropologists') reverse need to find utopia in the rural communities of Latin America. Each sees the other in their own cultural narratives. Each uses the other as unwitting symbols in ritual expressions of postmodern angst, one side yearning, the other falsely nostalgic. "They asked me to ride the white horse," said Rosa, "I don't know what the symbolism is, but it sounded great to me." It was a fair trade.

Although she found the ritual enchanting, Rosa did not linger long on her white horse. She turned once again to photography, feeling she "could do more as a journalist."

Rosa's story telling ability is one reason for her subsequent professional success. One of Rosa's stories is of a New Year's Eve spent with the FMLN. A fellow reporter persuaded Rosa to attend the guerrilla festivities.

Naturally, the two were stopped by a regional military commander on their way to the FMLN-held territories. Like an over-protective parent, the military official carefully explained the dangers of war to Rosa. Playing the obedient child, she promised to return early to the provincial capitol. Because of Rosa's charm and the holiday occasion, the journalists were allowed to pass on condition they return by eleven o'clock.

"It was a great dance," said Rosa, "It was wild seeing all of the compas just dancing and enjoying themselves." Rosa, ever the rebel, stayed for the entire night. Her colleague headed back before their curfew, however, in compliance with the commander's orders. Well into a New Year's Eve drinking bought, the commander either did not notice or care that Rosa had not returned as promised. Providing a happy ending, Rosa adds: "The photos of the dance sold really well."

Not all of Rosa's stories conclude happily, however. When I asked her to name the most meaningful photo she had ever taken, Rosa told me about an encounter with the *Brides of Death*, one of El Salvador's many death squads, one that worked closely with the military's first battalion. One day, Rosa was out shooting some downed telephone poles, results of FMLN sabotage. She was taken aside by a young man who asked her "Hey, listen, do you want to see what we've got?" Rosa continues:

> They went to the ditch and pulled out a dead body which they had covered with leaves. It was a guerrilla. They threw him up on the hood and then took out these black scarves and hung them underneath their hats. They said, *"Somos Los Novios de la Muerte"* (We are the Brides of Death). Those were supposed to be their veils. And they put the corpse up on the hood like it was a deer...[stuttering]...They posed with their rifles like they were very proud of their trophy.

Finishing the morbid tale, Rosa complained that the death squad issue was never adequately covered in the U.S. press. She listed that issue among other important, yet ignored stories, such as the presence of several hundred U.S. military advisors in El Salvador, a number well beyond the legal limit of fifty. "There were a lot of things," claimed Rosa, "that never came out."

Asked how she deals with fear, Rosa responded, "Sometimes, very badly. When I worked in El Salvador I can remember coming home on vacations and being good for about three days or so, but then starting to cry...at anything." Once, she became very angry at her father for rather innocently introducing Rosa to a Salvadoran man he had met. "How could you do this to me!" she screamed. Like most who return home from war, Rosa wanted to forget her experience for awhile, but could not. She concluded, "It does affect me very deeply."

Rosa was very proud of her investigative talents. She "went places that reporters didn't go," such as the time she rented a boat near Tiger Island and "pretended to fish" while taking pictures of an important news figure, or her visits to Honduran brothels to collect information about U.S. soldiers and Contras.

Rosa described her favored method of investigation:

> There was a remarkable story about a radar installation called *Cerro La [Hule]* right outside Tegucigalpa. It was top secret. It went berserk one night, starting to show blips on the screen. It made it look like there were tanks from Managua approaching Honduras. And so everyone went on alert, right? We had no idea about this until The Embassy held a mock election at the Hotel Honduras Maya one night—Daniel Ortega got one vote, a write in. But anyhow, first thing I met this Chaplain I hadn't seen for a while from the army base, and he said, "Boy Rosa, I can't tell you what was going on, but we sure had some stuff going on the other day outside Teguc [pronounced 'Tagoose,' refers to Tegucigalpa]." I said, "What do you mean? Outside Teguc could be Nicaragua?" And he said, "I really can't

talk about it. Let's just say a radar base." So I said, "Oh! Cerro La [Hule]!"

So I go to the next guy and said, "So, I hear there are some problems at Cerro La [Hule]?" He goes, "Ah listen, we can't talk about that. And anyhow, I think that it must have just been a mechanical failure. I mean, I can't really believe those tanks were headed this way." So I said, "Tanks!"

So then I go up to this public affairs guy, who is kind of drunk by this time, and I said, "So listen, I heard about the tanks at Cerro La [Hule]." He goes, "How did you hear about that? We have only been here like five minutes. Who told you?" I said, "Well, I can't tell you who told me." I said, "I just want to know if there is a picture opportunity for me." And he said, "Well, it could be if they shoot down one of those planes." And I said, "Planes too, huh?"

So then I went to one of the American Embassy guys and he said, "I just think it was a blip on the radar screen." He didn't even ask me how I knew. So the next morning the *New York Times* guy comes in and says, "Anything new?" I said, "Yeah, there is something sort of curious going on here." So he got in at 7:30 a.m., I had breakfast with him, and he went to The Embassy like at 8:00 a.m. or 8:30 a.m., something like that. The Embassy guy was just blown away that he had heard about this. In fact, some of the military guys later told me that [the reporter] must have heard about it through a leak in Washington.

"That kind of stuff was real fun," concluded Rosa.

After several years of successful work as a free-lancer, Rosa became the San Salvador Bureau Chief for a large international agency. Unfortunately, in a pivotal moment of her career, Rosa felt a need to quit her post after one of her Salvadoran staff members, a good friend, was killed covering battle. She had become very disenchanted with her agency, whose head office knew about the staff member's death a full day before informing her of the tragedy. They did not tell Rosa because they wanted her be well rested for the next day's election coverage.

Rosa and the rest of the corps were certain the Salvadoran journalist had been targeted by the military. Two ceramic hearts now rest on a shelf in the office were Rosa used to work, part of a monument to her fallen friend. Next to the hearts stands a toy soldier in meaningful juxtaposition, testament to that which cannot be explicitly stated in the agency's public space.

After the killing of her friend and coworker, Rosa left to get her "life balanced and become involved in social concerns." Rosa has now struck a more satisfying balance between the role of journalist and social worker. Most of her time is spent doing photo projects with children in Guatemala. She explains:

For a long time I was pointing and running from one problem to another and saying, "This is really awful. Can anybody do anything about this? I gotta move. I gotta take off. I gotta a story to do here!" Now I am putting something back in.

Rosa has not returned to El Salvador since a brief visit in 1989. "I just couldn't make myself go back," she explained.

Rosa's stories are equal part entertainment and cautionary tale. They serve as a means for Rosa to remind herself and others of where she has been, what she has accomplished, and where she never wishes to return. In their conflicted and sometimes terrifying beauty, Rosa's tales provide a glimpse into the war correspondents' collective heart and soul.

Structure

and

Practice

A TEAM, B TEAM

"It would be stupid to say that there are no favorites. There is usually a large overlap between the journalists who are large bureau chiefs and those who are ingratiating. If the Ambassador enjoys sitting with a reporter, he will get invited back. There is no real mystery to that."

—United States Information Service (USIS) Representative in El Salvador (interview)

Stringers are reporters who sell articles, radio pieces, and photos to a number of news organizations or "strings." The most common strings include medium-market newspapers (*San Diego Union, Philadelphia Inquirer*), larger institutions that lack Salvadoran bureaus (*CBS radio, BBC radio*), news organizations seeking to supplement staff coverage (*New York Times, Miami Herald*), and small-market, alternative media (*The Nation, Pacifica Radio, Catholic Reporter*).

Stringers harbor a great deal of animosity towards staff correspondents, whom they call the *A Team*. Their complaints are as follows: 1) staff correspondents are both physically and culturally removed from Salvadoran society, 2) *A Team* correspondents exploit stringers' knowledge and labor without offering adequate compensation and 3) staff correspondents rely much too heavily upon elite, propagandistic sources—especially U.S. State Department officials—and are, in turn, treated preferentially by them. While such complaints often take the form of gossip—"dirt" concerning *A Team* reporters—they cannot be completely dismissed as products of professional jealously. These tensions indicate the importance of the hierarchical stringer/staff system, an issue almost completely ignored by academic researchers despite the fact that it plays a fundamental role in structuring the activities of foreign correspondents and influences the news they write. The *A Team/B Team* structure is not only a question of professional status, but a political, economic, cultural, and ideological divide as well. Although the ratio of staff to stringers shifted over time, the dichotomous structure continued to be a fundamental part of SPECA life until the very end of the war.

The Embassy and the Press

As is true of U.S. foreign correspondence in general, the *A Team/ B Team* conflict was heavily influenced by the U.S. State Department. For SPECA reporters, the State Department is represented in the form of "The Embassy." Journalists speak of the U.S. mission, "The Embassy," as if there were no others in El Salvador. It is by far the single most important source of news for the U.S. press, and has a significant influence on the reporting of other nations' journalists as well.

SPECA journalists speak of The Embassy continually, many of them critical and resentful of its inevitable influence. Troy, an *A Team* journalist, said the following:

> Oh yeah, it is important in every way you can imagine. I can't think of another country, with the possible exception of Haiti, where the U.S. Embassy is anywhere near as important to a reporter.... I did a long interview with the Ambassador here, who compared himself with Henry Cabot Lodge in Vietnam as being this kind of guy who practically ran everything. I asked him what it was like to run everything. You would think that most diplomats would demure or say something to the contrary. [Ambassador] Walker, quite to the contrary, affirmed it, explaining how he was a guy who could pull a lot of strings here.

As the mouthpiece for U.S. policy, The Embassy is involved in almost every issue SPECA journalists cover.

Most editors demand that news stories include the perspectives, or at least the quoted statements, of official U.S. government sources. As a result of these pressures, intimate access to The Embassy is crucial to most SPECA journalists. Those who are able to get exclusive, quotable interviews with decision-making embassy staff have an advantage over their colleagues who must rely on the oblique, though ubiquitous, press hand-outs and infrequent embassy press conferences.

Cognizant of its worth to the SPECA community, The Embassy only provides interviews to certain reporters, namely those who can be trusted to use the information in a safe and sanctioned manner. Bob, a stringer who spent over seven years in El Salvador, explains:

> You get a certain access when you are a staff reporter for a major U.S.

paper that you don't get as a freelancer or someone who works for less prestigious papers.... Have you heard of the *A Team* and the *B Team*? It's very true. The Embassy will only invite certain people. The big boys will go to the little, intimate briefings. [U.S. Ambassador] Walker only does briefings with people that aren't going to disagree with him that much. They'll get more disagreements if [Ronald] or I are there. It's a question of them doing a triage with the most important papers they are trying to affect and those reporters with whom they get along best. It tends to work out that they get along better with those people because their minds are in the same place.

I interviewed two USIS press representatives, both of whom affirmed Bob's contention. The quote at the beginning of this chapter is extracted from one of those interviews.

I interviewed another State Department official, an amicable bureaucrat who said he earned a "grad level education in dealing with the press" while working in Panama during the 1989 U.S. invasion. He expressed a favorable view of staff correspondents:

They figure to be around a lot longer. They are less likely to burn you. They see people we can't and provide us with information. It is an exchange, a nice working relationship.

In other words, there is a coincidence of interests between The Embassy and the *A Team*. Given access to the valuable quotes of embassy decision-makers, *A Team* correspondents return the favor by allowing the State Department inordinate power to shape the news discourse (Herman and Chomsky 1988:18–25, Fishman 1980, Sigal 1986).

This professional "exchange" often develops into personal friendship. Pati, a Canadian reporter, explains that "it is impossible to isolate yourself and not identify with the people who you quote on a regular basis." Indeed, most USIS officials count several staff correspondents among their best friends, a natural outcome of their mutual "working relationship." (Sigal 1986:28)

USIS officials have a very different attitude towards stringers. "They are generally not as good," said one. "They are less prepared. They are trying to sell a story, which is more dangerous." The main "danger" he and his agency fear is that stringers will deal with State Department information in a critical, or at least idiosyncratic fashion. As information managers, they must carefully weigh the potential risks and benefits of providing access to journalists. For them the staffer/stringer dichotomy provides a convenient and fairly accurate guide for determining who can and cannot be trusted to represent State knowledge in sanctioned form. As will become clear in the following descriptions of each team, The Embassy's filtering process imbued the already contentious staffer/stringer structure with even greater cultural meaning.

A Team

Most SPECA staff journalists received their degrees from prestigious universities in the eastern United States or Britain, including Harvard, Cornell, Oxford, and Cambridge. Most of the *A Teams'* editors and sources were educated at similar institutions. President Christiani, for example, attended Harvard. Conversely, most stringers earned their degrees at public universities (Lichter et al. 1986:20–53).

The staff members identify themselves quite closely with their institutions. When asked to describe her past, Nell explained that she had attended "private schools in New England" before enrolling at a "good Ivy League university" and then, in fulfillment of her career plans, received a position at a "very prominent, large newspaper." Through her association with these "good" and "prominent" institutions, Nell has gained a greater sense of self worth, professional prestige, and inclusion in an elite clique. *A Team* journalists like Nell are cognizant, and sometimes even boastful of their institutional role in informing and influencing policy makers. Nell conceived of her work as an attempt to "bring these problems to life for an affluent, educated and possibly policy-making audience" (Bagdikian 1990:105–117, 195–207).

The *A Team* maintain constant contact with their editors and associate themselves closely with them (though a certain level of tension always exists between author and editor). Katherine, a staff correspondent, explains her relationship with her editors:

> Having been an editor, I think you are more inclined to write the story the way you think they are going to use it than trying to confront them, maybe
> …You get along better with them if you do that. It is self-defeating to fight them.

A Team journalists see editors as fellow professionals and ultimately part of the same team. Bob explained:

> Many journalists, if they tend to want to get ahead, basically will play along with the prejudices of their editors. Bit by bit they will learn to become like their editors. And, eventually, they will become their editors. The system rebuilds, re-cements, and re-propagates itself.

While stringers prefer to project an air of independence, the staff correspondents' professional identities are largely constructed in relation to their news institutions. Correspondents employed by the *New York Times*, for example, rarely refer to themselves as generic "journalists" or "foreign correspondents." Instead, a "*New York Times* correspondent" will almost always refer to herself as just that. This tendency is part of what other journalists call "the *New York Times* disease."

The "*New York Times* disease" also manifests itself in a sort of institutional solipsism. the *New York Times'* reporters enjoy quoting the behind-the-scenes maxim: "If the *Times* isn't there, it isn't news." This statement has a double meaning. On the surface it promotes the idea that the *New York Times* will cover all newsworthy events. Therefore, if something is not covered it is because the issue or event itself lacks intrinsic news value. That is not how the *New York Times* reporters use the phrase, however. For them, "If the *Times* isn't there, it isn't news," is a boastful and self-conscious realization that they, as an institution, play an instrumental role in defining the national, and sometimes international, news agenda. In a world of infinite issues and events, the *New York Times'* very presence often defines what is or isn't news. One reporter for the *New York Times* put it bluntly: "The *Times* has the attitude that if we weren't there, it didn't happen."

Rosenblum cites the example of the *New York Times'* R. W. Apple Jr., whose coverage of the war in Chad in the late 1960s caused the rest of the mainstream U.S. press to "catch up" on events there as well (1979:12). The European and African press had been writing about the Chadian conflict for several years, but the United States did not consider it a newsworthy story until Apple wrote of the war while touring Africa. In typical *Times* style, Apple boasted, "I discovered a war."

The *New York Times'* correspondents exhibited similar self-referential and agenda-setting tendencies in their coverage of the Salvadoran War. A parachuter for the *New York Times* interviewed FMLN Commander Jauquin Villalobos near the end of the war, portraying Villalobos' rather typical statements as a "striking departure" from the "Marxist rhetoric" of the past. Reporters more familiar with El Salvador were outraged. They knew Villalobos had been making such statements for several years (and that the FMLN was never simply a "Marxist" institution). Three days later another *New York Times* reporter contextualized Villalobos' statements in the "striking departure" frame as well. I asked why and he replied:

> There is a very clear reason. It had been on the front page of the *New York Times* two or three days earlier…[Jauquin Villalobos] could have been saying it for five years, but until it is in the *New York Times*, nobody believes it. The *Times* makes a story…Christiani even said that the only thing new [about Villalobos' statement] is that it appeared in the *New York Times*. He said that at a press conference. Which is true. The *Times'* editors are funny. They take the attitude, "Well, we don't necessarily have to be first. The important thing is that when we have it, then it is important."

In other words, the ideological shift may have not been a recent, nor even major change, but once printed in the *New York Times* it became reality.[1] Because the first *Times* correspondent had written in the "striking departure" frame, the second felt an obligation to do likewise. It had become *Times*-sanctioned truth.

The "*New York Times* disease," a virulent hubris more common than its label implies, manifests itself in additional ways. According to the stringers, staff correspondents "feel like they are purely objective, sort of above it all." They are "above it all," literally. Most of them live in the Escalon, a wealthy residential and shopping district which lies along the raised shelf leading up to Volcan San Salvador. The place is closer to Miami than the slums of San Salvador.

Their geographic isolation is matched by even greater social distance. The *A Team* members rarely mix with middle and lower class Salvadorans. "Those people who make it through the hoops and become staff," explained a stringer, "tend to be people who also get along better with other conservative people in the Salvadoran establishment." As usual, Paul put it more bluntly:

> They are married into the class system.... They live in scrumptious mansions just like the [U.S.]AID people, among the oligarchy. They have no contact with other classes, except their maids.[2]

This may be overstated. Not all staff journalists live in "scrumptious mansions." Furthermore, the *A Team*'s frenetic parachuting schedule is rarely as pleasant as the stringers contend. "I'm sick of living in hotels," complained Katherine, "It is hard on your health. I'm gaining weight."

Nevertheless, stringers perceive of *A Team* life as culturally distant and materially ideal. In their indignation, SPECA stringers not only demonstrate a strong disdain for *A Team* behavior, however, they also implicitly make a claim towards greater involvement with, and understanding of, the Salvadoran masses.

B Team

Staff and stringers are usually drawn to El Salvador for different reasons. Bob explains:

> Freelancers (stringers) tend to be in a country they like. They are interested in it and what is going on, whereas a staff correspondent may be put here when he wants to go to Paris. El Salvador is a stepping-stone for where he wants to go later in life.

Indeed, the two highest profile *A Team* correspondents were constantly complaining about their assignment.

Conversely, stringers choose their posts themselves (although there must be a market for their work). Thus, they "tend to be in a country they like." Several SPECA stringers were first drawn to El Salvador for non-journalistic reasons, such as human rights work, development, or tourism. Marla's first exposure to Central America came in college, where she met several Nicaraguans. A trip to Central America sparked an interest for Marla which "continued through to today." "You have to go where your personal *ganas* (desire) is," said Marla, "I think that ultimately it makes more sense to cover the story that you find most engaging, as opposed to a career decision." Others left positions at small market domestic newspapers in order to work internationally.

The stringers' interest in and dedication to Central America is so pervasive that many have lingered well beyond news editors' interest in the story. Cary is one of these. According to a housemate, every month for the last several years Cary has threatened to leave El Salvador for a more marketable story. Nevertheless, he remains with his community of Salvadoran friends and SPECA colleagues.

B Team reporters work, live, and play together. Cary described recreational life in the *B Team* community:

> We go out for meals in the evenings, sometimes with a group of other journalists. We go to the beach. In this household we [stringers] tend to go out and eat a lot together; go out and do things together with Shawn and other people. Yeah, it's quite a small community. We go play basketball together with some of the church people. The Mennonites are demons on the basketball court.

I occasionally accompanied the stringers in their recreational activities, including attending parties, watching sporting events, and mostly, sitting around the kitchen chatting. One Sunday morning, for example, I worked on the *New York Times* crossword puzzle with a few stringers (we failed miserably, despite the fact one was a *Times* stringer).

The *B Team* community is not only a professional collective, but a social and recreational network as well. As Cary's quote implies, the *B Team* community overlaps with other expatriate groups, such as the Mennonite "demons." While *A Team* journalists mainly hang out with local and foreign elites, the stringers tend to socialize with a slightly more diverse group including church workers, human rights activists, members of international solidarity groups, and a few local intellectuals.[3] These groups, like the stringers themselves, tend to have liberal to left political views.

While most of the stringers come to the country with liberal views, others gravitate toward those perspectives after dealing with the Salvadoran army and government. Tracy, a fixer, claimed that Cal, a wire service reporter, was more conservative than she because he had "only been in the country for a year." According to this popularly held view, the more time reporters spend in El Salvador the more liberal their political perspectives generally become. Michael, an *A Team* magazine correspondent, explained:

> Because stringers get to know a place so well they tend to become a little bit more liberal. A correspondent flies in and he's much more detached. I tend to have a much more—not conservative—but detached attitude. He [the stringer] sees all the abuse and so isn't so detached…. The service stringer's sell is familiarity. Complete familiarity can lead to pretty strong emotions

towards the story. The [staff] correspondent flits in and out.

In sum, a combination of factors—motivation, experience, and social environment—conspires to provide stringers with a more liberal outlook than their higher-status colleagues.

Although the stringers' personal politics tend to be more liberal, however, their news reports do not generally contain liberal biases.[4] Stringers must conform to the political and editorial wills of their clients. Bureaucratic exigencies and restrictive journalistic conventions generally prevail over individual politics. For this reason, they feel much more freedom when writing occasional pieces for alternative press organizations such as the *Village Voice, The Nation, The Progressive* and other institutions whose editorial politics mesh much more closely with their own. Unfortunately, these institutions cannot afford to pay very well and constitute a very small part of the overall news market.

Sometimes the difference between the two teams is not just *how*, but even *what* they see. An FMLN soldier flagged down a press vehicle during one pack outing. He exhorted the journalists—one staff correspondent and several stringers—to take an injured child to the hospital. The stringers were later surprised when the staffer wrote: "[A] mother carried her nine-year-old daughter in her arms, pleading with passing cars for a ride to a medical clinic." He was evidently unwilling to present an image editors might construe as favorable to the FMLN. He had to construct a more suitable reality.

Reporters who wish to rise in the press hierarchy must learn that sort of editorial discipline. The stringers are, for the most part, young reporters who will either leave the profession, gain one of the relatively few, underpaid positions in the alternative press, or become staffers themselves. Unfortunately, it is difficult for a stringer to become staff. "Having been a stringer actually hurts you," explained Adriana, "because you haven't been under the editor's constant eye."

For reporters, "the editor's constant eye" forms an inescapable center. Editors exercise control over their charges' postings, their writings, public exposure, and career-chances. For these and other reasons, editors can depend on staffers to perform their duties with relative compliance. Stringers, however, develop their craft slightly outside the boundaries of any single institution's gaze or disciplinary regime. This makes them "dangerous" and "subjective," two words often applied to stringers by the U.S. and Canadian editors I interviewed.

Nevertheless, it is occasionally possible for stringers to shed their stigmatized status and become staff correspondents. However, most stringers must greatly modify their writings, if not their attitudes, before making this upward leap. Capitalist enterprises, corporate media included, must make a profit to survive. Certain basic social conditions are necessary for the creation of profit, including a stable and easily controlled work force, access to cheap and plentiful resources, and high consumer demand. Generally speaking, the further right one goes on the western political spectrum, the greater the emphasis upon political programs that foster such conditions. Left political ideals—including conceptions of workers' rights, sustainable ecological systems, and non-consumerist values—are often, quite correctly, seen as anti-profit and anti-corporate points of view. Therefore, corporate media institutions, or at least the most influential functionaries therein (owners, management, editors) tend to embrace moderate capitalist ideals, while strongly rejecting leftist values. Reporters who either directly support or consistently fail to question the goals of the corporate system, have a much greater chance of success than those who, even occasionally, construct news stories with the potential to subvert the profit paradigm. U.S. governmental leaders have traditionally had the profit maximization of American corporations in mind when developing U.S. foreign policy toward Central America (Diskin 1983:xv–xxxv, Chomsky and Herman 1979:53–60, Gettleman et al 1986:9,12). A young reporter seeking success in the corporate press would be unwise to present significant challenge to either U.S. foreign policy, or to the U.S. corporations that control much of Central America. These institutional and political economic exigencies form a countervailing force to the "liberalizing" effects of life in the stringer community.

As a result of these pressures, stringers must usually move right to move up. Therefore, most stringers-turned-staff have been accused by other stringers of having modified their reporting in order to advance, of "selling out." Four ex-stringers were most often cited as examples, including two stringers-turned-staff for the *New York Times*, one *Washington Post* correspondent and a *Miami Herald* correspondent. "They began blaming the FMLN for everything," complained one of the stringers left behind, perhaps an unfair characterization, although their reporting certainly became more conservative after they made the transition from stringer to staff.

Stringers who submit reports to alternative press are particularly stigmatized by corporate media, even though it comprises a small part of their overall news output. Ronald, an intense and intelligent young stringer who writes regularly for alternative media, was rejected for a staff job at a U.S. daily for this very reason. The offending editor told Ronald he greatly respected his work, but that it was too "left-wing." "It is apparent that if performers are concerned with maintaining a line," argues Goffman, "they will select as teammates those who can be trusted to perform properly" (1959:91). The *A Team* and their bosses find Ronald's performance anything but proper.

The *A Team* correspondents vehemently disagree with the *B Team's* contention that ideological criteria are used in the staff hiring process. Troy explained:

Papers don't choose to send people here based on ideological disposition. I was never asked about politics. I was not involved in Latin American politics. I didn't speak Spanish. I considered myself innocent. Nobody could accuse me of anything.

This is probably true. The gatekeepers have little need to ask people like Troy about their politics. Politically moderate and compliant, Troy fits the needs of his news institution quite well. The hiring system acts as an ideological thermostat, allowing consenting and compliant reporters like Troy to enter while keeping dissenters like Ronald standing outside the company gates. In short, media corporations regulate their workforce, as must any successful corporation or governmental bureaucracy.

The Language of Team Competition

"All the agents in a given social formation share a set of basic perceptual schemes," explains Bourdieu, "which receive the beginnings of objectification in the pairs of antagonistic adjectives commonly used to classify and qualify persons or objects" (1984:468). This "network of oppositions" (high/low, unique/common, etc.) explains Bourdieu, "is the matrix of all the commonplaces which find such ready acceptance because behind them lies the whole of the social order" (468). Similarly, the A and B teams share a set of "antagonistic adjectives" ("antagonism" in this case meaning both binary opposition and actual hostility) through which they define each other, themselves, and their shared cultural/linguistic system.

Stringers usually categorize reporters in terms of employment status: "staff" vs. "stringers." On occasion, they refer to themselves as "independent journalists" or "freelancers," however, inverting the social order by invoking the journalistic ethic of independence. Conversely, this infers that staff are *dependent* upon and constrained by the institutions to which they belong.

When among their own, stringers often use the *A Team* label when referring to staffers, demonstrating both their hostility towards, and recognition of the status system that links the two teams into a single, albeit contested culture. Conversely, I never heard a staff correspondent use the terms *A Team/B Team*, although those terms were originally invented by a stringer-turned-staff reporter.

Staffers reserve the title "correspondent" for themselves, while labeling *B Team* journalists "stringers" or "part-timers." Through their appropriation of the generic term "correspondent," staff journalists accord themselves a much greater sense of importance while denigrating the stringer "part-timers" as less serious professionals. "Within the journalist community there is a pecking order," explained Janice. "They [staffers] think that they are the serious ones." The *A Team*'s terminology reflects this sense of superiority. An American news magazine journalist referred to a group of competing grant applicants as "just stringers, not professionals."

When asked to name the best reporters in Central America, staffers almost always cited fellow *A Team* journalists. Ironically, when asked to name the best articles written during the Salvadoran war, most *A Team* journalists cited those written by or in conjunction with stringers and free-lancers.[5] In abstract they think of themselves as the finest, if not the only, journalists working in the region. When asked to produce evidence of excellence, however, most could only remember work produced outside their exclusive clique.

For the most part, staffers ignored the existence of stringers, especially during our interviews. When making the point that journalists were quickly leaving El Salvador, a staff correspondent stated, "The *Miami Herald* doesn't have anyone here." "The *Herald* still has a stringer," I corrected him. "In fact, he has been receiving a byline." "Yeah, but they used to have a *correspondent*," replied the staffer. From the perspective of most *A Team* reporters, stringers simply do not count.

The *A Team*'s disregard is strongly contested. I received a serious rebuke from the aforementioned *Miami Herald* stringer when I asked him to compare "stringers vs. correspondents." He interrupted, angered by my juxtaposition of the terms "stringer" and "correspondent." "We are the real correspondents," he explained, "We are *permanently* stationed in El Salvador, 'corresponding' rather than parachuting." The stringer ridiculed staffers for their exclusive claim to the generic title. He called forth the mythical figure of Earnest Hemingway, the archetypal foreign correspondent-freelancer, iconic evidence that one need not be staff in order to earn the title "foreign correspondent."

To summarize, at different times and for different reasons stringers would invert the social order by elevating themselves to the prized status of "independent" journalists, level the field by referring to all reporters as "correspondents," or mock the rigid hierarchical arrangement using the *A Team/B Team* terminology. Normally, these expressions of group antagonism remained behind team lines, given public display only when SPECA debated critical problems like the salvoconducto system. On rare occasions, however, certain stringers have issued these complaints in public forums. *A Team* journalists were especially angered by an article Ronald published in the alternative press. Ronald criticized his higher status colleagues for having been out of the country during the start of the November 1989 FMLN offensive. He argued that the staff correspondents' physical absence served as evidence of journalistic complacency and effete distance from the conflict. As a result, Ronald was greatly admired by other stringers and universally disliked by the *A Team*. Many *A Team* journalists registered their contempt for the renegade reporter by using him as a negative example in discussions of press professionalism, repeatedly and purposely mispronouncing his last name.

Such name plays were common. Paul, a photographer who lived and worked alongside the *B Team*, played the same name-mutilation game as Ronald's detractors. Paul purposefully, and playfully, mispronounced the names of two *A Team* reporters whom he and his colleagues held in extremely low regard. He would often modify an *A Team* correspondent's name in such a way that it resembled a disliked government official (the matter of anonymity is unfortunate here, because some of the name-plays are quite clever). This playful manipulation of names elevates inter-team contempt from the level of personal dislike to that of professional disregard. To mangle a competitor's name is to trivialize her life's work. "In reporting," explains Shawn, "your name is all you've got." The byline is a precious commodity.

Motivated by this ongoing, if normally covert conflict, *B Team* reporters were constantly giving me "dirt" on *A Team* reporters. I told one that my goal was not to create an exposé, however, but instead a serious study of SPECA. I explained that I was not out to "burn" anyone. "You should," he replied. My work and presence became yet another site of symbolic contestation between the teams.

Interdependence and Ideological Control

Despite their mutual antagonism, *A* and *B Team* journalists are heavily interdependent. A great deal of international news is produced via their collaborative efforts. Most staff journalists rely heavily upon stringers for knowledge of ongoing events and to make contacts among sectors not readily accessible to their parachuting practice. "I am a correspondent," explained Michael, "but I rely on the stringer that lives here. He lives and breathes it."

The stringers provide their labor and knowledge to staffers in exchange for money, institutional resources (an office and secretary), and an opportunity to reach wider audiences. Paul, a veteran photographer, equated these relationships to international oil dependencies. Like oil-bearing, Third World nations, stringers need cash. Like First World industrial powers, staff correspondents need the reporting "resources" stringers possess: contacts, knowledge, and reporting skills.

Cary aids a parachuting staffer. Whenever his staff patron flies in, Cary provides him with an update, arranges necessary contacts among nongovernmental sectors (i.e., the FMLN or popular organizations) and provides logistical aid. Like most stringers, Cary feels inadequately compensated for his hard work and expertise.

Cary occasionally publishes his own articles in his staff patron's newspaper. He feels exploited in this role as well. As evidence, Cary displayed his check stubs. Most of the payments ranged between $25 and $80 per story. Cary held up one $60 stub, total recompense for an article that took several days of work. Such meager compensation is the norm. Stringers receive an average of $150.00 for each 900 word report. This is practically nothing when compared to a staff correspondent's salary, which is usually well over $50,000 a year. Distance and dispassion certainly have their rewards.

Shawn often collaborated with staff correspondents. He had a reputation for considerable knowledge, writing talent, and connections among FMLN and grass-roots opposition groups. Shawn's relationship with a severely challenged, yet highly placed staff reporter allowed him to have significant influence upon the reporting of a prominent national newspaper. It was rather easy to identify which elements of each story were written by Shawn, and which were written or distilled by his staff patron. Shawn's staff collaborator, a product of nepotism, had very poor writing skills and relatively little knowledge of Spanish. Despite his invaluable aid, however, Shawn received little credit or compensation.

A desire to reach larger audiences compels stringers to enter into these relationships despite the lack of financial and professional compensation. A *New York Times* staff correspondent boldly admitted having plagiarized one of Ronald's news reports, making the unrepentant admission in front of Ronald himself. Nevertheless, Ronald did nothing about it. He was angered by the theft, but glad to see his material reach a wider audience, regardless of attribution.

Usually, these inter-team relationships force stringers to work within more constrictive ideological parameters. By joining forces with staffers, they submit themselves to the same bureaucratic forces that control the *A Team*'s work, including more frequent contact with editors. The stringers are tempted to modify their work in order to get it past the editorial gatekeepers. The U.S. helicopter-downing article quoted in the Introduction is an example of such accommodation.

Another example is a report two stringer/staffer collaborators wrote about the death squads. The stringer discovered the basic facts of the story after being approached by an ex-assassin. He then completed most of the investigative work and constructed a compelling model of how the death squads were operating (and continue to operate). In order to get the story accepted and published, however, he felt compelled to join with a staff correspondent, a man whom other stringers referred to as an "Embassy reporter," claiming that he "dulled" the story. Conversely, staffers discussed the collaborative effort as if the stringer had little or nothing to do with it, giving almost full credit to their own teammate.

The *A Team* collaborator has since gone on to make a big name for himself, while the stringer is still just that. In this way, staff correspondents often accumulate professional capital from the unaccredited and under compensated labor of stringers. Deflated by a piece of shrapnel received during a mortar attack and a set of media clients who were stonewalling on payment of his medical bills, a tired stringer summarized the *B Team* plight: "Stringers are so exploited, Mark."

The Political Control of SPECA

As several reporters mentioned, SPECA is like a family. And like most families it is based on a contradictory structure of conflict and cooperation, its alliances shifting in response to the particular questions and interests of the moment. The patriarch of the corps-family is the SPECA president. Until 1992, the president had always been drawn from the *A Team*. During much of my research, the president was a bureau chief for a large international wire service based in the U.S. His predecessor was a U.S. staff correspondent, his successor a young British staffer.

Many stringers resented the *A Team's* effective control of SPECA. They accused successive presidents of using their position for advantage, creating and fostering important contacts under the auspices of SPECA business. One SPECA president confirmed this accusation. "The only advantage of being president of SPECA," he explained one day over lunch, "is the closer contact you get with important people." At the time, he was negotiating press access with Col. Carlos Amando Aviles Buitrago, head of the Salvadoran military's psychological operations unit and a key figure in the Jesuit murder case. After the SPECA negotiations had concluded, however, he wished to "have a beer with Aviles" in the hope of getting inside information about the UCA massacre. Not surprisingly, the president in question was also pushing a cautious line in the SPECA debate over press access. This was precisely the sort of accommodation and opportunism SPECA stringers suspected and resented.

The inter-team tensions were most pronounced during debates over the salvoconducto system. A particularly stormy debate took place February 5, 1991, shortly after several reporters were detained by the Salvadoran Army and refused access to FMLN-held territories. As usual, Bart (*A Team*) spoke most forcefully for the cautious position, while Bob (*B Team*) took the lead in arguing for more vigorous action on the part of the association. "We are not covering the war," said Bob, "we need to cover what is happening inside the country."

Bart, urging caution, suggested they write letters of protest to U.S. Embassy and Salvadoran military officials. Bob complained they would only get "pretty words" in return. Referring to similar, failed strategies in the past, Bob complained that governmental officials would only appear to compromise, sign documents, and then "do nothing," adding, "I don't believe in the American Embassy." Bob and others wanted SPECA's blessing to write about the salvoconducto system and urged the organization to take out *campo pagados* (paid advertisements in local papers) condemning the press controls.

Bart presented his position as the more "realistic" of the two. He pointed out that the U.S. military was doing the very same thing in the Persian

Gulf, employing highly restrictive rules to control press coverage. Bart argued the U.S. actions gave SPECA very little leverage when arguing for a loosening of restrictions in El Salvador. Bart's Salvadoran staff members agreed with his cautious position.

Shawn played upon Bart's realist language, agreeing that SPECA should "recognize reality," but adding, "We should also recognize that reality in public."

To the stringers' proposal—which Bart characterized as the "extreme position"—the *A Team* and their Salvadoran employees replied, "We are not a union." To the proposition that SPECA should publicize their opposition to the restrictions, Bart replied "It is not our job to hold press conferences." Although several trusted Salvadoran allies would soon turn on the *A Team* (see chapter 14), they backed the cautious line in this case, just as they had throughout the war. The Salvadorans were frustrated by the incessant debate, an unresolved argument they had sat through time and again at SPECA meetings. "It's always the same thing," whispered Elicia.

Corps relations and alliances were changing, however, as the war came to an end. As SPECA shrunk, the few remaining *A Team* journalists began mixing more with stringers in both work and recreational settings. Information and reporting decisions were being shared more frequently across team boundaries. The wire service bureau chiefs—who have always occupied a somewhat intermediate role between the two teams—began to spend most of their time with the dwindling pool of stringers. They no longer had the option of hanging out with *A Team* reporters, most of whom were no longer in El Salvador on a permanent basis.

The bureau chiefs and parachuting *A Team* journalists nevertheless continued to fulfill leadership roles, making decisions that filtered down through the entire corps. More than once, Bart was the ad hoc arbiter of newsworthiness. His decisions whether or not to attend particular events often influenced the stringers' reporting schedules, as did the parachute agenda of visiting staff. Despite their greater numbers, stringers continued to reluctantly follow in the wake of *A Team* reporting.

DISCIPLINE AND PUBLISH

"You cannot bash in the head of an American citizen without written permission from the State Department."

—Woody Allen in *Bananas*

In this chapter I will deal with the two most powerful institutional influences in the work of SPECA journalists: news organizations and the U.S. Embassy. My purpose is to provide a more complete understanding of the ways in which these and allied structures discipline journalistic labor.

According to a "Western Diplomat"

The U.S. State Department imposes strict guidelines of attribution that reporters must follow faithfully, or lose access to Embassy staff. These rules were explained to me in detail by a USIS Attaché. The first rule is that all interviews must be conducted under the rubric of "deep background." Under these conditions, quotes cannot be attributed directly to the source. In news reports, such information is preceded by phrases like "It is generally understood that…" or "It is widely believed…" Following the terms of deep background, the specific words of the State Department are posited as the general opinion of local society.

After conducting an interview, journalists may negotiate on a quote by quote basis to move information into the category of "background." Under the rules of background attribution, the source may be cited as "Western diplomat." Under that guise, actual quotations may be reproduced. Therefore, journalists always hope to be accorded the privilege of "background" status.

Background attribution assumes less generality. A "Western diplomat" is an actual person rather than an amorphous social collective as implied by the phrase, "It is widely believed." A greater sense of authority and credibility is implied in the expert testimony of a "Western diplomat." The great majority of statements attributed to "Western diplomats" in the U.S. press come directly from the State Department.

Beyond deep background and background, there is "on the record." Few journalists are granted this right to direct attribution and, once again, only on a quote by quote basis. The Embassy staffers reserve the right to choose which statements will actually be attributed to themselves. It is uncommon for a journalist outside the most trusted circle of *A Team* reporters to be accorded the privilege of directly quoting an interviewed Embassy official.

In our initial interviews, I asked journalists what readers should know in order to better understand the news coverage of El Salvador. Several cited the State Department rules of attribution. Bob answered:

> People should know about the incredible involvement of the U.S. Embassy and how, when they read a mainstream story and it says "Western diplomat," that three out of four times, or probably higher, that is going to be a U.S. official who has deliberately spoken on the record on *background* so he doesn't have to take responsibility for his views. Yet, he allows you to use his views under the rubric "Western diplomat," which gives the impression that the source is a non involved person—just a detached, objective diplomat who is speaking—when in fact it is someone who is a major player.

Stringers were not alone in complaining about Embassy influence. After volunteering that "a diplomat close to the [Salvadoran] government" quoted in one of her articles was in fact Ambassador "Bill" Walker, Katherine admitted she does "not like using The Embassy people that much." Unfortunately, she finds them "impossible to avoid in El Salvador, because they are key players" who are "running a war." She certainly did not frame the U.S. functionaries as "running a war" when writing news, however. In fact, she did not frame them at all. Their identities remained safely hidden behind misleading attributions, while their ideas framed the presentation of news subjects, like the FMLN.[1]

Despite their discomfort with the practice, reporters work extremely hard to obtain "inside" Embassy quotes, no matter how prefabricated and banal they may be (Sigal 1986:22, Smith 1980:64). The main reason journalists tolerate The Embassy's restrictive the rules of attribution, opacity, and obstructionism is the editors' preference, if not requirement, that official U.S. government positions be included in most news reports. Shawn explains:

> The "Western diplomat" attribution allows State Department officials to present themselves and present information in people's stories as if it is coming from a disinterested party; when, in the case of El Salvador, they are not disinterested (laugh).... Usually it is a case that you just need a quote. The fact of the matter is that you sometimes do it for editors.

As a result of this editorial pressure, SPECA reporters will print the words of State Department officials even when they know the information is inaccurate.[2] In 1938, *St. Louis Post-Dispatch* editor Oliver K. Bovard explained (Mott 1952:85):

> Here is a lie. I know it is a lie, but I must print it because it is spoken by a prominent public official. The public official's name and position make the lie news. Were the source some unknown person, I could and would gladly throw it in the wastebasket.

If editors feel that they "must" print such falsehoods, then reporters are obligated to do the same. Reporters are "tempted not to quote them," explained Paul, "but the editors won't run it."

The rules of objectivity, as currently conceived, further constrict the reporters' ability to qualify or contextualize the State Department frame. On several occasions the State Department charged FMLN guerrillas with carrying out or inventing atrocities which were, in reality, the work of the military or their closely affiliated death squads. This was The Embassy's strategy, for example, after the El Mozote massacre, UCA assassinations, and murder of Herbert Anaya Sanabria, President of the non-governmental Human Rights Commission.[3] Most reporters recognized The Embassy claims as propaganda, having heard the same false and diversionary charges in the past. They were unable to present that historical qualification, however, when reporting the recycled Embassy assertions, since that would be seen as "editorializing." This duplicitous process of editorial, state, and narrative disciplines creates a "string," in the words of a U.S. journalist working in Honduras, which "runs from the Administration and State Department through almost all news coverage."

Those willing to offend The Embassy have come under sharp attack from what Bob calls "the sleazy tactics" of the State Department. The Ambassador and his staff have made repeated calls to the top editors of newspapers for which Bob has submitted reports, and have even spoken with his publisher. Bob explains the effects of this flak:

> It weakens your credibility, especially if you are a stringer. The publication listens to this supposedly authoritative and professional State Department functionary calling up and saying, "Your reporter has made a whole bunch of mistakes and his reporting is tendentious and biased."

This is one reason reporters feel compelled to represent elite sources in a favorable light. Another is their need to maintain privileged access. "Journalists start to get into bed with their sources," explained Bob, "They have to start treating their sources in a respectful and non-confrontational manner to keep them."

For the same reasons, "other" Western diplomats are rarely quoted in U.S. news reports. I was chatting with a British stringer before the start of the Jesuit massacre trial when one of his compatriots, Charge d'Affaires Ian Murray, approached and greeted him by name. The stringer asked Murray for his impression of the trial. Without pause, the British official stated: "The trial doesn't mean anything. It does nothing to challenge the military or the government. It is just a show for the Americans." Murray was an outspoken critic of U.S. involvement in El Salvador, representing European antipathy for U.S. hegemony in Latin America.

Such views rarely appeared in U.S. news reports, however, even though they were spoken by "Western diplomats." The reporters were hesitant to violate the "Western Diplomat" rule—the appropriated space of the State Department—for fear of losing future access. Only those who were already disenfranchised from The Embassy and relatively free from editorial pressure could afford to violate this system of corporate, state, and narrative structures.

Brenda
"One answer to the problem of how to treat reporters is to treat them frequently."
—F.H. Brennan, *St. Louis Dispatch*

Brenda was SPECA's main State Department contact. As head of operations for USIS in El Salvador, Brenda managed to keep abreast of the journalists' work, maintaining a constant dialogue with staff and stringers alike. And she was in charge of propagating the official point of view of U.S. foreign policy or, at least, reducing the threat of challenges to that perspective.

Shari described an incident in which a television correspondent was influenced by Brenda's well trained tongue. The correspondent experienced the aftermath of a massacre. Salvadoran witnesses claimed the murders had been committed by the Salvadoran army. Nevertheless, Brenda managed to talk the journalist out of reporting the event as a massacre. She so disoriented the hapless parachuter with questions and assertions that he no longer felt comfortable describing it as a massacre or placing blame on the military. It became the word of Salvadoran witnesses versus that of a U.S. official. Following Brenda's interrogation, the correspondent ascribed the murders to El Salvador's nebulous "culture of violence," rather than the military unit fingered by eye witnesses.

The "culture of violence" thesis is particularly popular among parachuters and others with little familiarity of the social, political, economic, and cultural realities of El Salvador. Excerpts from a 1980 NBC report illustrate this frame (Anderson 1988:240):

> In the tortured country of El Salvador the violence and killing continue everyday, and it's random and senseless.
>   The Mayhem in El Salvador is all the more chilling because people never really know where it's coming from....

Similarly, one of my *A Team* subjects argued that "extreme violence is part of [the Salvadoran's] national character." She blames much of the killing on "rumor, cruelty, and ignorance" among the "largely illiterate" rural population. Within such a frame, acts of extreme violence appear insensate and the institutions which utilize terror are made to seem mere epiphenomenal by-products of the society's savage proclivities. The "culture of violence" is a vector of terror unrelated to political, economic, or international relations of domination (Hallin 1983:30–32).

Brenda's job was to foster such a frame. She was charged with the difficult task of placing her institution and the allied regime in a neutral middle space, a buffer between the horrific violence of the extreme left and right, the guerrillas and the death squads (Cooper 1986:32). The U.S. and its allies were represented as a unified force struggling to develop a civil society amongst the violence of outlaw extremists—a civilizing force in a primitive land.

Brenda was a constant fixture in the lives of the SPECA journalists. They spoke often of conversations with her. Shawn described one such exchange. Speaking with Brenda, Shawn compared the FMLN executions of U.S. military advisers and similar cases involving the murder of FMLN combatants. According to Shawn, Brenda then "hit the ceiling," screaming, "C'mon Shawn, you can't seriously be comparing that!" That was Brenda's job. She was the nagging voice of the State Department. While Ambassador Walker produced official public decrees, Brenda propagated doubt, insecurity, and a incessant stream of petty, behind-the-scenes flak.

"Editors Suck"
The rules of journalistic conduct are less formalized than those of other professions. There is no job description, formalized rules of conduct, written code of ethics, nor body through which a professional journalist becomes certified as such.[4] Journalists consider formal rules to be overly confining, and thus prefer to remain in a liminal professional category. What is lost in prestige and formal standards is recouped in professional autonomy, or at least a sense thereof.

This lack of formalized rules and conventions allows journalists to pretend, in abstract consideration, that there are none at all. Thus reporters often speak of their professional practices as if they have been individually designed from scratch, *ad hoc* creations developed outside of constraint or convention. While reporters often noted the severe limitations faced by colleagues, most claimed to have a great deal of autonomy in their own work. My initial interviews provided a space within which reporters felt free to present themselves in this autonomous frame, much as they do when speaking with each other and when writing autobiographical texts like those discussed in chapter 1. It was only in subsequent interviews, when I asked them to explain contradictions between their reports, their stated views, and actual practice, that journalists began to speak of the numerous people, institutions, and conventions that influenced their reporting. When faced with discrepancies in verbal, practical, and textual representation, most placed the blame on their editors.

Reporters conduct their work within extremely hierarchical bureaucracies (Gans 1979:83–87). Most of them are at the bottom of their respective organizations, beneath ascending levels of editors, managers, and owners. The field reporter must constantly defer to her immediate and ever-present boss, the editor. The professional promise of freedom—the cherished sense (and pretense) of autonomy—is contradicted in practice by realities of constraint and control.

Such is the recipe for frustration. These frustrations are most often projected upon the editor, the most obvious and immediate symbol of institutional discipline. Youthful reporters, those who have not completely acquiesced to the disciplines of mainstream press work, are particularly vigilant in fighting to maintain a space, however small, within which they may retain a sense of professional autonomy. It is the job of editors to collapse that space, to facilitate the assimilation of institutional ideology into the individual journalist's regimen. As a result, all reporters share a degree of antipathy towards editors.

Photographers exhibit a particularly strong distaste for them. Joe summarized his colleagues complaints: "Editors suck." Print journalists, while slightly more forgiving, are equally critical toward their editors. Shawn had this to say:

> The only good editor is a dead editor. It's like the lion and jaguar; they are
> the natural competition and enemy, even if they are a good editor. If you
> write something bad it is in your name, even if it is their fault.

Although they are less resistant to editorial influence and less in need of ideological correction, *A Team* correspondents nevertheless resent editorial control. Katherine complains that there are "some editors up there without much experience." One day, as if to confirm her claim, an editor called Katherine before eight o'clock in the morning to ask which story she would be covering that day. Katherine reminded him of the time difference, and said she would need a little more to find out what was going on. Not surprisingly, journalists often referred to editorial oversight as "harassment."

Wire services are especially editor-heavy (Rosenblum 1979:113). The wire service reporter not only has to deal with the local bureau chief, but also the regional editor in Mexico City, editors in New York, and finally, the publishers and editors of client institutions throughout the world. Wire reporters must write with all of these editorial levels in mind. A reporter who started his career with the Associated Press described the results of working underneath these multiple layers of filtering agents: "Working for the wire services you are just putting out stories you think editors might like." This is one reason why newspapers often hire wire service journalists. They are properly disciplined.

The most widely distributed U.S. news magazines are equally "editor-heavy." The editing process at *Newsweek* is typical. First, editors meet to decide which stories to pursue. Then, reporters, many of them stringers, provide appropriate copy to a desk editor in New York. Finally, the desk editor writes a news story using whatever aspects of the field reports he chooses, fitting the story into what editors and reporters alike call "Newsweekspeak."

Reporters and stringers are often frustrated by their lack of influence over news magazine articles. Jerry became quite angry when a news-magazine editor chose to represent the Jesuit murder trial as a "breakthrough." Jerry, who covered the trial and contributed information for the report, saw the event in a completely different light. The infuriated stringer asked his editor how the trial could be seen as a breakthrough when the judge had felt compelled to flee the country afterwards, seven of the nine defendants had been set free, and the probable intellectual authors of the crime were never even investigated. The editor's supercilious response: "You can't have everything now, can you?"

Terrence worked for a U.S. newsmagazine he called "notorious for the limited autonomy it affords to the people in the field." I asked Terrence if he had been kept from writing about certain issues for political reasons. "Oh yes, often," he replied, "I think everyone dealt with that. I dealt with it a little bit more because I was on staff.... My editors here didn't really care about helping me balance out what I would cover. They somewhat capriciously assigned which stories I would cover. I think that operationally I was handicapped."

Editors not only edit reports, but also decide proper placement for articles, anywhere from "Column One" to the back pages, where the story may be dwarfed by a Macy's ad. Editors often reject a reporter's work altogether. Likewise, editors influence the journalists' daily reporting agendas and geographic distribution as they cast their institutional "news net" across the world (Tuchman 1978:15–38). In addition to all of these functions, editors keep in constant contact with their correspondents, suggesting stories and discussing news concepts. They are not only "gate-keepers" (White 1950) but "overseers" as well. Editors not only filter out unwanted materials from the news hole, but actively involve themselves in the reporting process as well. "I tell the editor that *this, this*, and *this* is going on," explains Janice, "and he says that he wants *that*."

Occasionally, editors will even go so far as to request specific quotes. For example, in 1991 Jerry was called by a major U.S. news magazines to get an FMLN statement regarding their "sudden" move from Marxism. Jerry gave the editor a quick history lesson, explaining that the guerrillas had been making such comments since 1986, and had never simply been a Marxist movement. He offered to go back into his file and pull out a quote from past years regarding the FMLN's ideological tenets and trans-formations. The magazine editor was not concerned with history, how-ever. Other institutions, in particular the *New York Times*, were publishing stories about the FMLN's presumed ideological sea change. Therefore, Jerry's editor felt obligated to do likewise. Nevertheless, Jerry refused. He was among a small clique of stringers who repeatedly subverted their chances for advancement through small acts of institutional and ideolog-ical noncompliance. Such experiences have motivated Jerry to believe that "If you die they will say that you were the greatest. If not, you get no respect from editors. They don't give a shit."

Editors also perform the difficult task of writing headlines. Headlines are an extremely influential framing device that summarize, contextual-ize, and even replace news reports as hurried readers breeze through the morning paper. Reporters are often angered by headlines. For example, an editor entitled one of Shawn's articles, "HOPES RISE IN EL SAL-VADOR," even though the article clearly argued *against* an optimistic view of the negotiations. Furthermore, the article was edited in a manner that favored the optimism of the headline, contradicting the text Shawn originally submitted.

Further frustration is added by the fact that most editors know very lit-tle about Latin America and think of Latin American culture almost sole-ly in terms of violence. "Editors want bang bang," complained Michael, "If there is no bang bang, they figure, 'Why pay attention to it?' They are very Eurocentric. They don't appreciate Latin America for what it is." Similarly, Pati complained "editors…need to know that not everyone is carrying an AK-47 and wearing a red bandanna, and that just because a journalist is interviewing campesinos and guerrillas doesn't make them a communist."

U.S. editors normally gauge the newsworthiness of an international story by the amount of *public* governmental attention it is given (they gen-erally ignore covert action). Dell, an editor of a major U.S. daily, described the sorts of questions he asks each day when choosing a foreign story for the front page: "Is it just a story that will interest a narrow audience or is it something that could spread to a wider conflict, draw in the U.S. ...raise questions about our policy, raise questions about the Bush administration's stance?" This translates into severe limitations on reporters' abilities to cover other important aspects of Latin America. "You have to cover more than they want you to in New York," explained Paul, "because in New York they don't know jack shit about the country." However, "they" are the ones who select or reject Paul's photos. As Dell's comments make clear, they do so through a presidential filter (see chapter 10).

Most correspondents, especially the successful ones, produce the sorts of materials editors desire. Marla put it best when explaining her coverage of the elections. "As far as the editors are concerned," she complained, "which ultimately is the bottom line for us, the [1991] elections are very unimportant." The editorial "bottom line" represents a constant influence on reporters, staff and stringers alike. "After a while you know that editors can change things and there is nothing that you can do about it," submitted Shawn, "particularly when they don't even know who you are and they are 3000 miles away."

As a reporter for *Time* explained in *Deciding What's News*, "Every writer has a working knowledge of what his editor wants. Unless he's incorrigibly stubborn or independently wealthy, he tries to give it to him" (Gans 1979:102). Although editors are themselves subservient to a number of institutional superiors, they represent nearly absolute power from the perspective of the field journalist. It is little wonder reporters do not like to talk about them. The editors' existence serves as a reminder they work near the bottom of hierarchical organizations, and that the power of authorship does not flow from their pen, but from the structure as a whole.

The Ray Bonner Effect

Journalists who continue to breach the parameters of permissible discourse despite routine editorial attempts at correction, often receive punishment in the form of unwanted assignments, rejected reports, demotion, or even loss of a job. One of the most well known cases of journalistic censure involved Raymond Bonner of the *New York Times*. On January 27, 1982, Alma Guillermorpieto and Bonner published front page stories describing the aftermath of the now-infamous El Mozote massacre. At least seven hundred peasants were murdered at El Mozote, many of them children. Several of the corpses displayed signs of torture. The massacre was committed by the Atlacatl battalion, the officers of which were trained in the United States (Danner 1993).

Bonner's report of the El Mozote massacre was published one day before the Reagan administration was legally obliged to assess the human rights situation in El Salvador before Congress, making it a great embarrassment for U.S. foreign policy makers. The State Department claimed the massacres never took place. According to the administration's testimony before Congress, Embassy officials in El Salvador had visited the site and found no evidence of an attack or massacre. A decade later, those officials admitted they had lied to Congress. No U.S. officials had ventured anywhere near the site of El Mozote (Hertsgaard 1988:190).

Predictably, Guillermoprieto and Bonner came under attack from the U.S. government and conservative institutions like Accuracy In Media (AIM) and Freedom House (Hoyt 1993:33, Hertsgaard 1988:190). Perhaps most disturbing, however, was the flak generated by other media institutions.[5] The *Wall Street Journal* started the wave of criticism, claiming the reporters were duped by a "propaganda exercise" of the FMLN. The *Washington Post* editorial board rejected Guillermoprieto's evidence. They wrote an editorial endorsement of the Reagan administration's claim that things were improving in El Salvador. The day after the massacre reports were published, CBS devoted thirty seconds to the presidential affirmation, none to the El Mozote massacre.[6]

The editors of the *New York Times* responded to the flak by pressuring Bonner to moderate his reporting. When Bonner failed to do so, he was removed from the bureau. A little later he was demoted to the New York metropolitan desk. Finally, Bonner resigned on July 3, 1984. Another *New York Times* reporter explained, "The board came down hard on [executive editor] Abe Rosenthal, who was a conservative guy anyway, and he fired Ray." Perhaps during a moment of less intense governmental interest in El Salvador Bonner would have gotten away with reporting the truth, but not in the midst of a foreign policy crisis. As another reporter explained, "Bonner was crucified for telling the truth."

I visited the site of El Mozote exactly ten years after the massacre. An official investigation into the atrocity was just beginning. The bodies were bones by then, but the evidence was clear that hundreds had been killed. In a rash of news stories covering the excavations, Guillermoprieto and Bonner were publicly vindicated in the U.S. press. CBS's *Sixty Minutes* televised a powerful exposé of the event, including vivid descriptions of Bonner's treatment by the press, and a harsh condemnation of the Reagan administration's lies.[7] Unfortunately, the report was ten years too late.

According to many reporters working in the early eighties, Bonner's removal by the *New York Times* had a "chilling effect" on news coverage (Hertsgaard 1988:196–97, Parenti 1986:57). What little space had been opened for critical news reporting quickly slammed shut, leaving a brisk chill of caution as its legacy. Shari claimed that a conservative shift in the writings of several reporters, including a man whom she now calls an "arch enemy," was precipitated by Bonner's firing. She and others call this "the Ray Bonner effect." The Ray Bonner effect is manifested in an extreme, yet rational, fear of editorial retribution.

I do not believe that the Ray Bonner effect was as "chilling" as the critics have claimed. By the late 1980s and early 1990s most of the corps were only faintly aware of who Bonner was, let alone the events surrounding his removal. "I know Bonner was unhappy when he left here," said Jelisa, "but I don't know much more about him." I received many similar responses. By the latter half of the war Ray Bonner had pretty much fallen out of the consciousness of the press corps. The journalists were much less cognizant of the issue than were solidarity workers and others in the U.S. left who have made the Bonner case a cause célèbre.

This is not to say that reporting had become less controlled in later stages of the war. The same structures that led to Bonner's downfall were still firmly in place and new ones, like the salvoconducto system, had been developed. News institutions only show their punitive potential, however, when reporters repeatedly attempt to move beyond the boundaries of permissible discourse. Most correspondents do not. A confluence of organizational structures effect constant micro-corrections, keeping reporters within established parameters of political discourse without the need of overt censorship or retribution. Therefore, while many media critics are searching for conspiracy, they should be looking at continuity, the disciplinary structures that control reporters' work in seemingly petty ways—minor disciplines that are extremely effective in the aggregate.

One of the best ways to ensure reporters' compliance with institutional demands is to hire the right sort of people in the first place. Gans explains (1979:184):

> [J]ournalists with conscious values were in the minority, for the news media I studied seem to attract people who keep their values to themselves. Those unable to do so seldom look for work in these media, especially when their values are discordant; and those who come with discordant values do not remain long. But equally important, the national media, and journalism generally, appear to recruit people who do not hold strong values in the first place.

As a U.S. Marine-turned-lawyer-turned-stringer-turned-correspondent, Bonner was very unusual. The *New York Times* took a risk in hiring the untested stringer, and paid dearly. What they got was a reporter with strong ideas and values he was unwilling to compromise for the sake of career or country. Most media hires are much more willing to compromise their values, have relatively few conscious political values, or are in general political agreement with their institutions from the start. In other words, Bonner's experience could not have chilled the other staff correspondents because most of them were already cold. "I'm not sure if the other correspondents were scared off," agreed Bob, "or if Bonner was just the exception."

What I find most "chilling" about the Bonner affair is that most SPECA reporters were no longer aware of the issue by the latter half of the war. Several generations of correspondents had already come and gone between Bonner's dismissal in August 1982 and June 1990, when I arrived. Bonner's successors were increasingly unaware of those earlier epochs. There is a severe lack of institutional memory in the corps. It is a culture with much tradition, but little history. Ironically, those who do know about Bonner are generally not the hypothetically chilled journalists, but instead the most defiant members of the corps. Othello, who had covered virtually the entire war, summarized the Bonner case: "Your editors' desires are one of the most important things.... Bonner went against them, but how long did that last?" One need not remember the second issue, Bonner, in order to be "chilled" by the first.

The *New York Times* reporters who followed Bonner in the Salvadoran post were not so heavily sanctioned for their mistakes. For example, one of Bonner's successors reported a piece of propaganda created by the Salvadoran military's "Psychological Operations" unit, a division created and funded by the United States. During an election, COPREFA generated a rumor that peasants had been massacred by FMLN guerrillas. According to the story, the victims' voting cards had been stuffed into the corpses' mouths. The *New York Times'* journalist wrote about the fabricated event as fact without proper confirmation, thus transforming military propaganda into international news. Bringing the fiction full circle, the *New York Times* report was then used by the U.S. State Department as primary evidence in their public campaign to discredit the FMLN. Although Bonner was attacked as being "overly credulous" for reporting a massacre he personally verified, the "voting card" correspondent prospered despite reporting a brutal and tendentious fiction (Hertsgaard 1988:196–97). Lesson to the post-Bonner generation: err on the side of power.

Another post-Bonner correspondent for the *New York Times* received a lot of flak from angry readers:

> I don't know why people get so excited. My editor said not to worry because anybody working here is going to get a lot of flak. Very little of my mail is forwarded. I am always amazed that my editors never complain, and they get quite a bit of mail.

His editor even made jokes about the letters, passing them off as inconsequential (The *Los Angeles Times* correspondent in El Salvador does not read such letters either. In fact, he does not even read the *Los Angeles Times*). Very little feedback from readers reaches the insular world of the correspondent. While a few well-placed critics had the effect of displacing Bonner, significant amounts of criticism from the public sector (mainly the left) have had little effect upon the reporting of staff correspondents. The efficacy of flak generally increases in relation to the financial and political power of those who produce it (Herman and Chomsky 1988:26–28).

To conclude, there is a simple fact worth repeating: "Bonner was crucified for telling the truth." Bonner did not rise up through the proper channels and did not produce sanctioned truths. What he did was question the United States' role in El Salvador, if not the basic precept of U.S. media coverage—that the American government fulfills a positive role in the world community. Fortunately, for every dozen or so journalists willing to conform to the needs of power, there is someone like Ray Bonner who keeps asking the wrong questions, regardless of the costs.

THE
SOURCE WAR

"Today's news net is intended for big fish."

—Gaye Tuchman, in *Making News*

There is a clear distinction made between those Salvadorans who are considered sources and the great majority who are barely considered at all. Minor sources utilized by the foreign press in El Salvador include the Catholic Church and academics at the University of Central America (UCA). Even less common are sources from within the popular organizations, unions, peasant cooperatives and politically uninvolved members of the oligarchy. These sources figured much more prominently in stringers' reports than those of staff correspondents, although even stringers used these sectors rather sparingly.

The stringers were particularly fond of quoting one UCA intellectual, however, who was usually sourced under the anonymous attribution of "political analyst." Staff correspondents were much less likely to use academic sources, or "domes." Instead, the *A Team*'s "political analysts" are more often drawn from the U.S. diplomatic corps. Therefore, behind the vague attribution "political analyst" is an ongoing debate, a discursive battle between stringers and staffers. To the extent that U.S. reporters can inject any argument of their own into the news, it is through their choice of sources, selection of quotes, and textual juxtaposition thereof (see chapter 10). Their biases remain hidden within the opinions of sources. While editorial pressure greatly limits their choice of quotes and informants, they do manage to manifest some creativity in this regard.

The *B Team*, while forced to reproduce the dominant narrative, also attempted to subvert it through selective use of "political analysts." The following excerpt from a stringer's report illustrates this method of source-based subversion [emphasis added]:

> U.S. and Salvadoran officials categorically oppose recognition of rebel-held territory. "The rebels don't control any territory," says a U.S. Embassy official.
>
> But *analysts speculate* that rebels hold de facto control of at least one fifth of the countryside. Government soldiers frequently patrol rebel strongholds, but usually cannot remain without incurring heavy casualties.

These speculating "analysts" could be UCA academics or, most likely, other reporters. Whether derived from an actual source or not, such vague attributions are a means by which reporters subvert the institutionally-favored argument and interject their own points of view, or in this case, a well known point of fact. The author of the above report knew as well as anyone how much territory the FMLN controlled, but was unwilling to directly countermand the position of the "U.S. Embassy official." In order to comply with the rules of objective journalism, she had to use a surrogate voice to blunt the official's presentation.

Her, Rigoberta Menchu

Of course, most people never become news sources, either individually or under the auspices of collective representation (Gans 1980:8–15). Reporters are well aware of this, and most of them regret the oversight. Tabatha, a stringer, had this to say about reporters' neglect of "ordinary people":

> Reporters prefer sensationalism over the mundane present. They present El Salvador as more polarized than it really is. Those with despair, without political convictions, don't make good copy. They aren't considered "newsworthy."

In "Reporting and the Oppressed," Clifford Christians explains that reporters "find it extraordinarily difficult to remain inspired by the preferences, sentiments, and anxieties of the disadvantaged" (1986:119). That was certainly the tendency among SPECA reporters.

One of the clearest examples was an excursion eight SPECA journalists and I took to Guatemala (about twelve other international journalists joined us there). The object of coverage was *The Second Encounter of the 500 Years of Indigenous, Black and Popular Resistance Continental*

Campaign, the largest ever transnational meeting of indigenous leaders. The Encounter took place in Quetzaltenango, Guatemala, October 11–13, 1991. The march of 40,000 indigenous Guatemalans on the final day of the Encounter was the largest political demonstration since the early 1980s, a period when at least 100,000 people, mainly *indigenas*, were murdered in a governmentally sanctioned terror campaign (Simon 1987:13–15).

Nobel prize winner Rigoberta Menchu wrote: "What hurts Indians most is that our costumes are considered beautiful, but it's as if the person wearing it didn't exist" (1984:204). Unfortunately, most of the SPECA reporters demonstrated this racist mind-set during their coverage of the Encounter. They were more interested in the images of indigenas than in their thoughts, plans, and protests. Before reaching Quetzaltenango, several of the journalists told me they expected the Encounter to be "colorful," a particularly good photo story (Albers and James 1990, Krouse 1990). Visualizing American Indians as an exotic people who wear beautiful costumes, they took extra film along, hoping to take advantage of the timing of the event (the 499th anniversary of Columbus' landing) to market their work.

When demonstration day arrived, the news photographers could be seen weaving in and out of the marching mass, searching for the "colorful" Guatemalan clothing which was their quarry. Fortunately for them, there was plenty of *traje* on exhibit. The traditional blouses, skirts, and scarves worn by some participants were brilliantly visible against the larger, less colorful backfield of dusty brown dress pants, dirty white work shirts, weathered blouses, and an occasional Miami Dolphins or Kawasaki T-shirt. The photographers' challenge, therefore, was to isolate their traditional ideal from the less resplendent mass.

At one point, a group of journalists stood at the bottom of a hill, carefully examining the oncoming crowd. Suddenly, a brilliant patch of blue appeared, a group of about thirty women wearing new and carefully coordinated traje. Unlike most of the marchers, they had no Pepsi bottles, popsicles, or other stigmata of modernity. The photographers bolted from their waiting positions, the brightly plumaged prey fixed in their sights. They descended upon the women and began shooting.

The written news narratives were colorized as well. A parachuting North American wrote: "The marchers, the majority of them Guatemalan women dressed in the brightly colored skirts, shirts, and scarves of their native villages, marched slowly through the center of Quetzaltenango." Not only is this a conspicuously colorful description of the participants, it is a particularly insulting news narrative whose gaze trivializes the intended message of the participants. It is hard to imagine reporters covering the Republican National Convention in similar fashion: "The delegates, the majority of them inebriated white men dressed in drab suits,

ties, and dress shirts, stood in the center of the convention arena and vig-
orously applauded the speakers." The emphasis on superficial appearance injects a *National Geographic* motif into what is intended to be a
political news discourse.[1] Reporters ignored the fundamental causes and
contexts of the indigena demonstration.

Most of the journalists were disappointed, however, by the relative lack
of "color" at the conference and march. They became confused and professionally paralyzed when the Encounter could not be incorporated into
their simple, predetermined frames. One photographer dropped his plans
to shoot portraits of conference participants, because too few of the
Indians were wearing what he had visualized as "native costumes." He
was looking for what Elizabeth Edwards calls a "portrait type," the most
important characteristic being the "non-European nature of the subject"
(1990:242).

From its inception, the Encounter campaign was designed to be a coalition of the "indigenous, black, and popular resistance," primarily, but not
exclusively, an "indigenous movement" (*Diario Latino*, October 19,
1991:13).[2] Nevertheless, several reporters complained about the presence of nonindigenous delegates. One reporter asked, "Who are these
black guys?" referring to a group that did not seem sufficiently indigenous
to him. "Garifuna," I replied. To which he responded: "What?"[3] The
coalitional nature of the event disoriented the U.S. and British journalists, who arrived expecting an exclusively "native" event.

Several reporters complained about the political nature of the
Encounter. One blamed the popular organizations for their "politiciza-
tion of the ostensibly native conference," as if "native" and "political"
were incompatible terms. This wrought-from-without frame ignored the
fact that many popular organizations include significant indigenous mem-
berships (Barre 1989:17). Rigoberta Menchu—who is herself a union
organizer, popular organization leader, and indigena—tried to remind
journalists of that fact at a press conference. One of the journalists later
criticized Menchu's use of political class rhetoric, however, calling it "old"
and complaining that "it will never work with Indians." The next day, the
presence of 40,000 indigena demonstrators contradicted his claim (most
reporters I polled the day before expected fewer than 2,000 marchers).

The most striking feature of Encounter coverage, however, was the relative lack thereof. Despite the large number of journalists in attendance,
only a handful of reports were published or broadcast in the U.S. press.
The reporters' disorientation and disappointment were largely to blame.
Another cause was the absence of correspondents from the *New York
Times* and *Los Angeles Times*, both of whom had previously indicated they
were going to cover the Encounter. Lacking the sanction of the prestige
press, the stringers' reports received marginal placement in marginal newspapers.

When I returned to El Salvador I asked one of these reporters why he had failed to attend the event. The staffer explained he had not expected the conference to be of any significance, and complained that U.S. readers do not wish to read about "little brown people." However, since newspapers don't conduct public opinion polls measuring the popularity of "little brown people," one can justifiably assume that the staff reporter's assertion is instead a representation of his institution's agenda and, perhaps, his own value system.

The peaceful nature of the march further reduced its newsworthiness. I wasn't surprised when a group of journalists asked me to guide them to Quetzaltenango's army installation. They were hoping to see a confrontation as the marchers passed by the cuartel on their way back to the conference grounds. Fortunately, there would be no violent confrontations that day. For a brief and rare moment, there were no soldiers to be found on the streets of Xela. Unfortunately, from the perspective of journalists, Indians make better victims than political actors. Live body, no story.

A U.S. stringer who is permanently stationed in Guatemala City produced the greatest number of published Encounter reports. She only attended the opening ceremony of the conference, however, and missed the march altogether. Her work was vague, cliché ridden, and focused almost entirely upon the Colombian Quincentennial controversy. Conversely, Shawn's work was exceptional. Having lived in the area of Quetzaltenango for several years during the 1980s, Shawn was much more conversant in the greater range of issues discussed at the Encounter. Shawn persuaded an editor of a fairly prestigious North American newspaper to run his story.

I first met many of these same SPECA reporters at another Guatemalan event, the June, 1991 Summit of Central American Presidents. The same correspondents who discounted and ignored the voices of the Encounter participants, dutifully transcribed the words and perspectives of the officials attending the Summit, from Secretary of State James Baker III to the Central American Presidents themselves (for a comparative analysis of the Summit and Encounter, see Pedelty 1993). The same institutions which ignored the largest ever hemispheric meeting of indigenous peoples, gave considerable coverage to that rather uneventful, highly controlled, and fairly opaque Summit meeting. The *New York Times* alone produced four articles from the Antigua Summit, yet, as mentioned above, did not print one of the Encounter.

The neglect of non-elite sources in El Salvador is equally pronounced. That neglect is partly attributable to the salvoconducto system. Yet, the reporters were also to blame. Journalists were perfectly free to visit the extensive areas of countryside lying outside the conflicted zones. There they would have been able to cover peasant life, questions of land tenure, and many other rural dynamics which led to the war. For example, I visited a Salvadoran Cooperative Federation (FEDACOPADES) farm in Ahuachapan, an area far from the FMLN-held territories. Most of the cooperative's leadership had been "disappeared," presumably tortured and murdered. I learned a great deal talking to the survivors. One did not need to go to the restricted and conflicted areas of Morazan or Chalatenango to meet such people. Unfortunately, "ordinary people"—ranchers, peasants, surfers, carpenters, small business owners, or the maids who attend to the reporters' daily needs—are not considered relevant sources.

Issues involving nonviolent actions of Salvadoran grass roots organizations were also ignored. One such issue was the *toma de tierras* (taking of land) movement. The campaign was orchestrated by several campesino organizations who were asking that vacant land be turned over to landless peasants. The government reacted by militarizing the protest sites.

On one of my first nights in San Salvador, I was visiting a friend who worked for a human rights monitoring organization. She took me to a site where a group of Salvadorans had temporarily taken over a small parcel of land behind the Assembly building. The human rights observers at the site suggested I alert the press. I found Jerry and Marla and we drove back to the site. By that time, the group was surrounded by riot police in full gear. Unwisely, the protesters had selected a very dark area in which to take their stand. After the group backed down, agreeing to abandon the spot, Jerry and Marla interviewed the leaders of the demonstration. We then jumped back into Jerry's truck and went home. The reporters did not write about the incident, however, for two reasons. First, it was too common. Second, there was no violence.

In fact, only after two land rights movement workers had been brutally attacked did the U.S. press mention the toma de tierras campaign. One of the workers was mutilated, the other stabbed to death. In reporting the violence, however, the U.S. press still ignored the underlying issue of land distribution.

"The Blood Has to be Purged"

"We expect them [Salvadoran officials] to work toward the elimination of human rights."
—an accurate misstatement by U.S. Vice President Dan Quayle

Occasionally, U.S. operatives outside The Embassy serve as news informants. Many of them come into contact with reporters at the British Club, a refuge for British expatriates, employees of the U.S. government, arms dealers (a U.S. arms dealer was the British Club President in 1991), foreign businessmen, wire service reporters and photographers—expatriates all. The "expats" gather at the Club to play pool, watch sporting events, and drink while older British couples play countless rubbers of contract bridge, trying not to notice the ongoing erosion of their social environment.

The journalists who belonged to the British Club became quite close to the military and government agents with whom they played pool, dined, and watched sporting events on television. In fact, the military and paramilitary specialists were close enough to know about a case of "crabs" a SPECA photographer encountered at one of El Salvador's many brothels. They threw around jokes about the man's genitals as they played pool. The young photographer normally liked to be the center of their attention, but not in that way.

The reporters were careful not to burn these contacts, because they were valued informants, if not friends. I was surprised when a staff reporter abstained from using a valuable piece of information we received one night while playing pool at the club. After a helicopter went down over the *Cerron Grande* (Great Reservoir), a member of the U.S. diplomatic corps entered the room and told a friend, "We had another one [helicopter] shot down today." However, the journalist, like his colleagues, reported the crash as an accident.

Perhaps the reporters were better off ignoring the club's nefarious characters. One evening when a staffer and I were playing pool, a U.S. operative started telling me about his role in the reporter's recent investigations. The correspondent had broken a story about a secret U.N. proposal permanently ceding territory to the FMLN. While the correspondent in question repeatedly said, "Shut up, Mason!" the laughing, loose-lipped official explained how he was approached to verify the news report's validity *after* it was released. To the reporter's relief, Mason had told him, "Shit yes! Of course it's true!" Nevertheless, the report was publicly denied by both the U.N. and the U.S. Embassy (A U.S. embassy official privately congratulated the reporter, however, for doing "a great job of investigative reporting"). Even the reporter's editor called and asked, "What are you up to?" Mason took sadistic delight in the correspondent's discomfort. The truth had earned the club correspondent nothing but ridicule and professional censure.

The club denizens liked to make fun of reporters, especially when they were not around. They did not characterize them as prensa enemiga, but more as "pinko limp-dicks," in the words of an American Marine. These military and paramilitary men feel the press corps is hostile towards the Salvadoran military. In a vague reference to this, one said, "I have been in the helicopters with these guys, and let me tell you, there are no atheist reporters up there" (they had elevated cliché to a way of life). They believe the journalists would gain a greater understanding of the military's situation if they experienced more of their same fears and dangers. Like most news critics, they cannot understand why the media do not see the world as they do.

The club commandos are just a small part of the larger, hidden world of strategists and operatives working in El Salvador. U.S. covert operations specialists, U.S. military advisors, and Salvadoran death squad members, among others, survive by virtue of their secrecy. Their message is clear, their purposes known, but their identities remain safely hidden behind a veil of anonymity. For the most part, the press corps has allowed them to maintain that powerful privacy.

Vinicio, a U.S. military adviser, was one of these private men. I got to know him rather well. By the time I arrived, Vinicio had switched over to the "humanitarian" wing of the counterinsurgency effort. He was teaching hygiene and basic medical practices to rural Salvadorans. A grunt involved in the Vietnam war summarized similar U.S. policies in Southeast Asia: "Bomb 'em and feed 'em, bomb 'em and feed 'em" (Herr 1968:10). Vinicio had not always been part of the "feed 'em" wing of U.S. operations, however. He spent most of the war helping the Salvadoran military create a civil defense force and training the Salvadoran special forces. He has worked in all provinces except Morazan.

Speaking with a slight drawl, Vinicio listed all the journalists he had encountered at the British Club, evaluating each. He liked Bart and his reporting, found it to be fair and balanced. George was also "O.K." He disliked Shawn, however, who he felt was biased towards the FMLN. For him, Shawn typified all that was wrong with the American press.

Vinicio liked Joe, of course, because he was always good for a laugh or two. One night Vinicio, Joe, and I were watching a football game when several shots or firecrackers, or something of that nature, rang out near the British Club. "Those are just firecrackers," said Joe with an air of absolute certainty. The young war photographer, who was obviously attempting to impress us, claimed he could differentiate between gunshots and incendiaries, even at a distance. After Joe left, Vinicio turned to me and said, "I can't always tell the difference between firecrackers and gunshots, and I sure as hell don't think he can" (indeed, they turned out to be gunshots). Because of Joe and the Joe-like behavior of many war corespondents, Vinicio and other soldiers consider them amateurish, perhaps even half-men. They turn the serious business of armed conflict into a game, playing war by day, but whisking back to the hotel at night pretending to know the difference between firecrackers and gunshots.

On several occasions, I sat alone with Vinicio in a back room of the British Club, listening to his stories late at night after the other club members had left. He spoke with a slow, deliberate manner as he described a situation in La Union where his trainees turned out to be FMLN spies trying to earn a little free training. Vinicio said that he was "hurt" when one of his favorite trainees turned out to be a guerrilla infiltrater. Vinicio had become quite close to his Salvadoran charges.

Vinicio claimed to have proof that the massacred UCA Jesuits had provided weapons to the guerrillas and thus deserved to die. Like many of the Salvadoran oligarchs and right wing politicians, Vinicio overtly defended the UCA massacre. Nothing terribly new or surprising about that. What was surprising, or at least confusing, was the odd way Vinicio would end nearly every conversation, stating simply: "The blood has to be purged."

This "purge" thing caught my interest. Vinicio was being hauntingly obtuse about the issue, whatever it was. I did not want to scare him off, though, by seeming too interested in his ramblings, so each night I waited for him to take it further on his own. One night an AID worker joined us late at night in the TV room. He had just gotten in from replacing electrical poles the guerrillas had sabotaged in the countryside. The AID worker's presence provided the catalyst to further loosen the advisor's tongue. Having drunk a few too many beers, buoyed by the presence of his AID ally, Vinicio turned, looked me directly in the eye, and calmly stated, "Kill them all," as if issuing a direct order.

A U.S. military man saying "Kill them all." Incredible melodrama. Was he unable to concoct a more poetic line? At least in the movies they say clever things like, "God, I love the smell of napalm in the morning" (*Apocalypse Now*). But, "Kill them all?" After I laughed, drawing a big smile across Vinicio's face, I finally asked him, "What the hell are you talking about?" "Kill all the guerrillas," explained Vinicio, " As soon as they sign the shit and drop their guns. Our guys [Salvadoran soldiers] are gonna have to..." he paused to remember his best line, "The blood has to be purged."

For the Salvadoran military, this man represents the United States. It was he and his colleagues who were, according to successive presidential administrations, "professionalizing" the infamous Salvadoran armed forces throughout the war. Meanwhile, he was promoting the idea the military should murder all the guerrillas once peace was achieved. Of all the official U.S. views I have read while analyzing U.S. news reports, I have yet to see this one represented. Such voices have remained safely outside of the news discourse. Yet, in many ways, this man *is* the U.S. program. Beneath layers of official spokespeople—a public relations apparatus which, for many editors, institutions, and therefore reporters, is inviolate—function a cadre of men and machines which facilitate the killing by aiding both the military and death squads alike (Sundaram 1991, Pyes 1986).

Imagine the headline: U.S. MILITARY OFFICIALS ADVISE THE SALVADORAN ARMY TO 'KILL THEM ALL.' Framed in this way, the FMLN demands for safeguards would have seemed much more reasonable, more like a logical reaction to real threats than "obstructionism" or a "Gordian knot," as the FMLN proposals came to be called in the mainstream dailies. Reporting conventions disallow such subversion, however, no matter how accurate. The Salvadoran War was not officially a U.S. war, so the heavily involved U.S. military never became a major source for the mainstream press. Even though the U.S. government provided virtually all the funding, training, and strategy for the Salvadoran government and military, El Salvador was not to be presented as a U.S. military action. As a result, U.S. military officials were not considered central news sources. Whereas, the U.S. press coverage of the Persian Gulf War carried constant comment from the Pentagon and their field operatives (Fialka 1991), the U.S. military remained a silent, yet effective force throughout the Salvadoran War.

The reporters complied with the Pentagon's desire for silence, neither seeking out nor quoting U.S. military and covert operations officials. As with most foreign news in the U.S. press, coverage of the Salvadoran War was largely coverage of the U.S. State Department. Reporters have learned to accept that as a natural part of their professional practice, ignoring other, purposely ensconced State operatives.

A notable exception is John Carlin's classic article, "Just Little Brown Men," published in the British daily *The Independent* (December 29, 1988). The title of Carlin's article is a direct quote from a U.S. Marine Colonel, who excused the rampant human rights abuses in El Salvador with the dismissive statement, "Well, come on.... After all: its only little brown men shooting at little brown men." Carlin juxtaposes the Colonel's brutally frank views of the war with the sanitized claims of the U.S. State Department. Carlin made the contradictions between U.S. foreign policy and practice painfully clear by including the voice of the forgotten element: the American military men who represent the U.S. plan in its most honest form.

One day, a stringer handed me Carlin's article, calling it the finest piece written during the war. Many others agreed with her assessment of the unusual report. The stringers and internationals greatly admired Carlin and wished they could be more like him. However, most would no more think of quoting a U.S. military advisor than they would an Embassy secretary. Neither are officially sanctioned press sources. The boundaries are set, the rules put in place. Most reporters must respect these limitations, at least most of the time.

PRACTICE

"I just got back from Poland and I'm off to cover the Salvadoran elections. Can you spare twenty minutes to brief me?"

—NBC journalist (NACLA Report on the Americas 1983, 17 (4):1)

The Problem with Parachuting

Much of the Salvadoran war was reported by parachuters. The paratrooping reporters converged on El Salvador whenever a major news event took place, most notably the 1982, 1984, and 1989 elections and the 1989 FMLN offensive (Massing 1982, 1989). During the elections of 1989, for example, 784 reporters registered with COPREFA. SPECA, the permanent and semi-permanently stationed journalists, were overwhelmed on such occasions by descending hordes of transient correspondents.

Parachute journalists bring "fresh eyes" to the situation, taking notice of exotic and newsworthy issues the permanently stationed reporters have begun taking for granted (Rosenblum 1979:11). "Someone new says, 'Hey, wow, that's interesting!'" explained Cary. "Their first impressions may show what the audience will find interesting as well." The parachuters' lack of familiarity is also a major handicap, however. Elicia, a Salvadoran who works for a parachuting journalist, describes how her transient staff employer experiences events in El Salvador:

When something happens, like the El Zapote massacre, she

doesn't know a thing about it. She is in some other country. She reads about it there before coming here to cover it.

When you are traveling all the time you tend to be superficial," Harold lamented, "You have to be." Aside from a few "freelance" reporters who produce investigative articles for magazines like *Rolling Stone, Vogue,* the *New Yorker,* and alternative media, most parachuters do not have time for background research or independent investigation. In fact, parachute "research" usually consists of little more than reading news clippings, most of which are also written by parachuters.

Parachuters duplicate each others' work to an absurd degree. David, a fixer in Honduras, complained that "the big guns" he works for "parachute in and just rebottle the same story, watered down to the lowest common denominator." Adriana observed:

> Parachuters rely on the people here. Often a person gets known as a fixer. They all go to him and get the same story. I hear them say things to each other like, 'Hey, did you do your coffee story yet?' The *New York Times* does a story so the next guy has to do his story on the same thing.

Not only is parachute work derivative, it also tends to be highly ethnocentric (Rosenblum 1979:11). Traveling from culture to culture, the disoriented parachuters have a greater tendency to return to their own cultural values and social conditions when interpreting the world. Antonio Canas, a professor at the University of Central America, explains (interview):

> This problem relates to that of the elections. The press comes to the elections with the ideas of the home country, speaking of reforms—changing this or that person vs. changing the system itself. They speak of remedies. It is like giving the person an aspirin when there is something wrong with the entire nervous system. That is the nature of their profession, not to get to the bottom of problems.

Another disadvantage of parachuting is the visiting journalists' lack of contacts. During the 1989 offensive many parachuting staff correspondents were not able to gain access to areas occupied by the FMLN because they had not spent time in those neighborhoods previously. "Independent journalists that knew the people in the area were given access," explained Marla, "because prior to the offensive we had given time to that *barrio.*" Paul agreed, "They [parachuting staff correspondents] will not get interviews with the other side. They wouldn't know what to say to them."

A Canadian stringer criticized a parachuting compatriot who "invaded [her] turf" at a press conference:

> He doesn't even speak Spanish. A classic case of parachute journalism.... He

doesn't understand a word they are saying. How the hell is he going to write his story?.... He actually grabbed a journalist at the end to ask some questions. I thought that was really arrogant.

Likewise, Ronald faulted parachuters for "coming in here with their Banana Republic clothes and getting it all wrong." Percy, an *A Team* reporter who covered El Salvador during the mid-1980s, agreed:

Some correspondents are complete idiots. They would come in. They would go to the hotel. They would call six people. They didn't know shit. They had never been anywhere. If someone put a gun to their head after three years and said, 'Where is Perquin on the map?' they wouldn't know. They would go to the economics counselor at The Embassy who would say, 'Salvador is blah blah,' and they would write those stories and, I mean, they just sucked.

I had to laugh when Percy mentioned the part about Perquin. A few months prior, Lester—a parachuter whom other SPECA members referred to as a "Cowboy journalist"—had trouble remembering the name of the FMLN-occupied town, exclaiming: "Shit, six months to a year and I have already forgotten!" Having traveled throughout the rest of Central America and Mexico after concluding my research, I sympathize. There were times I would awake in a dingy, unfamiliar hotel room, trying hard to remember which country I was in. Roaming from country to country, culture to culture, one gets a little lost.

Parachuters experience a similar sense of vertigo, constantly decentered and uncertain. Most try to cure their dizziness with quick-source therapy, visiting bureaucratic centers of power that are all too willing to condense complex situations into easily digestible bites, the simplest terms and the most convenient definitions. For the U.S. parachuter, The Embassy is both willing and able to provide cultural reorientation. The parachuter leaves the United States only to arrive there again upon landing in San Salvador. The Camino Real Hotel completes the experience, allowing parachuters to remain nested within a first world cocoon while reporting the discordant realities of the third.

"Those in the field," argued David, "especially the Latin-Americans, are the first to be skeptical and know what is going on. Parachuters are the last." Katherine is one of "the last," a quintessential parachuter. She reports the basic details, misreports many of the facts, and rushes off to the next country before having a chance to sort through the issues and events she has encountered. Although Katherine is technically based in San Salvador, her reporting responsibilities are spread throughout the entire region. She laments, "Even if I went out and rented a big house I'd never be in it—it wouldn't make sense. I live for the work. Some people who are basically stringers can have a more sensible lifestyle." Katherine experienced a life of constant work, confusion, and frustration. She was sick almost every time I saw her, retreating to her room at the Camino every night after work. In foreign correspondence, this is considered success.

An article about a U.S. "idealist" running an aid project in El Salvador serves as a typical example of parachute journalism. The article lauds said idealist for his kind service to El Salvador and implies that he was having a tough time getting money from aid agencies. I knew the subject of the article quite well. He would hang out at the British Club almost nightly. His favorite hobby was describing sexual adventures with young prostitutes at great length—what one receives for $20, which brothels are best, etc. His detailed narratives even seemed to disturb the other club patrons.

The "idealist's" second favorite pastime was making racist jokes about Arabs during the Persian Gulf War. He passed much of his time with U.S. military and diplomatic staff, with whom he had very close relationships, sharing high fives and making not-so-subtle references concerning his support for the Salvadoran military. I would constantly ask his friends what they did, knowing the answer would be: "If I told you I would have to kill you" (a laughable affectation). He even made references about having been up in Salvadoran military helicopters. Perhaps he was not a spook, but he had a strong tendency to hang out with them. None of the permanently stationed SPECA reporters, especially the British Club members, would have written a favorable story about this well known figure. Only a parachuter, unfamiliar with the underbelly of U.S. aid operations, would present this man as a disconnected "idealist."

In sum, parachuting tends to be superficial and susceptible to propaganda. Unfortunately, it is how much of the world's news is covered.

Hard Work, Routine, Disease, and Insanity

There is a greater degree of routine in the lives of permanently stationed reporters. For example, almost all SPECA journalists wake up before 6:00 AM to listen to the morning news broadcast on local radio station YSU. If an important story breaks, journalists call each other to discuss the issue and to arrange transportation, if necessary. Stringers have an advantage in this regard, becasue they are already surrounded by colleagues at the morning breakfast table; stringers will often wait, however, to see if their higher status colleagues decide to cover a story before committing their own time to it.

Although foreign correspondents are free from the restrictive "beats" that pattern the work of domestic reporters, their lives are still ruled by deadlines.[1] News is typically gathered in the morning, written in the early afternoon, and filed late afternoon or early evening. The pace of work is erratic. News coverage cycles through periods of feast and famine as the news agenda shifts towards and away from Central America. The fickle nature of the international press agenda, combined with the tendency of major events to cluster, make it difficult for the SPECA journalists to predict when they will be working feverishly or when it might be possible to grab a couple weeks of vacation. Their life and work is an odd hybrid of timed work-discipline, and "task-orientation" (Thompson 1967). E. P. Thompson argues that "a community in which task-orientation is common appears to show least demarcation between 'work' and 'life'" (60). This is certainly true for SPECA. They are never really "off" duty. The corps' recreational time is full of news talk. Furthermore, news can happen at any time of day, interrupting the ostensible "off" time of a dinner, party, or sleep. At the same time, reporters are never completely "on" duty. They rarely act as if engaged in a serious professional endeavor, except when around sources. They often imbue their labor with a strong sense of play. The boundary between journalists' work and "free" time is extremely porous (see chapter 8).

Some journalists are more sedentary than others. David claims that, even at the height of news coverage of the Contra camps, important foreign correspondents in Honduras would conduct much of their coverage from the Terrace Cafe. He and his closest colleagues would joke, "At least they have moved to another table!" The same held true for Guatemala, where some journalists would spend a great deal of their time in comfortable outdoor cafes. I conducted an interview in one such locale. Fred and Clarice, my caffeinated interviewees, explained:

> This is *the* hang-out; *the* gossip spot in town. They'll know if there is going to be a coup two days ahead of time here. All the journalists just come here and hang out. It takes awhile to get them to trust you, but its really *the* place to hang out.

After a couple hours spent there, I had no doubt they were telling *the* truth.

SPECA journalists, however, spent little time hanging out in such places, perhaps because of the war or dearth of comfortable Salvadoran cafes. A few made *Mr. Donut* (one of many U.S. chains operating in El Salvador) their office away from home. Frances would sit for hours at the *Mr. Donut* on Calle Roosevelt, typing away on his laptop and drinking hot coffee while Salvadoran children watched him work.

Much of the time, however, the pace is frenetic. There are deadlines to worry about, competitors to match, flights to catch, visas to acquire, sources to contact, bills to pay, phones not working, power outages, and on top of all that, dysentery to deal with. One of the favorite pastimes among reporters working in El Salvador is discussing their ailments. Most SPECA reporters have had bouts of malaria, dengue fever, and/or hepatitis. Virtually all have acquired amoebas or some other form of dysentery-inducing parasite. For many, the latter is a semi-permanent condition. Joe joked, "We always ask each other what color our shit is." He once asked me the same question. I described my condition. He said, "Green shit? Smells bad?" I replied in the affirmative. Joe responded, "I get that once in a while. Right now my shit is Black." Disease and dysentery are as much a part of SPECA life as interviews and press conferences. The work is highly uncomfortable in this regard (I apologize for this unpleasant, though essential bit of ethnographic detail).

Terrence cited social isolation, however, rather than fear, work, or illness, as the greatest cause of stress. He described the difficulty of "getting a life out of work." Terrence said that he always felt as if he was "nowhere." Due to cultural and economic barriers, SPECA relations with the common citizenry are distant, at best. Harold, typical in this regard, complained he had nothing in common with the impoverished majority, and a great distaste for the feudal, wealthy minority. This left a small middle class and even smaller clique of local intellectuals. Middle class Salvadorans were usually too busy attempting to remain in their precarious position, however, and many of the intellectuals, especially those belonging to the National University, had either escaped to the mountains to join the FMLN or left the country altogether. Furthermore, the journalist's work allows for little contact with people outside the press and the small circles of power within which they circulate. Therefore, they spend most of their time with other SPECA reporters. They are a fairly isolated social group.

This sense of social distance leaves many ex-SPECA reporters with haunted feelings about the place, as if they were never really connected with it. I asked Percy to summarize his experience in El Salvador. He related a story which combined several of the themes I have mentioned thus far, including terror, boredom, absurdity, and finally, distance—all in a "wild day" covering the conflicted zones. He and his companion, Francine, were both "spaced out and punchy" as they drove towards a town in Northern San Miguel whose mayor was about to exhume several corpses from a well. Nearing the site, they encountered a group of women dressed in mourning clothes, the mothers of the deceased. Naturally, Percy stopped to offer them a ride. With the mothers on board, he proceeded to roll his Jeep into a ditch. Fortunately, no one was hurt. It was "boiling hot" and there was fighting in the area, but after all their other troubles, no one seemed to care. They were all intent on witnessing the grisly procedure to come. As the weary group arrived, the mayor was exhuming the remains of corpses from the well, placing them in plastic bags.

Percy paused at this point in his story, stating, "It got to you, the work-a-day aspect of the war." SPECA reporters were forced to normalize the abnormal and routinize the absurd, while being served constant reminders they were not really "in" on the events they covered. The foreign correspondents were geographically *proximate*, but culturally distanced.

Percy finished his story, describing the reporters' exit in detail. It was getting dark and it was a "bad area." As they rolled past one stretch of forest, they heard the disembodied voice of a small child float in through the Jeep's open windows. The soft voice simply said, "*Que les vayan bien*" ("that you would go well" or "good-bye"). Percy explained the significance of that memory:

> I couldn't take it. That has stayed with me. That was just like the weirdest sort of thing. I don't know how it translates, but Francine and I both were so (Percy paused, laughing nervously)...blown away by this. It just became part of our time in El Salvador, and there was just no way to tell this story in a way that made sense or write about or get it out of your system. It will always be in your system. There are a lot of things in El Salvador that came in through your eyes or in through some way that you just knew you would never be able to get rid of. I think that's why I and other people (long pause with the sentence dangling)—I was not a crazy person, but I saw people [journalists] who were.

Press work in El Salvador can drive you crazy, and the social isolation and distance of the work plays a large part in inducing that sense of insanity as one attempts to bring the preverbal truths of terror into a language which is absolutely inadequate.

Reporting is also, quite simply, hard work. Probably the most thankless job is left to the wire reporter, whose work is both frenetic and office-bound (Rosenblum 1979:27–28). As the title for Joe Morris' history of the United Press International (UPI) implies, the wire service reporter faces a *Deadline Every Minute* (1957). With thousands of clients around the world, wire service journalists work under deadline pressures which are, quite literally, constant. Wire service agencies demand that reporters file and update stories continually to meet the staggered deadlines of individual clients and provide fresher copy than competing services. Therefore, one reporter, usually the bureau chief, remains in the office nearly the entire day while other staff, mainly photographers, go out to cover events.

Minutes are money for the wire services. The Reuters bureau chief bragged that his company broke the Kuwaiti invasion story before any of the competition. A real scoop. They beat the other wire services by a whole five minutes.

One day I found Cal slaving away in his office, fuming at his editor. His boss had just called to demand more news output from the Salvadoran bureau. Cal complained he would therefore have to spend much more time in the office and rely even more heavily on official sources, especially those with the means to deliver information to his office or who could be reached via telephone. Cal, sensing he would be forced to do a more superficial job, complained he was being judged on the basis on volume and velocity, rather than quality.

As a result of deadline pressures, wire service reporters often harbor desires to become newspaper staff. "Wire people dream of working for a newspaper," George explained, "because your first deadline isn't until three in the afternoon." The deadline-effect is one reason why wire services report the news in an extremely superficial manner. They are an excellent source of headlines, a flag service for alerting the reader to the basic outlines of events and issues, but they are of little value for news consumers who want to better understand the structures, history, and significance of a situation. However, because staff-originated copy costs "ninety percent more than syndicated material," newspapers and other media are rapidly replacing their own foreign correspondents with wire service reporting, "the cheapest news possible" (Bagdikian 1974:195).

Other correspondents' deadlines vary in number and frequency. The *New York Times* is under heavy pressure to file daily. A staff correspondent for the *Los Angeles Times* is under less pressure, both due to the three hour time difference between New York and Los Angeles, and because the *Los Angeles Times* is a more feature-oriented newspaper than its east coast cousin. Often, the *Los Angeles Times* reporter will go for days without needing to meet a deadline.

Stringers' deadlines are even more varied. If important news is breaking, they may have to meet several strings' deadlines in one day. The typical stringer writes several stories, each differing only slightly, and then sells them as "Special to the Minneapolis Tribune," "Special to the San Francisco Examiner," and "Special" to whomever else will buy it. Conversely, if there is little breaking news and the stringer is working on a feature, she may feel no deadline pressure at all. In that case, economic exigency takes over as the major time-limiting factor. The stringer needs to sell a minimal number of stories in order to subsist.

A print and radio stringer described a typical day during the coverage of a breaking news story:

> If there is a big rebel attack overnight, I call up the [major string] and [a European radio network] and say this is happening. I watch the wire, go out and get information, and get back. I make a quick call to The Embassy and COPREFA to get a quote, or call the wire to get a quote. There is usually something on the radio. I then hammer out a minute and a half voice report for [a European radio network] and cut it down to a minute for [a U.S. radio network] and file that. I call the [major string] to find out how much they can take. They might take 800 words. I hammer out a story for them. By 3:00 PM I hope to file my initial story for the [newspaper], who have already saved space for it. If I have time I put together a longer story for [special news program on U.S. radio network] or if there is not time, they interview me. By 5:00 PM I try to file for [a West Coast U.S. newspaper]. I get an extra two hours for them. That's how I get through that lot. I am usually pretty nackered by then.

I became "pretty nackered" just observing the reporters' perpetual deadline dash.

The Second Floor

The primary location for the staff correspondents' work, and SPECA activity in general, was the second floor of the Camino Real Hotel. Most of the major bureaus were located there. Rather than isolated units, each office was part of a larger, communal space shared by all of SPECA. Rarely were office doors closed while journalists worked inside. Reuters reporters were almost as likely to be found in the Associated Press office as their own. Staff and camera crews for Visnews and CBS could be seen sitting around together, gambling in the hall, or commingling with the Televisa staff in their office. The second floor was public space.

Stringers were often part of the second floor scene as well. They visited the Camino while working with *A Team* correspondents, to use their offices while they were out of the country, or to chat with friends and colleagues. The wire service bureaus were an intermediate space, a comfortable place for both *A Team* and *B Team* journalists to drop in anytime. Likewise, the stringers' homes were important sites of communal corps activity.

The second floor and stringers' homes served several journalistic functions. The first, already mentioned, was that of providing professional meeting space for journalists to share ideas and coordinate reporting activities. Second, these were loci for information gathering. Every home and office had a radio with AM, FM, and short wave so that reporters could listen to the morning YSU broadcasts on the AM band and reports from Radio Farabundo Marti and Radio Venceremos on short wave and FM (Drucker 1984).

As mentioned earlier, the local press is a primary source of information for the foreign corps. "A lot of writers now a days just stay in the office," Joe observed, "They get news off of the radio or make a phone call." Indeed, when things are fairly slow, journalists often do little more than sit in their offices, eat, talk, and listen to the local radio broadcasts in case something should happen. "Some days you just sit and listen to the radio," explained Efrain, a Salvadoran working for an international wire, "YSU, to see what is going on."

Local television, while much less important, is another source of information for SPECA reporters. Most watch the evening news on Channel 12, which is especially useful for coverage of minor press conferences and events. They rely upon CNN to keep up with foreign news. The latter was a major source of frustration for SPECA journalists as they sat and watched the worlds' attention being directed elsewhere. It was especially frustrating for them during the Persian Gulf war, when news from the rest of the world, including El Salvador, was shoved aside almost completely. A few SPECA journalists found the frustration too great, finally leaving Central America to report on events in Saudi Arabia, Israel, and Iraq.

SPECA journalists read local newspapers as well, especially *Diario Latino* and *Diario de Hoy*, diametrically opposed organs. *Diario Latino* is the only alternative newspaper published in El Salvador. *Diario de Hoy*, on the other hand, has the largest readership in El Salvador and invariably represents the points of view of the far right. The *Diario Latino* staff and UCA authors satirize the *Diaro de Hoy* (daily journal), calling the right wing publication *"Diablo de Hoy"* (daily devil) (El Salvador Processo 1991:1–4). Reading both papers gave the journalists a better sense of what the organized left and the right were thinking, in addition to details concerning relatively minor issues and events.

SPECA journalists also receive press releases at their homes and offices. COPREFA news bulletins are delivered daily to the second floor offices, a counterbalance to information provided by FMLN radio. In one of the most interesting interviews I experienced, the colonel in charge of COPREFA explained his agency. He said that COPREFA was structured upon the model of Voice of America (VOA), the U.S. government's international radio network. He explained that COPREFA was created to combat "the very good propaganda campaign" of the FMLN.

The COPREFA chief also provided his interpretation of the history of El Salvador, the military, and the press. He represented the rising Salvadoran military elite, those who are slowly replacing the members of the *Tandona* —the military academy graduating class who have controlled the military for two decades. In his view, El Salvador was indeed a repressive, class-based society during the early part of the century. Such oppression and "marked distinctions," explained the officer, had lessened greatly, although there were still reasons for the people to rise up in the late 1970s. The "revolution as a foreign import" theory was, according to the COPREFA director, "more propaganda than truth." I was astonished by that last admission, as well as the colonel's confession that the army had once "considered the foreign press to be the 'enemy press.'" He also admitted "there was some truth in what [the foreign press] said about us." The COPREFA commander explained there were once real conditions of oppression, but also claimed the military had gone through fundamental changes during the war. Like most of his comrades, however, he believed the U.S.' low intensity war strategy had failed El Salvador by keeping the military from wiping out the FMLN, thus prolonging the war and his people's suffering.

In short, according to the head of COPREFA and the "liberal" wing of the army he represents, the oppression that once dominated El Salvador has now largely passed. This historical revision is much more sophisticated than the simple anti-communist line of ARENA. Armed with this more subtle method, what George called the "love bomb" approach, COPREFA had become a very sophisticated public relations tool for the military. Though most of the press greatly distrusts the army, many reporters believe the military has indeed become more democratic and professional.

In addition to COPREFA handouts, SPECA reporters also receive press releases from the Salvadoran government, political parties, the USIS, international human rights organizations, and grass roots opposition movements. The announcements involve upcoming news events, demonstrations, meetings, and press conferences. Of these various groups, the government, the USIS, and COPREFA produced the greatest volume of information.

The governing triumvirate also had much better press access throughout the war. Once I was sitting in the Reuters office when an emissary from the popular organizations appeared in the hall outside. She waited nervously at the door to be invited in. The journalists in the office failed to notice her, so she slowly approached me instead. The conversing journalists continued to ignore the young woman, while she offered me an envelope, thanked me politely and walked quickly from the room, no doubt relieved to be out of the foreign environs of the Camino Real. Conversely, one day as I was chatting with Harold, the ARENA press secretary wandered casually in to his office. She sat down with us and told Harold he would be granted an exclusive interview with President Christiani. I later interviewed her over breakfast. She was not difficult to find, her office was located at the center of the second floor, just across from Harold's. The Camino was a familiar environment for her and the powerful clique she represented.

These encounters symbolize the relationship between sources and the press. The "free market of ideas," like all markets, is owned by those with the greatest amount of capital, both cultural and economic. While the opposition must depend on the truth value of its arguments, power need only rely on the weight of its informational output and casual encounters with affines. While the Salvadoran Cooperative Federation (FEDECO-PADES) and other grass roots opposition volunteers pound out crude newsletters on old typewriters, the USIS, COPREFA, and Salvadoran government flood the press with millions of bits, bytes, and sheets of information. While such information may leave the SPECA journalists unimpressed, they heavily influence the editors and Washington beat reporters who write the major news columns, editorials and state-side reports concerning El Salvador. Therefore, it is best for U.S. SPECA reporters to channel a bit of that informational flood into their reporting as well. Furthermore, the ready-made information presents an extreme temptation to harried SPECA journalists, who do not always have time to collect their own body of information.

In addition to gathering information at their homes and offices, journalists also write, edit, and file reports there. Stringers write on their lap tops, cloistered away in their bedrooms while working under tight deadlines, or in the shared living space if less pressured. Staff correspondents write mainly at the office so that they can be close to the necessary resources, including Salvadoran aids and secretaries. As the site for these essential activities, the office scene was by far the most important space in SPECA culture. This is less true now that international coverage of Central America has fallen off dramatically and the second floor offices have been converted back to hotel rooms.

The Pseudo-Event as Press Ritual

O Ceremony, show me but thy worth!
What is thy soul of adoration?
Art though aught else but place, degree and form,
Creating awe and fear in other men?
—Shakespeare's King Henry V

Reporters evaluate, often on a collective basis, whether an event is newsworthy. The following chain of events is typical. Over a local radio broadcast, I heard the U.N. was going to escort a guerrilla leader to the Cuscatlan airport. During dinner at Shari's, I informed the gathered journalists from El Salvador, Japan, Mexico, and the U.S. about the upcoming event. Shari immediately called Jerry, who said he would check it out with others and call back. After a series of calls and discussions, the corps was able to garner the logistical details of the U.N. escort. Most of SPECA decided to cover the event. Car pools were formed and schedules set for the next day.

Though certain events will send reporters unreflexively running for coverage—*Coups and Earthquakes* come to mind (Rosenblum 1979)—most events are planned in advance, leaving the corps time to consider their newsworthiness. Daniel Boorstin refers to these planned occurrences, uncharitably, as "psuedo-events" (1964). A psuedo-event is any occurrence "planted primarily (not always exclusively) for the immediate purpose of being reported or reproduced" (1964:11). While I do not consider all such events "false" (psuedo), I believe Boorstin is correct in making the distinction between made-for-media rituals and other types of events.

"Ritual is an obsessive repetitive activity," explains Clyde Kluckhohn, "often a symbolic dramatization of the 'needs' of the society, whether 'economic,' 'biological,' 'social,' or 'sexual.' Mythology is the rationalization of these same needs, whether they are all expressed in overt ceremonials or not" (Kluckhohn in Doty 1986:75). The goal of the psuedo-event ritual is to bring political myth into practice, to posit a set of specific interests as the "needs" of society in general, to rationalize them (Kertzer 1988, Levi-Strauss 1967:205, Doty 1986:13–36). The psuedo-event serves as a bridge between the world of political myth and daily life, a play-acted attempt to manage the meta-frames upon which democratic power is predicated.[2] The mere telling of political ideas is inadequate. The performance of made-for-media rituals—press conferences, interviews, and photo opportunities—reanimate the meta-narratives in the micro-moment, making old into news.

The Press Conference as Drama

Tutela Legal, the human rights monitoring organization of the Catholic Church, held a press conference during the early part of my research. It was organized to publicize the El Zapote massacre through the testimony of the lone survivor. About fifteen local reporters where on hand, but only three SPECA journalists attended: Shawn, Bob, and Jerry. It was the most poorly attended press conference I witnessed during my time in El Salvador.

The press conference began with a short introduction by Monsignor Rosa Chavez. After his secular benediction, he sat down and the head of Tutela Legal, Maria Julia Hernandez, began to read the 81-year-old woman's testimony. As is true with all press conferences, Tutela Legal could have simply delivered the woman's words to the journalists' offices in a press release or given copies to them upon their arrival. However, that would have undermined the theatrical purpose of the ritual. Such information is most often held until the media ceremony is concluded. If distributed beforehand, it is usually "embargoed," given to reporters under condition it not be filed until the press conference, speech, or related psuedo-event has been performed.

After Maria Julia Hernandez finished reading the testimony, the 81-year-old woman spoke for herself. A hush fell over the small crowd as she boldly stated: "My children were killed by soldiers." She went on to describe how the judge pressured her to change her testimony. Finally, the elderly woman concluded her statement with an indictment of the Salvadoran justice system, stating that Salvadoran legal officials "do not want to see justice done."

Seventeen minutes of questions and answers followed. As was almost always the case, local reporters asked the first several questions. The initial part of the interrogation involved questions for Monsignor Chavez. Then a local reporter asked the prelate if it would be possible to direct a question at "her," meaning the elderly massacre survivor seated to his right. Chavez agreed and everyone's attention turned to the principal character. Others also queried the elderly woman. One reporter asked: "Are you afraid now that you have made this statement?" To which she simply replied "No."

As was clear in this case, press conferences are designed to provide a sense of action to the news narrative. The psuedo-event enables correspondents to report quotes with proximity, not just "he said...she said" but *how* and with what affect. Tutela Legal used the face-to-face event as a means to animate the otherwise lifeless facts and quotations found in standard press releases. The grandmotherly survivor of the massacre was brought before the reporters for just such an effect, and her presence was truly powerful. Once again, I use the term psuedo-event as a way to distinguish between the carefully planned media-oriented occurrences and others, not to denigrate all of them as "false." The fact the Tutela Legal conference was a ritual performance does not take away from its considerable truth value.

The psuedo-event is a ritual invention which meets the needs of all participants: the directors (institutional sponsors), actors (spokespeople), and audience (journalists as surrogate audience for the reader-citizenry). The press conference is a dramatic, ritualized, and embodied performance through which an institution's world view is made real. It is that view or "paradigm" which is truly in contention, not the factual matters relayed therein. The play is the thing. Therefore, political organizations must be dramaturgically adept and semioticly skilled if they are to succeed in modern politics and media.

Just as fictional drama is judged according to aesthetic and social criteria—as more or less "moving" and/or humanly relevant—reporters judge press conferences based on a set of culturally-specific performance values, including that of "authenticity." A good performance not only dazzles and flows, it also convinces the reporter that the spokespeople, and thus their message, are sincere. In the case of the Tutela Legal conference, the apparent conviction on the part of Monsignor Chavez was very effective (and affective). Shawn explains how the conference prompted him to do a lengthy follow-up report on the El Zapote massacre:

> What made me want to write the story is that the Church really wanted to go to the mattress on the case. It was amazing that Rosa Chavez would come out as strong as he did.... I think he is pretty good.... I mean, the man speaks in very measured terms and he doesn't get upset in public and he doesn't really go after the army but he'll talk about political violence and that stuff, but in this case he was just livid! You were at that press conference. I saw it as a real sea change in the position of not only the Church, but Rosa Chavez. They really wanted to take the army on in this one.

In other words, it was not just the informational content of the event, but Chavez' emotional tone and sense of conviction which moved Shawn to write the follow-up article.

The psuedo-event makes concepts "real," embodying abstract ideas in the comprehensible form of human actors and dialogue. Often, the press conference drama is a ritual reenactment of previously unwitnessed events. For reporters who covered the Tutela Legal conference, the issue was no longer just another case of statistical murder—part of the "75,000 dead"—but instead the massacre of a grandmother's entire family, a strong and kindly woman they were allowed to hear, see, and touch. Abstractions made flesh.

As Boorstin makes clear, psuedo-events have come to dominate news coverage (1964). Unfortunately, this has not greatly benefited marginal organizations like Tutela Legal. Those with the greatest cultural, political, and economic resources have colonized the journalists' time with an incessant array of arranged performances, forcing their opposition, like Tutela Legal, to do likewise. Unfortunately, power has better production values.

Pseudo-events have become an easy replacement for "organic" events, not to mention independent research and investigation. Psuedo-events are favored by news sources because they retain inordinate control of the performance vis-à-vis the journalist. Press conferences, in particular, allow organizations to maintain a great deal of temporal and spatial control over the communication process. Furthermore, the press conference format forces journalists to ask very simple questions. Each journalist knows that she will be allowed only one or two questions, and that her questions should be simple enough to allow for relatively short answers. Those asking complex and/or compound questions invade other journalists' time by compelling complicated and time consuming responses. Journalists abusing these basic rules of decorum receive censure from their colleagues, who demand equal time and access. Therefore, press conferences allow, if not require news makers to offer slogans or "sound bites" rather than involved and thoughtful responses. Simple questions demand simple answers. When performers wish to explain their positions more fully, they usually do so in the uncontested introduction period. In short, press conferences are, for the most part, an exercise of power.[3]

Manufacturing Consensus

In addition to press conferences, much of the news is derived from interviews. The interview is an efficient means of communication and the preferred method among journalists. In an interview, the reporter can delimit the range of issues herself, thus facilitating a more rapid and targeted exchange of information. Archival research, observation, and other information gathering techniques are much more difficult and time consuming.

Journalists use interviews as their primary means of validating information. A fact or statement is considered to be accurate, or at least publishable, if it has been repeated in separate interviews by reputable sources. This is usually what they mean by the term "confirmation." If the small community of sanctioned sources holds something to be true, then it is generally "confirmed" as such, whether or not the empirical evidence warrants such a conclusion.

In *Manufacturing the News*, Mark Fishman describes how the press "manufactured" a crime wave against the elderly in New York, based on anecdotal evidence and assertions that contradicted statistical reality (1980:4–10). While police records indicated that criminal acts against the elderly had actually *decreased*, the press nevertheless assembled a crime wave out of several isolated, albeit graphic, incidents. Immediately, this "crime wave" against the elderly became a major theme in local political and police circles. The police started a special monitoring unit for crimes against the elderly and the mayor's office made it a central cause of their administration. Fishman explains the self-perpetuating aspect of the crime wave coverage (1980:10):

> Thus, a week and a half after the coverage started, the police wire was steadily supplying fresh incidents almost every day. And when there was an occasional lack of crimes, there was plenty of activity among police, politicians, and community leaders to cover.

When the special monitoring stopped months later, so did the crime wave.

Fishman's example illustrates the incestuous nature of news knowledge. Reporters rarely step outside their source community or utilize other methods of information gathering, such as archival records, observation, or statistical sampling. This is not to say that SPECA reporters are overly credulous. They are quite aware that much of what they hear from sources is false. "This place is a real minefield to report," explained Cary, "Everyone lies to you. Everyone is a real expert at it after ten years of war." For the reporter, it often becomes a matter of which lies make the most newsworthy quotes.

With quote-bound journalism, other forms of knowledge become fairly irrelevant. Academic texts, for example, have little place in the modern journalist's preparatory arsenal. While they may use archival news clippings for contextual background, they rarely if ever read the works of academic researchers. Referring specifically to the use of academic research, David explained he was "surprised how little [journalists] are involved in outside intellectual endeavors." Indeed, "intellectual endeavors," including serious research, are "outside" the average journalist's reporting practice.[4] Rather than conceiving of reporting as an "intellectual" exercise, most journalists envision their labor as a set of basic work routines. Little methodological creativity is possible given the logistical constraints reporters must deal with every day. Get the quotes, write the story, have a beer. Repeat the same routine tomorrow.

That routine is rarely a solo effort, however. Most news is produced by committee. Journalists gather after witnessing an event to discuss and "negotiate" what they have seen. Like cops at a crash site, journalists are often faced with the daunting task of sifting through wildly divergent interpretations of events. For example, after a presidential press conference Cal, Jerry, and George discovered they had each translated the same statement in radically divergent ways. After discussion, they came to agreement on a single quote, which may or may not have resembled Christiani's original statement and intent. Consensual filtering of statements, events, and issues was the norm.

Reporters are usually in a tertiary relationship to the news events they cover. Since they are rarely at the scene of breaking events (e.g., battles, earthquakes, political negotiations) they must collect and evaluate others' interpretations thereof (Goldstein 1985:111). Given their emphasis upon elite sources, who themselves are usually hearing about events second- and third-hand, reporters are often evaluating others' interpretations of others' interpretations, and so on. The journalist must comb through complex layers of interpretation and representation, hoping to derive a more concretized sense of the original event. Psuedo-events are a great aid in this interpretive process. In psuedo-events, complex realities are filtered into simpler versions and usable bits, essential facts and quotes. Like legal trials, psuedo-events reduce complex realities into two-dimensional form, producing manageable outlines of complex issues. Journalists complete the process among themselves in intra-press negotiations, reducing "the story" to its most significant, or at least its most marketable, elements.

Cal explains one of the causes of "consensus news":

> There is a lot of peer pressure. If everybody else is covering a story—especially in a wire service—and you don't have it, then your clients are going to be angry. You have to cover consensus news.

The U.S. press, if not the international press system as a whole, is nothing if not duplicative. A television correspondent in Panama once received an angry call from his foreign desk after failing to duplicate a colleague's false report. Told the report was a lie, the desk manager shouted, "I don't care. You were scooped!"

As Todd Gitlin demonstrates in *Inside Prime Time*, "Safety first is the network rule" in entertainment programming (1983:63). This is true for news as well. Considerable deviation from the consensual line exposes a deviant news institution to heightened criticism from government, advertisers, and other organizations (Gitlin 1988:190–91, Herman and Chomsky 1988:26–28). The result is inter-institutional conformity and a high degree of ideological consensus.

The pack mentality starts at the top, gradually working its way down to those who do the footwork. Othello, a veteran radio reporter, provided a humorous anecdote concerning pack behavior during the early part of the war. One afternoon, journalists were sitting around the lobby bar of the Camino Real Hotel, waiting for something "big" to happen. Suddenly, the long wait was over. Two reporters darted from their table, running towards the door with an important mission in mind. The other reporters immediately leapt from their chairs, following their rushing colleagues into the parking lot. The two reporters got in their jeep and drove off while a caravan of anxious correspondents remained hot on their trail. First the pack turned right onto Boulevard de los Heroes, then right again on a side street, another right onto Calle Sisimiles, another right onto Boulevard de los Heroes and, finally, right back into the Camino Real. The flock had made a full circle, following their colleagues in and out of the hotel for no apparent reason. The twin leaders of the pack returned to their table, started reading the newspaper, and suppressed their urge to laugh as bemused colleagues filtered back into the air conditioned comfort of the Camino. The two had been conducting an experiment, one which quite successfully demonstrated the schooling-effect of modern journalism.

"The pack mentality," says Bob, is part of "the incredibly infantile competitiveness of U.S. journalism." Lester agrees:

> There is the same problem everywhere: a pack mentality. One of my greatest disappointments in my first several years overseas was, like everyone else, I thought that the foreign correspondent was the epitome of the craft. In fact, while there are tremendously brave, informed, brilliant, and talented people out there, the majority of correspondents are as bad as any reporters domestically. It's a cliché, but true—clichés are often true—they stay in the same place, stay in the same hotel, travel only with each other, talk to only each other.... In El Salvador they all live in Escalon—I live in Escalon—and they never go downtown or to other parts. All their friends, all the parties involve other foreign correspondents.

Teri, a Canadian correspondent, called the pack "a waste of energy." She gave several examples where the entire corps redundantly chased the same story, even single *aspects* thereof, while other events were happening "which would have been at least as important to cover." Massing calls this the "principle rule of the pack—that all journalists in town should chase the same predictable stories" (1989:42). That is perhaps the saddest aspect of the pack mentality, the hundreds of important issues ignored for the sake and safety of institutional duplication.

Warren, a wire service stringer, blames editorial pressure: "I constantly have to fight with my editors over getting 'scooped,' usually by Notimex [the Mexican wire service]. I tell them that I was there. He just saw it differently." Warren explained how his editors keep a constant account of his bureau's relative success. If his company begins losing out to other services, the blame is usually placed on Warren's reporting and any idiosyncrasies therein. As a result, Warren must constantly be aware of the pack line and agenda.

Pack reporting causes journalists to witness the same events, hear the same testimonies and, via group negotiation, frame them in a similar fashion. The consensual frame then becomes an objective standard. Divergent reporting will often be evaluated as "biased." There is ideological safety in numbers. Parachuting, psuedo-event packaging, and pack reporting are effective means for creating safe and fairly homogenous news.

RECREATIONAL RITUALS

"Along with the emotional problems they create, all cultures provide socially acceptable outlets or anodynes."

—Jules Henry (1963:26)

"We are not really *Latin* Americans, and we are not really Americans anymore," Lana said to Shari over breakfast, "so what are we?" Shari did not respond. There is no easy answer to that question. The expatriate press, like all cultures, is an amalgam of separate influences and experiences—part North American, part Latin American, part European, part upper class, part middle class, urban, educated, visual, verbal; the list continues. Out of that diverse mix comes a new and unique whole formed out of its separate parts, a foreign press corps culture.

In corps culture, both work and play are patterned by professional goals, with little distinction made between the two. Whereas, most workers "experience a distinction between their employer's time and their 'own' time" (Thompson 1967:61), the two are hopelessly merged in the life of the foreign correspondent. Bart explains:

It's not like there is a real distinction between work and free time.... I feel that it doesn't really exist for me here.... Here, it's not that I am so overwhelmed with work that I don't have free time, it's just that most of my free time seems to be dedicated with something to do with either journalism or journalists.

Whether they are Salvadoran, Japanese, or North American, the members of SPECA are, first and foremost, foreign correspondents. War correspondents, a special subspecies, are that much more distinguished by their professional identification. They work together, play together, eat together, live together, and often, sleep together. They are a community and a culture.

The preceding chapters dealt mainly with journalists' professional work. This chapter is about their professional play, the ways in which war correspondents recreate themselves through ritual. Not all recreational activities are rituals, however. Reporters play basketball, have semi-normal dating lives, go to the beach, listen to music, and are engaged in other activities that lack the social importance, repetition, standardization, and cultural meanings commonly defined as ritual (Doty 1986:1–40). If this were a simple "day in the life" study, I would write about such behaviors. Rather, I am trying to convey a sense of those activities that are more common, communal, and meaningful; in a word, ritual.

I will describe three particularly important recreational rites: the opinion and storytelling ritual, rituals of sexuality, and finally, ritual intoxication. I argue that many of these expressions represent alternative means of communication, spaces where reporters may act out their professional myths, identities deferred during normal work routines. Ritual fills this void between myth and practice, and in so doing, helps resolve the contradictions between them.

The Opinion and Storytelling Ritual

"The level of frustration was high, and frustrated people love to talk."
—Hortense Powdermaker (1950:6)

The more profound the disjunction between reporters' phenomenological knowledge of events and the texts they create, the greater their sense of frustration, anger, and alienation. Impassioned with purpose, but disciplined by practice, many reporters seek to find communicational outlets outside their news reporting. Conversations with friends and colleagues provide one such outlet. Several correspondents, especially the male stringers, project their opinions in very public and ritualized ways, especially when among other reporters. Terilyn noted this tendency among her male colleagues:

> I'm really amazed by the amount of machismo I see in the press corps here. And, it's not as simple as I thought at the offset. Many people don't fit into it, like Othello. But, there are all these other people who do, like Paul — who I think is wonderful. I guess I should define machismo. The womanizing and the drinking is one aspect of it…. The other side of it are the enormous egos, reflected in this egoistic mood, sitting there and pontificating about opinions all the time, and then saying the same things to

another person, and then another, and always the same thing!.... From what I can tell they are pontificating because they love to hear themselves speaking their opinion as if it is the last word. I sit there rolling my eyes, thinking, "I had to hear this two days ago. Do I have to hear it again? Can we talk about something else?"

She complained that Shawn, Cary, and Paul were particularly subject to this "egoistic mood."

Herbert Gans found the same tendency among domestic reporters: "From time to time, journalists have strong opinions about individual issues which they can neither express in their stories nor keep bottled up inside." Many of the frustrated journalists "express themselves in conversations" (Gans 1979:187). Gans found the opinions expressed in these discussions to be more critical than those contained in the journalists' published news reports. The same was true for SPECA. The war reporters expressed much more critical and combative views of U.S. intervention, the Salvadoran government, and the Salvadoran military during these backstage debates. By comparison, their written discourse is much more acritical, and homogeneous.

The opinion and storytelling ritual provides reporters a cultural space within which they may act out their war correspondent persona, projecting the intellectual authority and macho bravado which defines their lot. Reinventing the myths of war correspondents past—"In the great line of Crane, Orwell, and Hemingway" (Herr's back cover)—they fit their new experiences into the narrative structure of traditional war correspondent legends. There are two major types of stories told in these sessions. The first are those trumpeting the heroism of a journalist, usually the speaker herself. The second type highlight the failures of others.

The stories in the first category usually begin with the reporter-protagonist choosing to enter a dangerous situation, followed by the intervention of authority and/or sudden violence, and serious threats to the reporter-protagonist's life. An act of unusual intelligence and/or bravery on the part of the reporter-protagonist leads to a narrow escape in the end. These stories were most common among war photographers.

If the war correspondent narrative sounds like the plot to a classic western film (or *Star Trek* episode), it is because they are derived from the same cultural meta-narrative: the fiercely independent, intelligent, and brave male, who by virtue of those qualities is able to overcome seemingly insurmountable obstacles. That mythological narrative is an idealized description of American conceptions of masculinity, detailing the initiation process through which that status is achieved. In the specific case of war correspondents, these legends describe the initiation of neophyte reporters into the world of seasoned, veteran professionals. For several SPECA correspondents, the Salvador experience seemed to be nothing but an attempt to gather such experiences and tales, to participate in the grand narrative of modern war. They were out to overcome and conquer their fears, if not the war itself. It was a personal test judged by corps colleagues.

Therefore, war correspondents make a fetish of combat. Without it, there is nothing to distinguish their work from others. They would be nothing but *plain* correspondents. In order to promote and celebrate their role, they collect and practice stories of war, telling them to each other and whoever else will listen. The following story is typical.

During the FMLN offensive of November 1989, Paul was working in an embattled area of San Salvador when approached by a mother whose baby had been hit by shrapnel. She begged Paul to drive her and the child to the hospital. He agreed. Paul began to drive out of the zone, choosing the safest route away from the fighting. Unfortunately, the mother demanded they take the most direct path to the hospital. Although he knew it was a mistake, Paul yielded to his passenger's request. They were then captured by the military. The soldiers "were really pissed off," said Paul, "because half of the them had been wiped out that day." The soldiers charged Paul with working for the FMLN and prepared to execute him.

Paul believes he would have been shot, were it not for the subsequent actions of the woman. Her baby died that moment and she "went crazy," screaming at the soldiers and accusing them of killing her child. They took pity on her and agreed to simply arrest Paul. They took him to the military police headquarters and interrogated him. Paul then did what he called "a Ronald number," shouting that he was a journalist and should not be treated in such a manner. The official in charge explained that they would not interrogate him any further, but that he had better be careful not to insult soldiers in the future. It turns out that the soldiers had mistaken Paul for Ronald, who had insulted several military men that same day.

Notice how Paul, the protagonist, demonstrates a great degree of willful agency, how he is almost completely autonomous in his decision-making process, and independent in his actions, unfettered by anything but environmental obstacles. There are physical impediments—roadblocks, warriors, weapons—but no disciplinary constraints (e.g., deadlines, editors, conventions). He risks danger for the sake of the truth and an injured child. In selecting such a story for public consumption, Paul reduces all the normal complexities to a morality tale involving good guys (reporter and peasants) and bad guys (the military). There are no ideological vagaries nor contradictions to muddy the white warrior's struggle against the forces of evil. Most importantly, good triumphs in the end. Paul escapes with body intact and a further claim to legendary status.

I admire Paul, however, for being one of the few whose legendary projections are matched by practice. He really does work, think, and act fairly independently, a pro-social existentialist in a world full of conformists of one stripe or another. Paul is unusual. So were Hemingway and Orwell.

Though they are promoted as exemplars of the profession, they are aberrations rather than models of typical war correspondent behavior. Unlike Paul, most journalists who invoke the names and legends of great correspondents past do not act in a similar fashion. But it is not necessarily the truth value of these stories that matters here, but rather the telling itself. In selecting these particular stories for the ritualized exchange, the reporters betray a strong desire for validation from the rest of the corps. By selecting and projecting their finest moments, they hope to be judged worthy of the mythological tradition to which they belong.

Many of these stories involve an injury incurred by the speaker and/or the death of an associate. Fortunately, during the period of my research only two SPECA members were injured and none were killed. Both of the wounded reporters fell victim to the same attack. One received relatively superficial wounds on his leg. The other suffered more serious injuries, including a "sucking" chest wound (hole in chest wall from trauma of gunshot or stabbing, where air is forced into and out of the wound, if victim is still alive), and still has a small piece of shrapnel lodged in his chest.

The two were talking with some villagers in Chalatenango province when suddenly a mortar hit, fired from twelve kilometers away. They were not directly targeted for attack, given the great distance, but the event nevertheless served to change their feelings about the war. One said he was "taught the lesson of risk evaluation," implying he would be much more careful in the future. He also gained "a better feeling about what it is like to be a civilian in a war zone."

The other was moved to hate the army even more than he did before the attack. After being dressed in the field, he was rushed to a hospital in San Salvador. On the way, the group was stopped and detained twice by military officials. At one point they were pinned down behind a gun battle for two hours. Later, at a reten the wounded reporters and the uninjured radio journalist accompanying them were told to get out of the truck, their press passes confiscated. The commander in charge told them he did not believe they were really journalists. Such threatening encounters hardly ingratiated the press with the military, but may have been part of the reason army actions and offensives were consistently left out of the news (In fact, the military would often make certain such incidents would not be publicized. Once, after a National Police guard came across my press registration, silence became the condition of my release. I had to promise I would not write about the threats he made or money he stole from me.)

Fortunately, the wounded reporter made it back to San Salvador in time. As he was being prepped for surgery, the gathered corps came rushing in to get the injured man's story. The doctor asked the encroaching reporters: "Do you want him to live or do you want the news!" "Don't ask them that, Doctor!" shouted the wounded journalist. Later, only half jokingly, he called his fellow journalists "vultures."

Once healed, the more seriously injured of the two wrote about the incident. He handed me an eight page, single-spaced narrative that begins: "A sucking chest wound is nature's way of telling you that you've been in a firefight," a Marine corps proverb. The narrative is written in second person perspective:

> Ka-boooooom!!!!!!!!! A sharp, surgical piercing that you almost don't feel slices into you just before the sound and the impact of the explosion blasts you full in the chest....
>
> Just as the surging, awful WHY ME's? begin to well up inside you, a subconscious terrible fear takes over, the unthinkable fear of every man in combat, the unspeakable horror, of what they call THE WOUND. Because if you survive, you can live with it whatever it is, but oh, God, NO, anything, but NOT THOSE!!

I heard the reporter repeat the story several times, and later heard pieces of it repeated by reporters as far away as Guatemala. The story was told with uncanny precision each time, emphasizing the actual moment the mortar shell hit, the military detention, and his painful operation. Mostly left out was the stringer's subsequent struggle to get his clients to pay for his medical bills and the criticisms of colleagues, who argued the protagonist should have hit the ground when warned of incoming mortar fire (the audio of the tape, according to a friend of the injured journalists, includes a child shouting the equivalent of "incoming"). Once again, it is not the veracity of the claims but rather the editorial comment that interests me. The injured storyteller is projecting himself as the archetype war correspondent, discarding elements of the story that might detract from the intended image of overcoming adversity.

Many stories trumpet the journalists' clever means of overcoming press obstacles. I was told how members of the Honduran corps fooled Contra camp guards by posing as CIA agents, of a reporter escaping death by hiding in a chicken shed, and dozens of other parables where the protagonist-journalist deceived authority and/or defeated danger. Reacting to a set of allegorical tales Michele and Joe were telling one day, Jerry chided: "These stories get better every time they are told." He then told me two of his own.

In addition to anecdotes, the corps also accumulates and displays material representations of war. The macabre collection included parts of recently downed U.S. helicopters on display in the CBS, Visnews, and Agence France Press (AFP) bureaus. SPECA's predecessors in Vietnam went so far as posting Viet Cong body parts in their offices (Rosenblum 1979:60). These gruesome assemblages symbolize the reporters' symbiotic relationship with war, fitting fetishes to their verbal narratives.

As mentioned earlier, the offensive was a definitive moment for the corps, a time when true war correspondents became known as such, and others were marked as failures and cowards. Anecdotes concerning these "failures" made up a significant part of another category of stories: tales defining exemplary practice via negative example. Those who risked their lives to cover events like the 1989 offensive, mainly the *B Team*, photographers, internationals, and some Salvadorans, castigated those who failed to venture far from the hotel, mainly the *A Team* and other parachuters. Dozens of stories were told of parachuters who did little more than jog back and forth between the Camino Real and The Embassy.

One network television correspondent, whom I will call Al, continues to be a prominent subject of SPECA stories and those told in other Latin American corps. According to several SPECA reporters, including members of his own crew, Al never stepped foot outside the Camino while covering the 1989 offensive. He was too frightened to even walk out to the protected poolside where TV correspondents do their obligatory stand-up shots against the garden backdrop of jungle-like foliage. Likewise, during the Panama invasion Al was to be found in the towel room of the Panama City Marriot. As a result, he has earned the nickname "Action Al."

A member of Action Al's staff had this to say about his coverage: "He didn't know what was going on. He just sat there by the computer. The producer checks the material. Al doesn't even *see* the material before he reads it on the air." One of the reporter's crews, having witnessed a promotional commercial which posited Al as the epitome of foreign correspondence, produced a video spoofing his reporting. Al was one of the highest paid reporters in Latin America and also one of its biggest laughingstocks.

Al's producer was no better. Early on in the offensive, his camera crew came in from the streets claiming the army had not regained control of the city. Despite his hotel-bound vantage point, the producer overruled them, going with The Embassy version of events over the eyewitness evidence of his own crew. "It doesn't matter what I think," complained one of the Salvadoran crew members after the incident. Like most mainstream U.S. media, the producer's news broadcast claimed the army had retaken the city. Days later, the FMLN overtook even more territory, including the neighborhood of Escalon where President Christiani's house is located. Although the producer only left the Camino Real once during the 1989 FMLN offensive, he still had the gall to send his Salvadoran camera crew back out whenever they failed to produce proximate footage of the fighting.

The stringers' tales of *A Team* failures during the 1989 offensive all led to the same punch line: the latter group's premature claim the military had retaken San Salvador. After I asked a stringer for copies of her stories, one of Bart's FMLN offensive reports—complete with the aforementioned miscue—was slipped into the same packet. I assume the story was placed there as editorial comment on her *A Team* colleagues' lack of awareness.

Stringers enjoy telling stories about the *A Team*'s journalistic missteps and cultural distance from the conflict, parables that include an *A Team* couple who spent a fortune importing 100 pounds of U.S. dog food so they would not have to subject their pooch to a Salvadoran brand, or a TV network correspondent who tramped through a bombing site to examine crystal dishes in a gallery window. These stories of *A Team* failure and excess were part of a team-building process for the stringers. By detailing others' inadequate behaviors, the tellers of the failure were implicitly claiming that their own practices were adequate, if not exceptional.

Team unity was not always in evidence, however. As described earlier, the realities of war lead to group solidarity (pack reporting) and stress (fear of spies in the corps). So too, there is an element of competition involved in the opinion and storytelling ritual. I witnessed an unusually clear example of this in Guatemala when a photo agency mistakenly dispatched two photographers to the same site. One of them was Paul, the other a U.S. journalist who flew in from France. A turf war ensued as each competed to produce better photos and to more greatly impress their colleagues. Paul made the most of his status as a war correspondent, throwing out even more vulgarities and anecdotes than usual. His competitor projected an air of sophistication, mouthing obscure literary references and other pedantic non sequiturs. When I asked the young photographer about his nationality, he replied, "American, but many people consider me European."

This duel illustrates competing themes in foreign correspondence: the down-and-dirty war reporter vs. the refined world traveler, two halves of the foreign correspondent mystique. Paul was cognizant of that dichotomy, and worked to undermine his competitors' performance at every opening. Calling his competitor "ignorant," he later provided this following piece of evidence: "He said that the Sri Lankan war is over, but it's not."

Terilyn, a neophyte reporter, found equal fascination in the quarrel:

This weekend it was fascinating seeing the degree of professional jealousy when you get a whole bunch of press people together. When we were at the Boniface [hotel] that day when you and Shari were having lunch, I was just wide-eyed, sitting back and watching the interchange between Shawn and Paul and these other guys.... Paul was surprised to see this guy who usually works in France, so we had turf issues going on. It was really fascinating. You could just see professional jealousy and an incredible level of commentary. A sentence would be said, and underneath it would be a whole other sentence.

When the duel had concluded, Paul declared victory. The agency used his photos instead of his parachuting opponent's. Much to Paul's delight, his competitor used the wrong type of film. He was still very angry, however, at the other photographer, whom he called a "jerk," and at the agency for breaking their exclusive commitment to his work in the region.

In much the same manner anthropologists use "literary allusions and baroque rhetorical forms" as "weapons" in their professional disputes (Murphy 1990:332), war correspondents brandish claims to privileged information, knowledge of political intrigue, and tales of battlefield bravery in their quest to gain competitive advantage vis-à-vis their war corps colleagues. It is, quite simply, a matter of bragging. Of course, they were not only bragging to each other, but to me as well. After I warned a stringer of an encounter with the National Security Police outside the Camino (they detained, threatened, and robbed me, referring to me as *pelon* or "baldy," an insult I was getting used to hearing in El Salvador), the reporter responded with a display of macho bravado, bragging he would walk right by the men. "If they do that to me," he boasted, "I'll have my *urbano* (urban guerrilla) buddies kill them."

As Terilyn stated, ritual opinion and storytelling is a "macho" thing—mainly, but not exclusively, male. The performers in the opinion ritual and competition tended to be men. Aside from Rosa, female journalists were rarely as vociferous as their male colleagues. They would usually be present as participant-observers to the ritual, an audience of which the men were no doubt highly aware (Rosenblum 1979:52–53).

Female correspondents tended to deal with fear and terror in a less public and boisterous manner. Whereas, the men would use cock-sure posturing and competitive conversation as a means to express their relationship to war, the women in SPECA generally preferred to speak to the issue of terror in a more direct manner. The female reporter accompanying the two men wounded in the aforementioned mortar attack, for example, reacted to the experience differently from her male colleagues. She asked her wounded colleagues to get together with her to talk about the incident. The most seriously wounded reporter, author of the "NOT THOSE" narrative, declined, criticizing her for proposing "some work through it shit." "It's no big deal," he explained, "You have to expect it going in. If you're not prepared for it, you should be in a different job." Months later, the female correspondent left the world of journalism while her male critic, ever the war correspondent, was wearing his wound like a badge of distinction. Obviously, the injury was a "big deal" to him, but not one a self-respecting war correspondent would "work through" in a thoughtful dialogue with friends. The wounded man was fond of repeating the claim: "The only therapy for journalists is detox."

It was hard not to be a little bit put off by the macho pretense of it all, as were most of the women. I am hesitant to call such behavior "emotional sublimation" or to label the ritual itself a dysfunctional communication process. It is merely the reporters' means of relating to reality and to each other. As the wounded man's behavior demonstrates, the opinion and storytelling ritual is a means by which reporters salvage a sense of self worth and make an appeal for acceptance into their social group.

War as "Fun"

Many SPECA journalists referred to battle coverage as "fun." Like amateur rock climbers and bungee jumpers, war correspondents gain a sense of challenge, danger and pleasure protected by the twin virtues of distance and choice. Herbert Gans determined most reporters in his study "did not become journalists to advocate values or reform society," but were instead drawn by "the opportunity to be in the midst of exciting activities without having to be involved" (1979:185). That holds true for international war correspondents as well.

Contemporary capitalism is predicated upon consumption, the creation of ever greater needs, desires, and experiences. However, it is also predicated upon contradictory work practices that are routinized, specialized, and bureaucratized. Therefore, consumer capitalist culture impels us to be ascetic workers by day, aesthetic consumers by night. "Fun" is the disciplinary complement to work. As Henry explains, "[I]n fun the American saves part of his Self from the system that consumes him. Fun, in its rather unique American form, is grim resolve" (Henry 1963:43). That "grim resolve" is shared by war correspondents. They use both fun and fantasy to escape their stultifying structural realities and fulfill mythical imperatives.

The war correspondents' practice was permeated and mediated by currents of pop culture. As Herr explains, "We'd all seen too many movies, stayed too long in Television City, years of media glut had made certain connections difficult" (1968:209). Even for Salvadoran journalists, real violence and fictional media representations were hopelessly intertwined. "You sometimes forget that you are in a real war," said Sergio, a Salvadoran journalist, "It seems more like you are watching a movie." Indeed, such distinctions become difficult for those of us whose childhoods were spent swimming through images of media violence. One day, as I got out of a taxi in downtown San Salvador, I saw a large pack of high school boys screaming around the corner, chased by another boy shooting a pistol into the air and shouting threats. I looked up at the scene in the same manner one watches television after a long day of work, minimally distracted but not thoughtfully engaged. Even before the bizarre tableau departed around the corner, I returned to my conversation with the driver. The elder gentleman stood in front of me staring curiously into my eyes as if to say "Didn't you see that, gringo?" In that and other instances I did "see" it, but I am not sure I really experienced it.

One of my oddest experiences was being held at gunpoint outside a movie theater showing "The Silence of the Lambs." I was told to throw down my bag as two soldiers pointed their rifles at my head. They were making threatening comments. One was clicking his trigger. Fortunately, a young officer ran over and screamed for the older grunts to let me go. I then went inside to see the movie. I remember the movie much more vividly than the incident outside. The film seemed, and still seems, much more "real."

John Tomlinson explains, "reality must always be partly a function of our past experiences which generally, in modern cultures, include experiences of media texts" (1991:63). Contemporary correspondents, like most of us, are so heavily socialized and immersed within media representations of violence that their ability to distinguish such images from those encountered on the street or battlefield becomes nearly impossible. Real life and "reel life" have become hopelessly, and perhaps dangerously, intertwined in the late twentieth century. Real violence, like its imaginary counterpart, has become a form of personal entertainment.

The 1989 offensive, which most described as "fun," was one of those rare moments when SPECA journalists were able to live-out childhood fantasies, war movies, and professional identities in an all-too-brief orgy of playtime war. It is little wonder that legends of "The Offensive" dominated the SPECA storytelling ritual.

Phillip Knightley captures the entertainment ethos of war correspondence in "War is Fun," the concluding chapter to *The First Casualty* (1975:401–425). Knightley describes the way in which many journalists covering Vietnam had a "flip, throwaway attitude towards the war." "No one wants to admit it," said one "but there is a lot of sex appeal and a lot of fun in weapons" (419). "I think that Vietnam is what we had instead of happy childhoods," stated another (401).

El Salvador is what SPECA correspondents had instead of Vietnam. The post-Vietnam critiques of Knightley, Herr and others have added yet another layer of representation to SPECA's mythic image of the war and their role therein. Having emerged from Southeast Asia with mixed feelings of anger, accomplishment, maturity, mental instability, and above all, guilt, these journalists' texts add new levels of complexity and meaning to the war correspondents' collective persona. Having read the works of these correspondent-confessors, the SPECA reporters borrow an artificially constructed, ironic sensibility in representing their own practice. In interpersonal communication and daily work, they enliven their experience of 1990s El Salvador with cultural artifacts borrowed from 1960s Vietnam. They replay terms and vignettes gleaned from Herr, Knightley, and Francis Ford Coppola (*Apocalypse Now*) in much the same way children mouth war movie clichés and play-act scenes that transform frozen Iowa playgrounds into the tropical beachheads of World War IIs South

Pacific and other "theaters" of operation.

Likewise, legends of past Salvador reporters were integrated into the myth-time experience of 1990s SPECA reporters, images most often received via the mediation of Stone, Didion, or Bonner. The SPECA reporters of late war El Salvador exhibited a keen sense of nostalgia for realities they had never experienced. Ironically, those few journalists who had been in El Salvador throughout the entire war were much less likely to slip into the clichés of the "Salvador" days. They held less romantic views of the early war, a time when over 200 corpses per week were showing up on the streets, hills, and body dumps surrounding San Salvador. For these tragic few, there was neither fun nor fantasy to reward their work, just a pile of bad memories. As opposed to the show-and-tell tendencies of the rest of the corps, these few veterans preferred to keep their stories to themselves.

Ritualized Sexual Practices

Some SPECA journalists, particularly male staff correspondents and photographers, participate conspicuously in prostitution. Following the tradition of war correspondents past, they construct their professional identities through sexual adventure. Furthermore, through such adventures they recoup a sense of power, compensating for that which is ceded daily to censoring (neutering?) structures. In other words, they may not be allowed to write like Mr. Hemingway, but they can at least attempt to live like him. Therefore, it is only natural the world's oldest profession would intersect with one of its most frustrating.

Marla is angered by the cavalier attitudes of the male reporters towards sex and prostitution:

> Seeing prostitutes is something that is boasted about—not across the board, and more so among *A Team* reporters than independent reporters—but I wouldn't expect to have to sit through a conversation of that sort in the U.S. Just the fact that it is taking place is outrageous.

One night over dinner a staff correspondent told me about his experiences with various prostitutes, the first of many such conversations I took part in. He said he would never go to prostitutes in the U.S., but that it was acceptable to do so in El Salvador where, he claims, it is an accepted part of the culture.[1] Like freshman university students allowed to drink and "party" for the first time, these men suddenly felt free to indulge their sexual fantasies without fear of social censure.

One photographer said he liked to cycle back and forth between Salvadoran prostitutes and U.S. lovers. He referred to U.S. women as "independent" and Salvadoran women as "weak." After an "independent woman" he would be in the mood for a "weak" one, and vice versa. Though he was more explicit about it than most, this was a common dynamic. Reporters are attracted by the relative "weakness" of Salvadoran women. Sex is a source of personal empowerment, a means of reaffirming their potency via the reproduction of others' powerlessness.

One staff correspondent offered another reason for visiting prostitutes. "The war excites your life juices," he explained, "Your body understands the danger and says, 'Use me while you can.'" Not all of his relationships were with prostitutes, however, and in one tragic case, this correspondent's "life juices" got out of hand. He was forced to leave the country months later when the head of El Salvador's notorious National Police, a jealous ex-boyfriend of his Salvadoran lover, placed a bomb in his car. Luckily, no one was injured in the explosion. Weeks before the bombing, the reporter complained, "My dating life is unstable."

The bombing incident was covered by SPECA reporters until they learned of the troubling circumstances surrounding the event. That is unfortunate, for as Othello later pointed out, the bombing incident says much about El Salvador. "In the U.S.," said Othello, "if you like a cheerleader and so does the local cop, the cop probably won't kill you." Having survived and fled the country, however, Othello's young colleague will no doubt one day tell the story himself, perhaps in the traditional, heroic prose of war biography.

Although most reporters openly discussed their sexual exploits with prostitutes, they still exhibited a certain sense of shame. One wire service bureau chief dealt with his latent guilt by obtaining a department store job for his favored prostitute. Perhaps he honestly felt an obligation to help this woman. Or, perhaps he wanted to reserve her for himself alone, the ultimate act of machismo. I didn't know and didn't ask. I do know that he was disappointed when she returned to prostitution, unable to make a decent living as a store clerk.

Whatever their attitudes, the foreign correspondents engage in the same sort of sexual tourism put on naked display at places like the British Club, where American military advisers and AID workers sit around bragging about their encounters with Salvadoran *putas* (prostitutes), collapsing the bodies "self, social, and politic" (Scheper-Hughes and Lock 1987) in an ongoing orgy of neocolonialist domination (Sturdevant and Stoltzfus 1992). A good journalist, explains Adriana, tries to "establish a human relationship with the subject." Conversely, these correspondents establish a relationship of intimate exploitation and "dispassionate" power. Whereas, healthy sexuality involves a narrowing of social distance, the correspondents' sexual activities are ritual reenactments of the war itself, symbolic of the staff correspondents' relationship to the Salvadoran people in general. In the words of Michael Taussig, "[T]he victimizer needs the victim to create truth, objectifying fantasy in the discourse of the other" (1987:8). Through sexual exploitation, journalists "mimic the savagery they have imputed" to their Salvadoran victims as they passionately participate in the same culture of violence they coldly condemn in their reporting (1987:3-36).

I use the term "violence" guardedly, in recognition that prostitution need not be exploitative. However, the contract made between prostitute and client—as that between Salvadoran worker and employer, conscript and officer, peasant and landowner, maid and master—is formed within a context of gross social inequality. What is given is not offered under conditions of equity, but those of coercion and violence.[2]

Drugs and Alcohol

"Truth is the first casualty of war. Sobriety is the second."
—Frank "Hawkeye" Pierce from the television series *M.A.S.H.*

Thus far I have upheld the reputation of war correspondents as opinionated and *machista*. Indeed, I may have gone too far, since only about half of the corps members manifest both tendencies. Most SPECA women, for example, are neither conspicuously vocal concerning their political views or war exploits, and do not publicize their sexual practices in the same manner as many of the aforementioned men (see chapter 14). Having said that, however, I must go on to partially confirm another aspect of the war correspondent stereotype: that of the hard-drinking and harried foreign reporter. As the always-honest Efrain admitted, "We drink a lot, almost everyone."

As an Anthropologist, I saw my task as understanding the function of such things in the lives of my subjects. Therefore, I did my best to emulate Napoleon Chagnon and the other anthropologists who have shared experiences of ritual intoxication with their subjects (Chagnon 1968: 206–13). Unfortunately, because I only drink alcohol occasionally, I was not qualified for the task. While conducting a lunch interview with a British journalist, for example, we (mainly he) drank two bottles of wine in quick succession. As my questions became slurred and nonsensical, his answers only increased in clarity and insight. The popular depressant did not seem to have a dampening effect on this young Brit, nor the other journalists.

Other drugs, such as marijuana, seemed to serve an entirely different social purpose: communal sedation and escape. Gatherings involving marijuana were much quieter and less intense than the boisterous drinking sessions. One evening, for example, we gathered at a reporter's home to watch a World Series baseball game on television. As the evening began, the reporters were frenetic in their movements and conversation, as usual. They began the evening by debriefing a colleague who had just returned from Mexico City, where the recent negotiations between the FMLN and Salvadoran government were taking place. They then proceeded to fill their colleague in on events he had missed while away.

During the early innings, the pace of conversation matched that of the journalists' normal "work day"—fast, frenetic, and without pause for reflection. Then the pot brownies arrived, and the conversations turned from the "who, what, where, and hows" of recent events to matters of nonprofessional interest. The rate of conversation dropped off considerably and the element of showmanship disappeared almost completely. The marijuana ritual provided reporters with a much needed break from the mad dash intensity of their work.

The "down time" was a means of escape, not just from the work day, but from the nagging doubts, fears, and lies of press work. Herr explains how marijuana is used by war correspondents to avoid nightmares and memories (Herr 1968:33):

> In Saigon I always went to sleep stoned so I almost always lost my dreams, probably just as well, sock in deep and dim under that information and get whatever rest you could, wake up tapped of all images but the ones remembered from the day or the week before, with only the taste of a bad dream in your mouth like you'd been chewing on a roll of dirty pennies in your sleep. I'd watch grunts asleep putting out the REM's like a firefight in the dark, I'm sure it was the same with me. They'd say (I'd ask) that they didn't remember their dreams either when they were in the zone, but on R&R or in the hospital their dreaming would be constant, open, violent, clear....

Indeed, I encountered many such dreams among the corps (see Alonzo's dream, chapter 12). SPECA dreams, however, while certainly "constant" and "violent," where rarely so "clear."

Joe dreams that his bed is surrounded by land mines, a nightmare generated out of a real life hike he once took with Salvadoran troops in the conflicted zones. The hike, like the dreams, took place at night. Joe would often wake up in a cold sweat, disoriented. Meanwhile, once out of bed most of Joe's time was spent begging his bureau chief to let him visit the zones, hopelessly appealing to military officials to let him pass, or desperately searching for the elusive hit-and-run skirmishes that characterized the war. Joe's dreams, and those of his colleagues, represent their obsessive and contradictory relationship to the war. Like land mines around a comfortable bed, the war surrounded the SPECA reporters, but never really included them. Confusion and contradiction, fear and fascination—these are the demons and dreams that SPECA correspondents attempted to escape through sedation.[3]

In sum, marijuana was used to escape, not just from the terror, but the monotony and myriad lies reporters faced daily from their sources, and occasionally, themselves. Even escape was a group function, however. Most of the corps members displayed an almost pathological fear of being alone. Very few worked alone, and even fewer played alone. Harold is different, however. Harold is "burned-out."

Burn-out

In a telling exchange, a U.S. military adviser shouted at Michele, "You are earning money off of human misery." "That makes two of us," she shouted back. Indeed, violence is the war correspondents' primary commodity. Therefore, journalists often hope for the violence they cover to intensify. The corps constantly deliberated over the potential for further major guerrilla offensives. They wanted them. They needed them. At a Summit of Central American Presidents in June, 1990, a reporter stated, "I wish the *g's* (guerrillas) would hit this thing." Similarly, a photographer said she wished the police would "use tear gas or something" while covering a demonstration in San Salvador. During the signing of the Esquipulas II peace accords in 1987, reporters joked the presidential signatories should be required to reimburse the press corps for lost wages. Peace is good for humanity, but bad for war reporters. "You can either be a foreign correspondent," said Shawn, "or a human being."

Asked why journalists emphasize bodies and battles, Joe responded, "That is war. That is the news. That is why we are here." "If no one is killing each other," said Joe, "I ain't happy. I would get bored and quit. Any journalist that says they don't want to see things get worse is full of shit." Even the Salvadoran journalists in SPECA were, at best, ambivalent about the continuance of violence in their homeland. Several feared the end of the war because it would bring the end of their jobs as well. While at one level they wanted to see their country at peace, they also needed to feed their families. There was similar ambivalence among the stringers. One of them expressed "mixed feelings" about peace. She mentioned an FMLN friend who had been killed and another who had been tortured. Her sympathies lay with the guerrillas. She admitted a desire to see the FMLN stage another offensive in 1991, just as they had in 1989. To conclude her lament, she explained that an offensive would allow her and other stringers to pick up some much needed clients as well. It is difficult to separate the interwoven personal, political, financial, and professional motivations involved.

As in all professions where one sustains prolonged contact with human misery, the degree of frustration and eventual exhaustion is very high among war correspondents. As a result, few war correspondents remain in that role forever. Many stringers go back to their home countries and find positions in the domestic press. Only a few fortunate ones gain permanent foreign staff positions. A tiny minority become true "freelancers," earning relatively large advances to complete feature pieces for magazines or books. Many others leave the profession altogether, either sated by their short stints as war correspondents, or more often, frustrated by lack of advancement and job security. Some join other expatriate professions, such as human rights or international development.

Most staff correspondents either continue on in that role or eventually become editors. Only a few SPECA staffers expressed a desire to abandon journalism. One of the exceptions, a journalist who has been working on a book about Central America for over eight years, wants to leave the profession and try development work for awhile, where he feels one can make more of a difference. Another has published two novels, and would like to write fiction full time. Such cases are rare, however. Few staff correspondents leave the profession.

While few staff correspondents leave, many "burn-out." "The job takes a staggering toll in mental anguish," explains Rosenblum, "emotional stress and sheer physical energy" (1979:171). For many, the cumulative experience of covering wars and other forms of violence leads to psychic-numbing. They begin to conceptualize violence as normal, natural, and inevitable. These reporters tend to become cynical, not just about violence and human nature, but about their job as well. Whereas some cub reporters and stringers may be willing to risk their lives to get at hidden truths, most staff correspondents give up on such quixotic notions early, assuming they had them to start with.

After constant acquiescence to editorial demands, most veteran correspondents eventually adopt institutional perspectives as their own. Years of working in bureaucratic milieu serve to domesticate them, to discipline their labor and their minds. Herr recalls "how embittering" it became for the mainstream correspondents in Vietnam, "because they worked in the news media, for organizations that were ultimately reverential toward the institutions involved: the Office of the President, the Military, America and war and, most of all, the empty technology that characterized Vietnam" (1968: 214).

When the news frame is already decided in "offices thousands of miles away" (Herr 1968:214), career comfort and advancement become the primary and, often times, only issues worth considering for the foreign correspondent. What to print or broadcast becomes a matter of acting in a manner dominant institutions will find correct, or at least adequate. Indeed, adequacy is the rallying sigh of the burned-out reporter. The smoldering fire may occasionally ignite for an inspired feature or critical report, but is most often suppressed by a flood of bureaucratic inertia. Harold is the perfect example. "I don't give a shit about what happens to this place," Harold often stated, "Nothing ever really changes in any of these countries. After a while, you feel like you are writing the same story over and over again."

Bored with "writing the same story over and over again," Harold breached the most important taboo in journalism. He fabricated a story. The story in question was based on a trip Harold took to Morazon. According to the photographer who guided him to Morazon and facilitated his interviews, Harold fretted the entire way to the conflicted zone, fearing rain would come and wash out the bridges behind them, trapping them in the area overnight. Harold had only visited the controlled territories on a few occasions, and was unfamiliar with the guerrillas. According to the photographer, Harold's interviews with the guerrillas were extremely quick and superficial.

The incidents he reported in the subsequent article were pure fabrication. The article involved a detailed description of a Catholic mass officiated by well known liberation theologians. Harold maintained a supercilious tone regarding liberation theology throughout his report, the sort of cartoonish condescension that passes for analysis in much of the U.S. press. More problematic than his sophomoric analysis, however, were the "facts" of the story. In reality, the mass never happened.

Harold's colleagues were troubled by the story, complaining that it did not seem plausible. Their suspicions were later confirmed by the photographer who facilitated Harold's excursion. She explained that Harold had invented the story and, as a result, considered the seasoned staffer to be "mentally imbalanced." Ironically, Harold once told me "an awful lot of it comes out of your mind." I do not know if Harold's "it" is a reference to reality or the news reporting thereof. Either Harold is a solipsist or a willful inventor.

Harold's Morazon guide claims the errant reporter based his story on a popular book about liberation theology. Indeed, Harold told me he had read three or four books on liberation theology in preparation for the story, though he could not remember the names of any of them. Perhaps Harold's textual and phenomenological realities had merged to such a degree he truly could not separate the two. However, I sense that Harold can still tell the difference between fact and fiction, but does not feel that it really matters. That would certainly be the case for his readers, for whom the fictional mass certainly seemed "real."

The guerrillas Harold interviewed wrote an angry letter to the editor. They were still angry months later when I visited them. They asked my photographer guide if I could be trusted. After she answered in the affirmative, the comandante in charge replied, "That is what you said about the other one." They let me enter anyway. The guerrillas with whom I came into contact always seemed resigned to their fate. "We know there are spies all over," a guerrilla leader told me later, "but there is little we can do about them."

There was also little they could do about Harold's reporting. Their letter was never published, nor did Harold receive sanction, perhaps because it was, according to Harold himself, "one of the few stories suggested by my bosses." Perhaps the fictitious guerrilla mass was created as part of an effort to please said "bosses" with an acceptably compelling narrative.

Despite the lack of direct sanction, however, Harold encountered what he referred to as "flak" for publishing the story. He called it "the most controversial story I've written in the years I've been here." He continued:

I suppose I did the right thing. I received a huge number of letters from both sides that said I didn't have a clue what I was talking about…. It caused an awful storm.

Harold was obviously nervous about the story when I asked him about it later over lunch. "Has anybody told you anything startling?" he inquired. I responded, "Yes." That did not seem to set him at ease, although he continued to be a very giving, if highly cynical informant.

Another reporter at Harold's news institution referred to him as "an old curmudgeon." She and others were embarrassed by Harold's presence in the corps, and angered by his relative success. Perhaps they were frightened as well. Harold was, in Herr's words, "the sort of old reporter that most young reporters…were afraid of becoming someday" (Herr 1968:221). Harold was embittered, bored, frustrated, and quite simply, burned-out.

While the burned-out reporter is usually a veteran correspondent, the process that brings one to Harold's condition is cumulative, taking hold to some degree in nearly every member of the corps. Alonzo, a Salvadoran journalist, described the onset of burn-out as a fever:

It [reporting war] has killed something in my mind. I can't sleep. I can't talk with people that don't think like me. I don't have a good time with people that just talk shit [normal conversation]. The normal ways of the journalist are not normal…. If you don't have good morals, you become neurotic. Some get drunk, some take drugs. A lot go to Gloria's House, to see prostitutes.

Journalists are in constant danger of losing their "morals," of losing their sense of humanity and themselves. It is tempting, therefore, to claim that the myths and rituals I have described are means of rehumanization, rituals of regeneration or even "purification." The truth is much more complicated, however. Alcohol, drugs, prostitutes, and their concomitant rituals, are at the same time relief, self-abuse, and willful participation in the violence that surrounds the corps.[4]

Most reporters do not conceive of institutional frameworks as ideologically organized nor endemic to the system. They see them as separated aberrations—a bad editor here, lack of space for an article there—which if reformed would allow for truly independent practice. The macro structures are both represented in and obfuscated by a set of petty micro structures and activities that make it seem as though all restrictions are interpersonal ("Editors suck"), or at worst, organizational (The Embassy). Most correspondents fail to consciously recognize how their very practices and philosophies are organized by and for institutional structures and ideologies, apparatuses which comprise a system of power beyond editors and other petty disciplines.

The professional myths of journalism encourage this cognitive dissonance. In practice, reporters lives and texts are utterly dependent upon institutional structures. The cultural ethos that binds them together as a community, however, the collective myth of independence, allows them to recreate their sense of identity outside the repressive practice. (Culture allows us all that comfort.) Only a few journalists, the dissidents and cynics, pause for concentrated reflection upon the disunity of professional ideal and practice.

Yet, these cultural anodynes only satisfy at the surface. Most of the time, the journalists appeared to be rather dissatisfied with their working existence. The corps is, in this sense, what Edward Sapir refers to as a "spurious" culture, not "harmonious, balanced, and self-satisfactory" (1949:90).[5] Herr states (1968:187):

> I never knew a member of the Vietnam press corps who was insensible to what happened when the words 'war' and 'correspondent' got joined. The glamour of it was possibly empty and lunatic, but there were times when it was all you had, a benign infection that ravaged all but your worst fears and deepest depressions.

Stripped of purpose by a set of institutional structures which transform them, professional journalists, into mere scribes ("an official public secretary or clerk"), all that remains is a shared fantasy, a role-playing exercise in futility, a "benign infection."

Yet, that fantasy counts for something. These and other social rituals make the fantastic myths of war correspondence seem real, or at least realizable, by separating identity from practice. The war correspondents' cultural identity is formed and reconstructed mainly within the free play of ritual and popular culture, as separated from the contradictory and destabilizing circumstances of daily work. The "grim resolve" of myth, ritual, and "fun" provides reward for the grim realities of practice. Together, myth and practice, or "mythical practice," form a complete and effective discipline.

WAR PHOTOGRAPHY

"We don't take sides. We just take pictures."

—*Life* magazine advertisement

Thus far I have emphasized print, TV, and radio reporting. Although the comments of photographers have appeared throughout, I have not dealt directly with their unique practice and problems. This chapter fills that void, providing a description of three field trips into the FMLN-controlled territories, each with a different news photographer.

Images of Comandante Carmelo

Paul was the first journalist to take me along to the conflicted zones. We visited eastern Usulatan, a lush mountainous area ninety kilometers east of San Salvador. When we arrived, an FMLN brigade was encamped on the outskirts of San Francisco de Javier, a village surrounded by small fields and dense forest. Most of the compas were lying in hammocks and listening to American rock music on commercial radio, forsaking the rebel broadcasts of Radio Venceremos. The commander of the battalion was about twenty years old. It was difficult to judge the guerrillas' ages, however, since even the kids look old. Cliché but true.

The battalion's communications specialist was a young woman, probably in her early 20s. She radioed ahead to gain permission for our visit. Paul asked the radio operator to inform them that "El Gordo" (the fat man) was requesting a meeting with the local subcommander. Paul, unlike most of the corps, had extensive contacts among the guerrillas.

We were sent ahead, told to go about a kilometer around the bend, turn left at the two tallest trees, and proceed another half mile or so from there. "See?" asked the young soldier, "those two trees over there. You can see them from here." He also told us what kind of trees they were. Paul and I looked at each other, confused. We could not discern two "tall trees" amongst the thick matte of forest, nor had we heard of the species to which he referred. Realizing we were hopelessly confused, the compa told us a guide would meet us further down the road.

Halfway around the bend, we met a kind old man who gave us further directions. We then met up with our FMLN guide, who took us on a quick hike up the steep mountainside. A torrential rain started at that point. The thick dusty soil quickly turned to mud slop as we tried to keep up with our silent guide. Paul, several years my senior, and about sixty pounds larger, was fighting desperately for breath by the time we reached our destination far up the mountain. Our guide appeared to be seriously concerned when he finally noticed Paul's condition, perhaps envisioning the difficulties of explaining to his superiors how he accidentally killed one of the Gringo *periodistas* put in his charge. Fortunately, Paul hauled himself up the mountain with great determination, and recovered quickly once we reached our final destination. As for me, I was just happy to be out of the city and breathing fresh air again. The cool deciduous forests of Usulatan are about as far from San Salvador as one can get.

Paul found the hike well worth the effort. Meeting with the subcommander at the main FMLN camp, were two of the highest level commanders in the FMLN, Frederico and Carmelo. They were the real thing, not the "comandantes" found in many news texts (often low ranking battalion leaders), but actual members of the elite inner circle of strategists who managed the rebel coalition's political and military activities. Paul was ecstatic over his luck, having stumbled onto a guerrilla "mini-summit." As we were walking out of the camp, he turned to me wide eyed and exclaimed, "That was fucking incredible. That man [Carmelo] is a "General." I have been here for years and never met him."

I was more impressed with Carmelo's warm presence than his elevated rank. While I did not fully appreciate Carmelo's status and fame until later when telling other members of the corps about the visit, I was immediately won over by his kindness. Most of the leaders I had observed in El Salvador, as elsewhere, were the types of people who promote themselves and their ideological products with aggressive fervor. Conversely, Carmelo seemed almost shy.

Unlike almost all of the other leaders of his rank, Carmelo is of peasant stock. As Carmelo explained in a later interview, he was raised in a large and impoverished family in Meanguera, a small town in the north-eastern province of Morazon. His parents demanded that each of their children attend school regularly, and hoped several of them would learn a specialized trade. As a result, Carmelo started his adult working life as a tailor. Growing up a member of a Christian base community, Carmelo would attend catechism every Thursday, during which community members would study and interpret the bible as it related to the problems of their own lives and the plight of the poor in general. Carmelo explained:

> We learned that the problem of poverty, the *cause* of poverty, is not that of the individual, but of the society itself. It was there that we became not just a group of individuals discussing religious ideas, but instead a community searching for solutions to its problems. For example, we would pool our money for those who had the least resources and those who were ill. With this community organization we built houses for the homeless and bought medicine for the sick.

Through their practical search for solutions, Carmelo and many of his compatriots began to discover and confront the fundamental sources of injustice:

> We were becoming filled with a consciousness of the problem of social injustice, of the differences which exist between the capital class and the great majority of people. We were becoming aware that it wasn't enough to be working to help each other in the community. For example, I was working as a tailor. Any extra money that I made was given to the community. I began to realize, however, that my gift of a *peso* to another *miserable* wasn't going to solve the problem. We would both merely be equally broke. What was needed to resolve the problem was a structural change.

In other words, the motivational force behind the proto-FMLN social movement, at least in terms of a revolutionary base, was the need for justice in the form of work, food, housing, and medicine, guided by a set of Christian principals.

Carmelo explained that peaceful, democratic routes toward social change were blocked by the allied force of the oligarchy, the government, and the military. Thus, "the only alternative was armed struggle." He explained:

> The oligarchy had the executive, military, judicial, and economic power and would not permit anyone to modify that power structure. When they stole the elections from the Christian Democrats [in 1972], who at the time won the election based upon their support from the majority who were seeking change, the only alternative was to turn to the use of force. Likewise, the terror wrought by the armed forces in the countryside and the repression of workers in the city was generating a spiral of violence which forced the people to react. The people that were incorporating into the armed

opposition were aware that it was very possible that they would lose their lives. When people decide to go forward despite that risk, there is obviously a very strong motivation.

Carmelo had a profound impact upon me, partly because he was so personable, partly because I could relate to his view, but also because he was so very different from the dominant media image of the FMLN. Not once in our conversations did Carmelo utter the name Marx. One can hardly say the same for the U.S. media, whose obsession with communism tends to paint most resistance to the capitalist metropole, especially insurgent movements, in broad red brush strokes. Carmelo very charitably refers to this as "a misunderstanding of the origins of the conflict."

Carmelo, Frederico, Paul, and I sat in the small guerrilla camp and chatted, while the young men and women in the local battalion stared at their leader with awe and affection. After our discussion began to fade, Paul asked if he could take some photos of Carmelo. The unassuming rebel commander seemed surprised by Paul's request, as if he could not understand why anyone would want to take his picture. Carmelo agreed, but wanted to take off his campesino or "cowboy" hat first. He asked a compa to lend him an olive-drab military cap. Comandante Carmelo felt he should be in complete military uniform for the photo.

"I prefer the cowboy hat," I blurted out without proper forethought. The cap seemed uncharacteristically martial, thus unrepresentative of Carmelo's pleasant face-to-face demeanor. Furthermore, Carmelo seemed to be playing into the American stereotype of the Marxist guerrilla: an interloper feared by, and alienated from the local population. Reacting to my remark, Carmelo reached for his cowboy hat. "Wear whatever you like," Paul quickly interjected. Paul was shocked I would converse with an FMLN comandante in such a familiar way. I could not help myself. I really did find Carmelo to be familiar. Frankly, he reminded me of the men I worked with while I was growing up in Iowa, the cattlemen and workers at my father's stock auction market, work-strengthened and life-educated "peasants" like Carmelo. Fortunately, Carmelo did not seem to mind my indiscretion, nor take it as a sign of disrespect. Nevertheless, I was very embarrassed and tried to minimize my role in future press-source interactions.

After the photo session, Carmelo mentioned that his troops had recently downed a helicopter in a nearby ravine. Naturally, Paul wanted to photograph the site. At the conclusion of our interview and photo session, Carmelo asked three young compas to walk us to the crash, two compas in front and one in back to guard against attack or an errant trip over a land mine. We reached the wreck after a short walk. It was an American military helicopter. The *compas* told us how they had caught the helicopter crew unaware, trapping them in a cross fire from each side of the steep ravine. The airmen had been scouring the high grasses of the valley floor for rebels, foolishly lowering their craft to hill level. After a grizzly replay of events, we were guided down to the helicopter. There was a sign that read "danger" on the fuselage and a red arrow pointing to what had been the helicopter's tail before it was sheared off in the crash.

Paul asked the guerrillas to pose with their trophy. They lined up, a grim look souring each young face. I was starting to feel the same way myself. I kept imagining the terror of crashing, perhaps even surviving, and then.... But, not today, Paul was shouting at them to "smile!" I was beginning to wonder how far he would take this thing. Why not have them reenact the battle? How about asking the young female guerrilla to strike a suggestive pose over the fuselage? Paul's work-with-me protestations seemed grossly incongruous with the rest of the scene. Perhaps he was self-consciously attempting to counter the dominant media image of the "threatening" guerrilla, the "lawless" leftist who aggressively "confronts the viewer" in most news photographs (Anderson 1988:256-57). Paul would instead present a band of friendly and triumphant guerrillas to the news reader.

At first, the subjects refused to smile. However, even the famous flag raising photo taken at Iwo Jima required a second take. After repeated requests, two of the compas finally broke into wide grins. The third, a young man dressed in black fatigues and carrying an M-16, maintained a blank stare. I was not sure if he was unwilling to smile or had simply forgotten how. Perhaps he could not forget what it is really like when people get shot out of helicopters, or worse, shot at *from* them. I have a copy of one of the shots Paul took that day. It is a haunting juxtaposition of levity and terror: the three stooges kill a helicopter. Paul, I am guessing, was soliciting a look of triumph from the young rebels. What he got instead was a look of bemused embarrassment. The two "smiling guerrillas" look into the camera with clownish and apologetic grins, as if to say, "I'm sorry. Was that your helicopter?" The third face is simply vacant. The photo image does not look much like the Usulatan I experienced, but that is the beauty of photography, and memory—objects selected and arranged as needed. Suspect images.

After the photo shoot was over, the three compas escorted us to a dirt road and provided directions back to San Francisco de Javier. One walked a bit further with us until we picked up the main path to the village. Soon after leaving our guerrilla guide, we crossed paths with a priest riding a motorbike. He stopped to chat, leaving us with a warning: "Watch out for the bees!" The Africanized "killer bees" had been very active in El Salvador in 1991, just one more plague to bear. Of course, I immediately thought of the killer bees sketch on *Saturday Night Live*, John Belushi, Elliot Gould, and Dan Akroyd dressed up in bee suits, acting as a stereotypical band of gun-toting Latin American revolutionaries. Such is the patrimony of the postmodern, a media match for every "real" event; even a motorcycle-riding priest in a war zone.

Further on, Paul and I noticed we were being followed by two young men. As I turned to look at them they swerved off the path. I next saw their heads bobbing over the top of the hill, looking at us with great interest. Paul reached for his Mace, while I emitted a nervous chuckle. Fortunately, they simply disappeared. Paul guessed they were probably part of the civilian militia, local people aligned with the FMLN who were only activated when and if major offensives came to pass. In this case, the two men were probably just curious. Once back in the village, we drank warm Pepsi and joked with a couple of women sitting next to Paul's car. Then, exercising the ultimate privilege of both war reporting and ethnography, we left.

The sun was setting as we drove out of San Francisco de Javier. It was dark as we approached the Puente de Oro bridge, which made Paul nervous. This, in turn, made me nervous. As we sped along, the hot wind blasting our tired faces, a body appeared in the headlights. The man's legs were stuck halfway onto the road. It was not a very safe place to sleep. But, he was probably not asleep. I looked at Paul. "I don't want to stop," he said, "but I will if you do." I felt as though we should. I was still thinking in U.S. terms, however. I was acting as if this was unusual, something to be remedied through official channels—the police, etc. I felt that we should stop, but I knew there was nothing we would be able to do anyway. With silence I deferred to Paul's judgment, and we kept going. He did not mention "it" again. Either corpses were so commonplace for him that it was not worth mentioning, or like me, Paul would rather pretend he had never seen the man/corpse/whatever. After all, we had been passing people walking by the side of the road all along. Surely someone would have stopped if there was something left to be done. Surely... maybe... probably not.

Regardless of the trip's inauspicious conclusion, I felt I had learned quite a lot about El Salvador. I cannot say the same for most of the trips I took with the "pack." In certain ways, Paul's method is very anthropological. Like an ethnographer, he usually goes into the field alone, rather then surrounded by a phalanx of associates. He takes great interest in people and issues, regardless of their potential newsworthiness. Paul is unusual in this and other ways. One of the few journalists who refused to acquiesce to editorial interests, he has repeatedly submitted photos to editors of Salvadoran troops giving the "sieg heil" salute, even though editors flatly rejected them every time. "The soldiers are always doing it," said Paul, "I've sent lots of photos. Why doesn't that get published? If they are still doing that, there's something wrong here!" That seemed to be what kept Paul going despite his frustration of dealing with editors he considered "pea brains who can't walk and chew gum at the same time." Paul had an incurable need to show the world "there's something wrong here!"

Joe in El Mozote

"In the beginning every photographer and journalist who goes to war does not go already activated against the inhumanity of war. He goes with excitement, almost love for war. He goes to test himself, to see if he has got the courage."
—Don McCullin, in Jorge Lewinski's *A History of War Photography*

No journalist becomes a war correspondent without some attraction to war and violence. For several of the photographers I studied, it was the adventure of battle that first attracted them to the profession. Joe became a war photographer because "it's one of the few jobs left in the world where there's still adventure.... It gets your adrenaline flowing.... There's not much you can do today where a company pays for you to go off and do crazy things." El Salvador interests Joe because "it's a war. They are killing each other.... I like war stuff. I like guns and stuff." He refers to war as "exciting" and "fun," and even claims to enjoy being detained and threatened. Joe worries he will not be able to "beat the excitement level" in his next posting and complains he no longer receives the same level of "adrenaline rush" covering combat. He was constantly searching for a better high. For Joe, war is an addiction.

Joe is not alone. Paul called covering war "addictive...kind of habit forming." John Hoagland, a photographer killed covering the Salvadoran conflict, referred to war as "poor man's cocaine" (*San Francisco Chronicle* March 29,1984:27). The photographers' high is very different from that described in the preceding chapter. The main difference between war photography and other media is that photographers, in the words of several SPECA journalists, "have to be there." "We have to be in the place where things actually happen," explained Paco, "A newspaper reporter that wants to write about combat can just sit and listen to the radio." Pedro, another Salvadoran photographer, compared the "cold note" of print and radio journalism with the more personal, corporeal, and "warm" experience of battle photography.

The photographers' proximity to danger adds a daredevil mystique to their work and earns them a special niche in the profession. As Robin Anderson explains in his definitive study of photographic coverage of the Salvadoran war, "there is a tendency to think of the photographer as a hero" (1988:237). While the center of the journalistic world belongs to print correspondents, war photographers have created their own group identity on the margins. Photographers endure the danger, dengue, and low pay of their down-and-dirty role in return for an elevated awe and respect from others both within and outside the journalistic community.

The following quote by war photographer Don McCullin illustrates his transition from "little man" to war photographer (Lewinski 1978:9):

> I started off as such a simple, little man once upon a time. I just wanted to walk around and photograph people in the streets with my camera. And I seemed to find myself being arrested, beaten around sometimes by soldiers, being accused in Africa of being a mercenary, and locked up. And I, over and over, ask myself—You are supposed to be a photographer, why are you in jail in Africa, why are you afraid, why are you saying a prayer with some other men in prison, and why is the man next to you sliding down a wall with dried blood on his head? And, at the end of the day, you have lived more in one day than some people would live in their whole lives.

The legendary war photographer sacrifices everything, including life itself, to shoot the ultimate photograph. One of the most powerful scenes of the film *Salvador* is that in which photographer John Cassady (an amalgam of John Sullivan and other real life war photographers) dies photographing a plane bombing Santa Ana. His last words spoken through a blood-stained smile: "I got the shot. Take it to New York." Such are the legends and myths (literally, origin stories) that inspire others to join the profession and make similar sacrifices for their art. Every true war photographer wants to be like Cassady; to be remembered as more than a *plain* photographer.

The sacrifice myths provide a subtext for myriad minor legends. Almost all of the photographers in SPECA have at least one such story attached to their professional persona. William is particularly fabled. His story is that of a surfer-turned-war-photographer, a man who will stop at practically nothing to get the best shot. Although he spends most of his time in Central America, he will travel wherever there is a war, including the Persian Gulf. During that conflict, William ran in to trouble with the U.S. military and further enhanced his legend in the process. The fabled episode began when William stole a U.S. military uniform. He then camouflaged a rented car in order to fool Egyptian troops into letting him photograph them, troops who were technically off-limits to journalists covering the heavily censored war (Fialka 1991). According to his colleagues, William pulled this stunt almost immediately after being released from arrest for a prior breach of media restrictions. "William works with a clear and controlled insanity," commented George, "He is a star." Shari, however, considers William "psychopathic, the way he looks for blood." The two claims are hardly contradictory. A blood obsession lies at the base of many "star" photo careers.

Photographers are not really considered "reporters" by other types of correspondents. Because of the widespread visual bias—the sense that "seeing is believing"—photographic work is conceived of as little more than mechanized technique, a means of "capturing" reality. Writing automatically implies a process of creative construction, of authorship. Therefore, objective codes are required to domesticate and regulate it. Photography, however, is considered objective by definition. Photographic reality is not constructed, or so goes the story, it is "taken." Therefore, rather than being considered visual *authors* (as they are in truth), photographers are held to be mere craftsmen, simple technicians.

While this popular bias reduces the photographers' journalistic status, it is also quite liberating. Whereas, the correspondent must maintain a serious and objective performance, signs of obedience to an objective professional standard, photographers may be more creative in their public presentation without risking the dreaded stigma of "bias." As a result, photographers are free to imbue their very serious and dangerous labor with a greater sense of playfulness. Whereas, reporters must often remain controlled, composed, dispassionate, and, in a word, "professional," photographers present themselves in wildly divergent ways, with little concern for appearances. As long as they get the good pictures, nothing else matters. Correspondents dress up. Photographers dress down. While correspondents worry about wearing the right tie to a presidential interview, photographers are more concerned about having enough room in their vest pockets and bags for extra film, filters, flash, and beef jerky. Reporters must gain their sources trust and respect, photographers only need to *shoot* them.

Liberated from confining norms of behavior, yet forced to become intimate with danger, war photographers have both the freedom and need to express themselves in ways others might consider "crazy." The word "insane" was often used by other correspondents when referring to news photographers. As David explained, "Reporters tend to think of photographers as the ones screaming by the pool."

Joe not only accepts, but promotes this image of insanity whenever possible. When not "screaming by the pool," Joe is entertaining the corps in some equally bizarre fashion. He loves being considered a "crazy motherfucker." Imitating the dialogue of bad war movies, Joe often brags about his talents, his unique ability to "blow away" the competition.

Joe also plays upon the popular image of war photography to enhance his romantic chances:

> You saw the movie *Under Fire*, with Nick Nolte, the *Salvador* movie, and *The Year of Living Dangerously*. People get Hollywoodized, ya know. Every time I go back to the States and I'd be in a bar trying to pick up women or something like that, they say, "What do you do?" I say, "I'm a photographer in Central America." You gotta make it sound good. I say, "I'm a combat photographer."

Unfortunately, Joe is rarely successful in his quest to turn identity into intimacy. Women tend not to believe him when he claims to be a combat photographer:

> They say, "Yeah, right!" And they leave. They say, "This guy's full of shit."

> The people who know what I do think that it is this amazing thing. They have these visions from Hollywood.

I asked him to explain how real photo journalism differs from the Hollywood version:

> It has been really slow the last six months. Eighty percent of the time I sit watching my cable TV and drinking by the pool.

Joe does not allow reality to get in the way of public perception, however. He plays the role of war photographer with great flair. He asked that I ascribe him one of two pseudonyms: "Furious Man" or "Santiago Joe Otto." Joe's colleagues apply less flattering titles to the eager young shootist, nicknames like "Sparky," mocking his obvious attempts to earn a reputation.

Joe, often bored and frustrated, was sometimes forced to "baby-sit" the office while others were out of the country. I would find him pacing back and forth, muttering obscene comments about his boss and the competition, just dying to be turned loose again. Joe used the down time to clean out his agency office, play pool at the British Club, watch what he calls "bad movies" (he and George watched the movie "Roadhouse" over twenty times in a single month) and complain a lot.

Most of the time I was in El Salvador Joe was grumbling about being held back by his agency. He felt he had proven himself in Panama and now he wanted to make his mark in El Salvador as well. According to Joe, photographers for other major agencies had been "killing" his company, selling more photos to the major U.S. dailies. Likewise, the war was coming to an end. Soon, there would be no opportunity to get the perfect combat shot he had been searching for.

Joe complained that most supposed "combat" news photos are of soldiers firing at nothing at all. He wanted an authentic and perfect shot, one with all of the action and drama of a real gun battle. He would need to get out into the countryside more often to find that perfect shot. Eventually, his boss obliged him. They drove to an area of impending battle, and Joe finally got what he had been looking for. While the other correspondent crouched in a doorway, Joe moved out onto the street and started shooting. The result was a magnificent photo. Several Salvadoran troops are seen in the foreground of the shot, firing upon the advancing enemy while another attempts to haul a wounded comrade to safety. Words do not do justice. The image was displayed across the front page of a nationally distributed U.S. newspaper. By the standard criteria of war photography (blood, guts, and action) it is a classic. Congratulations were extended everywhere Joe went in the days immediately following the publication of his prize photo. In a suspect wave of humility Joe claimed, "I didn't even think it was that good of a photo." I must admit that I was both happy and relieved for Joe. He had finally gained his main goal, the perfect combat photo. Better yet, he was not killed getting it.

Joe is of the school who believe that photographic work is by definition objective, as long as images are not "staged." Such photographers support their objectivist perspective with the claim, "I just take pictures." Yet, as demonstrated earlier, Joe's selection of images is extremely influenced by organizational and institutional criteria. He not only "takes" pictures, he authors them. In her brilliant critique *On Photography*, Susan Sontag argues that "in deciding how a picture should look, in preferring one exposure to another, photographers are always imposing standards on their subjects" (1977:6). Joe was certainly no exception to this rule.

One of the most telling examples in Joe's work was a photograph he took of an FMLN arms cache. Having been taken to the site by a representative of the Salvadoran government, Joe dutifully photographed the booty and delivered the images to his home office. Joe knows such weapons are news, whereas the billions of dollars of U.S.-supplied weaponry put on display by the Salvadoran army in parades and offensives, is not. Joe was angry after sending the photos of the rebel weapons, however. He did not initially recognize the Russian made SAM-14 missiles in the cache, and therefore, failed to alert his editors to the greater significance of the story. "It would have been a scoop if I had recognized them sooner!" he exclaimed. Joe knows images of Russian involvement are more newsworthy than those which symbolize U.S. intervention. It is true that Joe just takes pictures. It is also true, however, that those pictures are selected according to ideological criteria.

Photographers are able to retreat to the objective pretense because much of their audience shares their same belief that photography cannot lie. "[A] photograph—any photograph," Sontag explains, "seems to have a more innocent, and therefore more accurate, relation to visible reality than do other mimetic objects" (1977:6). Photographs have a nearly incontestable "presumption of veracity" (6). Therefore, even though the application of news "frames" should be particularly obvious in photography, people tend to accept photographic images as objective and authentic "pieces" of the world (4).

Joe took a photo in Lima, Peru, soon after a bomb blast. The photo, which was displayed prominently on the front page of a U.S. newspaper, shows a group of men and women running frantically towards the camera. The man in the foreground is raising his arm, a wild look of fear and panic on his face. The caption implies the photo subjects are fleeing Sendero Luminoso guerrillas. There would be no reason for the reader to assume otherwise. In reality, the frightened man was hitting Joe with a stick just outside view of the photo frame, trying to keep the young photographer from taking his family's picture. In addition to illustrating the creative aspect of photographic authorship, the above example also demonstrates the news camera's status as "a tool of power" (Sontag 1977:8), a weapon far more powerful than a peasant's stick.

Yet, in certain ways, photographers are just one link in a complex chain of objectification. News photographers are at the mercy of the editors and institutions to whom they sell their work. The editors choose which photos to run, write the final captions, and most importantly, match photo images with news stories (Langton 1991:104–105). "Few journalists," writes Gisele Freund in *Photography and Society*, "are able to impose their own points of view. It takes very little on the part of an editor to give photographs a meaning diametrically opposed to the photographer's intention" (1980:162) (Hallin 1983:32–33).

Even the most well known news photographers are relatively powerless when dealing with the mainstream press. Gloria Emerson described the editorial frustrations of noted photographer Susan Meiselas: "Meiselas suffers because she cannot protect or control her own work. Rolls of film must be shipped to New York without her seeing them, pictures are chosen by others, often to run with words she would not choose" (1984:170). However, Meiselas, like Paul, does her best to send only those photos which are least susceptible to propagandistic manipulation by editors, those which best represent her understanding of the subject. "There are all these photographs I don't take everyday," explained Meiselas, "because these are experiences I feel are so terribly reduced in a photograph" (171).

Unfortunately, news photography is extremely competitive, forcing most photographers to acquiesce to editorial demand. News organs have hundreds of photos to choose from every day. During 1991, editors interested in El Salvador were able to select photographs from AP, Reuters, AFP, Gamma Liaison, Blackstar, Magnum, CIPA, and Impact Visuals, not to mention freelance work.[1] It is a buyers' market. Photographers learn to produce the types of photos editors prefer or else loose out to their competition.

Two categories of photos dominate that competition. The first category is that of politics, mainly images of psuedo-events. The other major genre of news photos is what journalists refer to as "blood." Blood is a euphemism for any war scene, especially those involving bodies, and quite literally, blood. Michele lists the types of photos that sell best: "Assassinations, bombings, funerals, and press conferences. Those that go along with the biggest stories." The most common query from Paul's boss' is "How many bodies?" "She actually asks that," said the exasperated photographer, "I say, 'Only five.' She says, 'That's not enough.'"

"Foreign news," explains Gans, "is limited to violent political disorder" (1979:53). This was certainly true during the Salvadoran war. Of the twenty-four photos of El Salvador published in 1985 in *Time*, *Newsweek*, and *U.S. News and World Report*, eighteen are of people primarily involved in military events (mostly victims of FMLN actions), four are of people primarily involved in electoral politics, while only two are of some other segment of social life.[2] Not one member of an opposition group or human rights organization is presented. Of the twenty-three stories run in the magazines in 1985, fourteen (61%) concern FMLN aggressions (five about the kidnap and release of President Duarte's daughter, four about an attack on a cafe killing four U.S. Marines, and five about other FMLN military actions) and four (17%) concerned an electoral victory by the U.S.-backed Christian Democrat Party. None of the five (22%) remaining magazine stories concerned the military actions or human rights abuses of the Salvadoran armed forces. This tableau of war and politics is the end result of an institutional frame-fitting process that defines news as political and military crisis.

In other words, Joe was made for the job. Whereas, Paul and like-minded humanists are constantly frustrated by the violent appetites of their editors, Joe's greatest frustration is that his agency will not turn him loose to capture more of the violence, blood, and gore. Some concerned photographers do side projects, mainly photo essays and museum exhibitions, to publicly display the images that are culled out of their news work.[3] Joe has no need for that. "They tell me I should do a photo essay," said Joe, "I don't know why." Whatever else one might say of Joe, he is truly at home in his work.

My most memorable excursion with Joe was a trip to the site of El Mozote. As mentioned in chapter 6, the El Mozote massacre occurred in January of 1982. Somewhere between 700 and 1,000 people were killed there by army troops. A decade later, when the official investigation of the atrocity began, Joe and I drove to the site with Fernando, a Salvadoran photographer. The rest of SPECA were waiting for the forensic excavations to begin, so that they could take better "bone pictures."

Joe was excited about seeing the site. Joe's interest was not generated by the massacre, however. He doubted that it ever happened. Instead, Joe was excited because he wanted to defecate on the site. Joe exclaimed: "I can't wait to tell all the liberals that I took a shit at Mozote." Joe disliked the "liberals" preoccupation with El Mozote.

When we arrived, a large group had gathered around the judge heading the investigation. As usual, Maria Julia Hernandez of Tutela Legal was there as well. As soon as the photographers and I arrived, a walk-through tour began of the massacre sight, guided by the sole survivor, Rufina Amaya. As Amaya walked the group around to each burial site, the judge overseeing the investigation asked her several questions, including the number of bodies she estimated to have been buried in each grave.

Soon after the tour began, Joe peeled away from the group. He was not there for talk. He wanted pictures. As I was listening to Amaya tell her story under the intimidating gaze of the judge, I saw Joe off to the left. He was staring at a stack of bones. Joe motioned for me to join him. Upon approaching I saw he was holding a small, clean white pelvis bone from a child's body. A little shocked, Joe asked: "Is this really a human bone?" Before he could finish the sentence, I told him a bit too brusquely it was a child's pelvis bone. It was definitely human, a pelvis bone or "Os Innominatum" ("nameless bone," so named because it looks like nothing else). On this specimen, the lower loop or "Os Pubis" was broken off, perhaps because it had not fully fused with the other parts of the bone, the Ischium and Ilium. Therefore, it belonged to a young adolescent or pre-pubescent. Whatever the case, it was a human pelvis bone. It had once belonged to a human pelvis. That was the hard thing to take in. It seems impossible, too horrible to imagine, too real to believe.

Joe put the bone back on the stack and took a few photos. Then, "Santiago Joe" asked if I thought it would be alright to "take a few of the small ones to make a necklace?" I walked away without answering. I do not know if Joe was serious. My guess is that he was play acting, a callused performance meant to hide his fear and shock. A 23-year-old kid with an ulcer. No wonder.

Joe and I left El Mozote as the tour began winding down. On the way home we discussed Joe's philosophical views, his reading habits, and whatever else there was to take our minds off the bones. Some were stacked, but most were just tossed aside in the grass. Others were poking out of the earth, disembodied, disinterred. For some reason, it is easier to get a corpse out of your mind than a skeleton.

When we returned, Joe was making plans to send a "great photo" with the pelvis bone in the foreground and the crowd of investigators further back. He was talked out of it, however, by a group of SPECA reporters who felt that we were being duped. They argued there should not have been bones just sitting around the site. Shawn made the same point to me later. I replied in anger: "What do you think they did, bring in a truckful of bones and toss them around for visitors? Do you think the FMLN has been stashing a bone archives somewhere in Morazan?" Having worked as an archaeologist, I can state with assurance the remains were not placed there for the occasion, at least not the partially buried ones. The dirt and rock around them had not been disturbed for some time. However, the stringers had convinced themselves that some sort of fraud had taken place. They were certain that all of the bones should have been underground, though they had never been to El Mozote themselves. They were obviously compensating for the fact they had missed an opportunity to take their own bone photos in conjunction with the news event. Made uncertain by his colleagues' comments, however, Joe did not send the bone photo. Instead, he submitted an image of a small monument marking the massacre site. Joe, the objectivist, bent to social pressure.

Joe is well-liked. He is considered an excellent practitioner of the craft, although professionally immature. "You can tell if someone doesn't give a fuck about the country," explained Warren, "You can see that in Joe's photographs." Joe projects an air of callousness, referring to human bodies as "just dead things." I believe that Joe does care, however. He is just young and confused. At twenty-three he has already seen too many bodies and too many bones. Of course, that is what he came to Central America to experience, to gain the power and identity one receives in association with violence and terror. But, in the slight pauses and rare moments of quiet, I could see the little kid's pelvis stuck inside Joe's eyes, mingled with his other nightmares. "Whatever their surface callousness," said Rosenblum about war photographers, "it does get to them" (1979:69). I am convinced "it" gets to Joe as well.

Dancing in Perquin

Shari is a veteran news photographer. She has worked in the region for over a decade. "I got assigned to the story because no man wanted it," explained Shari, "It wasn't a big story. Later," she laughs, "it became a big story, and the editors started saying, 'Who is this girl covering the war?'"

My research started with Shari. I was hanging out at the Presidential Summit in Antigua, afraid to approach any of the reporters, when Shari came over and asked what I was doing there. After I explained my research interests, she invited me to San Salvador for a visit. Often, when my research was slowing down, whenever I was seeing and hearing the same things repeated *ad nauseam*, Shari would invite me to dine with a parachuting correspondent or go along on a reporting excursion, breathing new life into my work.

The most memorable excursion with Shari was to Perquin, the de facto guerrilla capital in Morazon province. We were joined by Emilio, a local radio reporter with some international experience, Janice, previously introduced, and Maria, another "international." I was driving, so the soldier in charge of the reten asked me where we were going. I panicked and said, "San Salvador." (I have never been very good under pressure, which is one of the many reasons I would make a horrible journalist). Shari, herself rather high strung after ten years of war reporting, giggled in the back seat. Fortunately, she and Emilio took over, explaining that we were simply going to visit Ciudad Segundo Montes, a repopulation center on the road to Perquin. Of course, the soldier knew we were headed to Perquin, but agreed to play along. He did a superficial search of the bags in the trunk and sent us to the local cuartel in San Francisco de Gotera, the provincial capital. After several hours, we were given permission to go through.

Nearing Perquin, we passed through Ciudad Segundo Montes. This repopulation center became news in 1991 when residents accused army troops of killing 500 of their chickens in a bomb attack. The military claimed the chickens were caught in a cross fire between their soldiers and FMLN troops hiding out in Ciudad Segundo Montes. The repopulation committee, however, swore the FMLN had been nowhere near the sight of the attack. From what I was able to ascertain, both positions contained partial truths. The FMLN had evidently been through the repopulation center the day of the chicken massacre. In fact, most of the repopulation community is made up of FMLN sympathizers. According to Joe, several inhabitants told Bart there was a battle taking place when the chickens were killed, and that the number of chicken deaths was exaggerated. On the other hand, one does not accidentally kill an entire flock of chickens in a cross fire. The army was obviously gunning for them, just as they purposely burned down hundreds of saplings the repopulation community had planted in the nearby hillsides. The First Lady of France, Danielle Mitterrand, gave extra legs to the chicken story with a donation for the express purpose of replacing the slain fowl. The chicken-martyrs became symbols of the armies continued harassment.

This bizarre chain of events is emblematic of the propaganda battle waged during the latter part of the war. Almost everyone in El Salvador, journalists included, were aware that the citizens of Ciudad Segundo Montes overwhelmingly supported the FMLN. When the people of the center were caught off guard, FMLN banners could often be seen hanging in and near the community. To admit such allegiance would be to invite death, however. Therefore, they usually lied about such things when asked by reporters and other outsiders. They had to. Therefore, rather than openly admit their allegiances and more fundamental grievances, the people of Ciudad Segundo Montes had to filter their opposition through the international language of "human rights," a limited discourse that only acknowledges acts of immediate and explosive violence: imprisonment, torture, and murder. There was plenty of that still happening in other parts of El Salvador near the end of the war, but not necessarily in or around Ciudad Segundo Montes. They had the protection of the FMLN. The army knew that abuses of FMLN supporters would be avenged, and therefore, tended to avoid directly harming the inhabitants of Ciudad Segundo Montes. As a result, dead chickens became symbols of injustice. Dead chickens became news.

Further up the road from Ciudad Segundo Montes, Perquin is nested high in the mountains of Morazan, surrounded by lush pine forests. The army's defoliation program had not completely obliterated the natural beauty of the place. Upon arrival, we walked around the main square of the town. A brilliant mural with images of the slain Jesuits graced the church facing the square. According to Shari, the last time the army overtook Perquin they did not touch the mural. Unfortunately, it was damaged in an attack just a few months later.

Many of the buildings in Perquin have been reduced to bombed-out ruins. The people of Perquin, Chalatenango, and other conflicted zones were constantly ready for the sky to give way to bullets, bombs, and fire. The local kids are more aware of the various types and capabilities of U.S. aircraft than they are of traditional farming methods. They are acutely aware, for example, that U.S.-supplied Hughes 500 aircraft have the ability to "spray some 6,000 bullets a minute" at their targets and know how to best react upon seeing one (McConahay 1986:238). Walking through Perquin, I was amazed that these "targets" had survived over a decade of such terror.

After we milled about the town talking with guerrillas and local townspeople, we interviewed a local ERP comandante. As dusk approached, we met another FMLN leader, Santiago, the legendary head of Radio Venceremos. Santiago, prematurely gray and frighteningly thin, was worn out from a day of hard work, but managed to spare a couple of hours to eat and talk with us. At his side was an attractive teen-age compa. She reminded me of Mariposa (butterfly), a woman whom Santiago and the other Venceremos workers fought over in the earlier years of the rebel radio, as told in *Las Mil y Unas Historia de Radio Venceremos* (One Thousand and One Stories About Radio Venceremos), an engaging history of the guerrilla radio station expertly written by a Venceremos staff member (Lopez Vigil 1991). Santiago is a central, heroic figure in that text.

During our interview, Santiago spoke of the need for FMLN radio to become "more professional" as it entered the political arena. He claimed their function would be less propagandistic, and more informational than during the war. Santiago explained the FMLN would need to learn from the international media (they had been telling U.S. journalists that for most of the war, see Drucker 1984:46). That was just what Shari wanted to hear. She smiled and nodded. Santiago was scoring points with at least one of the reporters.

When a group of law students from the National University arrived, Santiago excused himself and walked outside to deliver a speech on the state of the struggle and the place of students in the new El Salvador. The rhetoric was cliché, and the "impromptu" speech obviously rehearsed. One of the law students, a reporter for her school newspaper, approached Santiago after his performance. She joined us as we continued to speak with the legendary Venezuelan.

I asked Santiago to say a little bit more about the difference between propaganda and professional journalism. The question obviously perturbed him. Interested in my question, the young law student jumped into the discussion, criticizing the concept of objective journalism. Santiago, who had been trying to maintain the "learning from the foreign media" line, looked crushed. The student and I were unwittingly subverting his sales pitch.

I felt very bad for having done this to Santiago. This was not the kind of issue Santiago wanted to deal with after a week of being shot at and bombed while trying to keep a radio program going, so I apologized for the question. The law student, however, ripe with energy, kept the issue alive as our entire troupe walked to the door with Santiago. Later that night, I apologized again to the rebel radio hero.

I must admit, however, that I did not like Santiago all that much. I found him to be the opposite of Carmelo and other rebels I met, whose honesty and dedication warmed one to their cause. Santiago, a Venezuelan internationalist, had a disturbing air of self-importance. During my time in El Salvador I became close to several Salvadorans who bravely worked to keep the guerrillas going through all the years of war, not by carrying guns, but through clandestine work in the city. I told one of them my impression of Santiago. "That is right," he smiled, "He is the perfect man for the job." Indeed, Santiago is the consummate propagandist, an essential component of any political struggle, armed or otherwise.

Janice was also turned off by Santiago's rhetoric. She felt there was something both fossilized and forced about Santiago's presentation. I was pleasantly surprised by the candor of two lower level rebel commanders, however, as they addressed the law students the next morning. They explained the current state of the struggle, mapped out the FMLN's political plans, and provided a very frank historical account of the Salvadoran insurgency. They told the students that, in 1982, after having failed in the first of several "final offensives," the rebel organization had been decimated and demoralized. They explained how the government's plan of elections and terror had exacted a significant toll on their recruitment and battlefield possibilities. It was not until a long term strategy was adopted, explained the rebel teachers, that the guerrillas' fortunes changed. In the question and answer period that followed, a student asked the rebel leaders if he and his peers should "incorporate" into the FMLN. One of the rebel leaders laughed and said he hoped the negotiations would succeed and that nobody would ever have to incorporate again.

After we shuffled out of the make-shift classroom, Emilio turned to me and whispered: "We had no idea." Neither Emilio nor the other journalists were aware the FMLN had once reached such a low point. It was never easy gauging FMLN strength. For example, the FMLN's most successful offensive, that of November, 1989, occurred right after "a spate of stories suggesting that the FMLN was on the verge of defeat" (Anderson 1990:4). Ironically, the major news foci, political machinations and battlefield fortunes, were the least accessible aspects of the war.

More memorable than Santiago's propaganda or the commanders' frank assessment, however, was a lively dance held the night of our visit. A FMLN band played while area residents, compas, the law students, ourselves, and visiting members of the German Green Party danced, drank, and celebrated. I am not certain what we were celebrating, but neither was anybody else. But that did not stop us from having a great time.

Many of the younger compas stood around the edges of the open air structure, awed by the undulating mass of green and black, punctuated by the students' colorful garb. Two boys sitting next to me, no older than twelve, were examining a grenade. One handed the instrument to his friend, who studied it and gauged its weight by tossing it five or six inches into the air. My second reaction was to scold them (my first was to hit the deck). I saved myself embarrassment by doing neither. A better response would be to scold the militarists and bureaucrats who stole these kids' childhood years.

I was inching away from the young warriors when the aforementioned law-student-reporter hauled me onto the dance floor. As I was being dragged through the crowd, I saw Emilio on stage recording the event on video, smiling as he scanned the sea of olive green ballerinas bobbing up and down to the intoxicating beat. There was a pervasive air of freedom and release as we took refuge a million miles from the oppressive fear and frustration of greater El Salvador.

The next day we talked about the experience as we drove back to San Salvador. Each of the journalists was affected in a slightly different way. The visit engendered a sense of pride, awe, and joy in Emilio. As a city-bound Salvadoran and local radio reporter, he had rarely experienced the countryside during the war. Shari's attitude was a cross between personal affection and awe. She was a little defensive, therefore, when Janice began criticizing Santiago's rhetoric. It seemed a personal issue for her, more than a question of politics or ideology.

Maria, like Janice, was inspired by the insurgents' history and accomplishments, but critical of certain aspects of their organization. Maria was profoundly affected months later, for example, after witnessing the aftermath of a guerrilla attack in San Salvador. A few civilians, including a child, had accidentally been killed in an FMLN assault on a military cuartel. During dinner that night, Maria shouted "How could they do that! They know it will happen when they use that type of bomb. I expect more out of them," she said, as if betrayed by a good friend. Like many stringers and internationals, Maria's critique was developed out of sympathy for the rebel cause. After spending time with the "gs" it was hard not to feel some sort of personal attachment to them. Only a true ideologue could remain completely dispassionate in El Salvador.

The day after we returned from Perquin, I visited Harold in his Camino Real office. Shari had arrived earlier, and was busy listening to one of his "I-couldn't-give-a-shit" commentaries. As Shari and I sat and listened, Harold proceeded to tell us about Radio Venceremos, which he claimed was broadcast from Nicaragua.[4] We sat and listened in silence to his misinformed monologue, neither of us having the heart to interrupt or correct him. The SPECA journalists had different ways of experiencing the war: from behind a desk as in Harold's case, or in the middle of cross-fire, from the bottom of a wine bottle, among a pack of peers, or all alone. Of all the techniques I observed, however, I found the "ethnographic" methods of Shari and Paul the most sound.

Text

and

Representation

THE NARRATIVE STRUCTURE AND AGENDA OF OBJECTIVE JOURNALISM

Thus far I have detailed five disciplinary apparatuses, which, as a loose coalition of influences, have resulted in a description of the Salvadoran war that both legitimated and obfuscated U.S. foreign policy and the Salvadoran power structure: military restrictions on SPECA movements, the hierarchical structure of the corps, elite sources, media institutions, and reporting conventions. In this chapter I will describe a sixth and final disciplinary structure: the objective news narrative.

Objectivity

The journalistic ideal of objectivity developed in the last century, but was not the dominant philosophy of U.S. reporting until after World War II (Schudson 1978:3–11). As the dominant mode of U.S. journalism, this philosophy largely separates the American press from others. Most of the worlds' press are comprised of news organs either openly affiliated with political parties or otherwise identified with overt ideological positions. Decreasingly common totalitarian press systems, such as those of China and Cuba, represent the extreme case. More prevalent are the pluralist presses of Europe, Latin America, and much of the rest of the world. Whereas, in the United States most newspapers and networks are subsidiaries of oligopolies, sharing a philosophy of ideological independence, most of the worlds' press work under no such pretense (Gans 1979:190). A visitor to Paris, Madrid, or Mexico City will be exposed to a large range of competing dailies, each representing different political, social, and cultural perspectives.

Journalists from other countries find the Americans' obsession with objectivity odd, and quite naive. Most of them reject the concept. Alonzo explains:

> The conception of objectivity depends on the school were someone has been formed. For American journalists, in their schools they are taught that they have to be objective in their writing, or objective in their approach to phenomena. But, in reality, objectivity doesn't exist.

As will be demonstrated in Section Four, most of the Salvadorans and internationals of SPECA work under very different professional codes than their U.S. colleagues.

It is easiest to define objectivity in negative terms—what the professional code of objectivity excludes. First, emotion is taboo. "I don't care what happens here," a U.S. staff correspondent was fond of saying, "I can't care." Emotional concern is anathema to objective journalism. In fact, objective journalists will argue quite passionately on the side of dispassionate journalism.

Second, politics are not considered objective. "Some [journalists] are extreme liberals," complained Joe, "but, others are *fair*." As Joe's comment indicates, a reporter cannot be overtly political and still be considered "fair" and objective. This is especially true for those reporters whose views lie outside the liberal-conservative spectrum which dominates the U.S. ideo-scape.

Objectivity is supposed to be value-free (Gans 1979:182–203, Schudson 1978:5). One cannot work under the rule of theoretical paradigms or other explicit value systems and still be considered an objective journalist. Likewise, one should not belong to a politically contentious organization, such as a grass roots political organization or labor union. Shawn, although himself a common target of such attacks, argued that the leader of *Diario Latino* "shouldn't be head editor because he is a unionist and therefore cannot be a fair editor." As Shawn's statement indicates, only the most powerful and/or populated social and political groups (e.g., the Democratic and Republican parties) are considered legitimate within the objective code. Shawn never recognized such a conflict of interest for his U.S. editors, however, who are at the same time both business managers and journalists.

Without explicit values, politics, or emotion, what is left? Fact. As Michael Schudson explains, the American journalists' "belief in objectivity is a faith in 'fact,' a distrust of 'values,' and a commitment to their seg-regation (1978:5)." Journalists turn fact into fetish. They believe facts speak for themselves; that facts are found, not created, and that they are communicable without placement in ordered and "valued" systems of meaning. Discovered and verified, facts magically transform the corre-spondents' prose into objective text. By making fetish of fact, the journal-ists are able to deny, disguise and disown the analytical frames that pattern their presentations. The inevitable ideological orderings or "frames" they utilize to make facts comprehensible and communicate them to the audi-ence are made that much more powerful through encryption.

In other words, objective journalism *is* a political perspective. As in academia, it is a perspective most closely associated with political cen-trism. Paul explains, "I have heard the journalists that pride themselves on being objective say things that make me think that, politically, they are centrist." Troy, who resides quite comfortably in that central location, was one of many who juxtaposed the "left leaning bias" of stringers and internationals with the more "even-handed" work of "those in the main-stream." Looking out from the center, the left (and extreme right) appear subjective, value-laden, and thus "biased," whereas those in the "main-stream" consider themselves and their texts objectively unencumbered.

Those labeled as "leftists" resent these distinctions. Pati, a stigmatized Canadian, complained that "reporters are only perceived of as biased if they are left wing." "Having been labeled a leftist journalist, I think that objectivity is a conservative perspective." Pati is "really careful, because the editors are reading my stories twice and trying to figure out where they are coming from."

Harold, like most staff correspondents, claims to occupy a neutral, and objective center. Conversely, he and his colleagues often charge the less establishment-oriented stringers of harboring political bias. He complains that Ronald, for example, "came down here with a program." Harold claims to have no such agenda. Like many mainstream journalists, he enjoys pointing out that his work has been attacked by both left and right wing critics. He claims this as proof that he is neither, and that he is, there-fore, objective. For Harold and his colleagues, centrism equals objectiv-ity (Hallin 1983:32–33).

As a centrist perspective, objective journalism also rejects right wing extremism (Gans 1980:30–31). Those on the right recognize and resent this distinction. Gerardo, described by SPECA members as an "ultra-right-ist," complains:

> You're a scientist. I am talking to a scientist, not a half baked stringer. You know that in science there is no such thing as objectivity. Everything is governed by actions and reactions and the receptor has as much to do with the reality as (pause), well, there is no such thing as reality.... If I were an idiot, or a cretin or something I would come off and say, 'Oh yeah, I'm

objective.' But, let's get down to brass tacks. If you are going to write a paper, that is going to be judged by men of great intelligence—and not by stupid idiots who work on newspapers—and you are going to talk about objectivity, you will soon realize that there is no such thing…there is something wrong with the evaluation, with the norm, with the standard.

Those outside that "standard"—right, left or otherwise—were much more likely to take a critical view of the objective code.

"The journalist who arrives here needs to locate himself," argued a Salvadoran journalism professor, "and understand that the situation and the vision one has is going to depend upon one's own ideological perspective and that of the agency as well." Such reflexive analysis is anathema to objective journalism, however. The U.S. correspondent sees his primary duty as that of *not* becoming located and *not* having an ideological perspective—objectivity as absence. This apparent paradox—self-conscious nonreflexivity—is made possible by a set of paradigms and practices which have come to define what is, and what is not, objective practice. By becoming conscious of these conventions, journalists are able to remain unconscious of the deeper cultural values and political ideologies that pattern their work. As a result, the paradigmatic regimes of liberal capitalism (I will refrain from calling this "late capitalism"), have become synonymous with objective reality. Thus, for the press, the end of communism and the apparent global spread of consumer capitalism were heralded as the "end of ideology." For the centrist journalist, capitalism is not ideology, but instead a neutral and natural condition, an objective truth.

Even in the U.S., however, objective journalism's hold is neither absolute nor unchanging. Though it is still official doctrine (the *public* face of U.S. journalism is still "objective") U.S. reporters have come to question the ideal of objectivity, especially since the sixties and the advent of "new journalism" (Dennis and Rivers 1974, Iyengar and Kinder 1987:132, Johnson 1978, Smith 1980). Although investigative and "new" journalism have both failed to enter the mainstream press, their presence on the margins of the discipline have caused mainstream reporters to question and reinterpret their positivistic tradition. As a result, objectivist press doctrine has been slightly weakened or, at least, reformed (Smith 1980).

The current thinking was summarized by Bart:

I believe that objectivity is an ideal. It's an unattainable ideal. But, it should be held out as an ideal that should be striven for. My view of objectivity is that people know in their own minds when they are reflecting what they see and when they are trying to kind of make what they see fit into some sort of scheme that they already have in their head.

Cal agrees "the reporter should strive towards objectivity" even though it is a "a utopian goal." Most U.S. and associated British reporters in

SPECA, stringers and staff alike, made similar paradoxical statements about striving towards the nebulous and unattainable "it" of objectivity. If nothing else, their employers demand a certain level of obedience to the positivistic paradox. A Reuters journalist explains:

> As a correspondent for Reuters I am still guided by Reuters' policy, which doesn't change. Objectivity, impartiality and even-handedness are the absolute basics to anchor a news story.... If they felt I wasn't doing that I'd get sacked.

Objectivity remains the standard by which journalists are judged.

Balance and Fairness

Mainstream reporters consider emotions, politics, and theoretical paradigms to be contagions which obfuscate, rather than facilitate, their process of discovery. Yet, in addition to their supposed rejection of values, theory, and ideology—objectivity as absence—there is also a creative aspect to latter day positivism. A number of practices and textual forms have been developed to provide journalists with a standard by which to differentiate objective and tendentious reporting. "Balance" and "fairness" are the most important of these neopositivist principles. "What objectivity has come to mean in terms of U.S. journalism," complained Bob, "is that you approach the subject with a sense of balance."

Balanced reports exhibit a very specific narrative structure. A balanced news report is one that represents the views of opposing parties arranged in a structured debate. Hypothetically, a reporter interviews the leader of one "side," such as Juaquin Villalobos, then asks a spokesperson for another, such as President Christiani, for rebuttal. The two are juxtaposed in a dialogue facilitated by the journalist. Reporters for U.S. institutions are considered remiss if they do not provide at least passing recognition of countervailing sentiments, regardless of the nature of the opposing claims. Speaking of the assassination of Salvadoran human rights worker Herbert Anaya Sanabrias, Michele explained:

> The government fabricated the story. Yet, you have to give equal importance to the witnesses of both sides. You must listen to both. It is a standard we have to maintain.

As a result, the "rigid formulae of so-called objectivity," as noted by journalist Eric Sevareid, "have given the lie the same prominence and impact that truth is given" (Lent 1983:47).

In practice, however, balance has come to mean much more than an exposition of opposing sentiments. In the case of El Salvador, many reporters purposely balanced their presentation of facts and events as well, complementing each report favoring the guerrillas with one favoring the Salvadoran government. Sam explains (italics mine):

In a war situation, where it is one side against the other, if you pick a topic that one side can't help looking good on, you should balance that by *finding* things that balance that so that you are showing both the positive and negative sides over a period of time.

Bob critiqued this conception of balance:

There is no doubt about it, the majority of human rights abuse in El Salvador was committed by the army. But what a lot of journalists did—especially those who were the most career oriented and ambitious journalists—they would say, openly, "Well, I've written an article hitting the army, now I have to write something hitting the guerrillas." I have heard at least three mainstream journalists, one for the *Wall Street Journal,* one for the *Washington Post,* and one for the *Miami Herald* say that. They are saying that both because they want to appear objective and because—if the army comes at them and says, "well you said this about us, but you are not criticizing the guerrillas,"—they can say, "oh yeah, I criticize the guerrillas as well." And it also pleases their editors as well, it shows that they don't have any sympathies.

But, what if the truth of the matter is that 85 to 95% of the abuses are being done by the army and 10 to 15% by the guerrillas?.... Are you going to mention an equal number of incidents for each side? It shouldn't be balanced because the situation isn't balanced.

As Bob explained, the equalization tactic is a means of professional, and even physical survival. The "balance" reporters do not deny this. Harold, who also openly admits to balancing his work in this fashion, agreed that it is "a matter of self-preservation to be seen that way."

The objective reporters equalized the violence of the left and right, placing the United States and the Salvadoran government in a neutral middle space between those "violent extremes." This artificially constructed ethic of balance is found in the U.S. press' standard death toll statistic. The following statement is typical: "The war has killed an estimated 75,000 people and displaced up to one million of the country's five million people" (AP July 11, 1991). That statistic, rarely qualified with explanation of cause or agency, mistakenly implies that most of the 75,000 victims died in battle ("the *war* has killed..."). The standard statistic also fails to explain who did most of the killing and dying, as if both sides were equally at fault.[1] In truth, the great majority of the victims were civilians killed by the military and closely related "death squads" (Cockburn 1989:438, Popkin 1991:60–63). According to the nongovernmental Human Rights Commission of El Salvador, this severe imbalance continued during the war's final years. In 1990, for example, the military murdered 1,005 civilians, while the FMLN killed twenty-seven (McKerrow 1991:15). Reading the standard statistic, however, one is merely informed that some 75,000 died, period. That statement is, at best, misleading.

The obtuse "75,000 dead" statistic was sometimes inserted by editors. "Some asshole [editor] keeps putting that in there," complained Bart when asked about his use of the balance stat. He pointed out the fact that nobody, including editors and reporters, really knows how many have died. The "75,000" statistic is a variable approximation, a collective guess by human rights workers and journalists. Pati explains:

> In every story about El Salvador it is written: "the eleven year old war in El Salvador has taken 75,000 lives." It is very arbitrary when it goes up every year by 5000.

Cal explains how he inherited the statistic:

> When I came down here my frame of reference was what my service was already saying about El Salvador, which pretty much fit the frame of reference of what everybody else was writing about El Salvador. Any reporter that comes down here has that structure, that media image of El Salvador, things that have been repeated over and over again. When you first get here that is a real help. More than 70,000 people, depending on what service you read, have died in this conflict, you know, but I haven't counted them all.

Nobody has counted them all. The real number could be a bit higher or, maybe, as Harold claims, "The death toll estimates are blown way out of proportion." Either way, objective journalism demands precision, especially in the reporting of facts, so 75,000 it is. What that actually means is another issue. The objective news presentation must appear accurate, and above all, balanced.

Objective texts must also appear "fair." According to most *A Team* journalists, a fair report is one that represents sources' perspectives accurately and without judgment. Because most of the journalists' sources are elites, this concept of fairness allows those in power inordinate influence over the creation of news frames (Hallin 1983:7–21). Their framing terms and assertions are allowed to pass without analytical oversight or qualification. Therefore, only when elite sources are in disagreement does the news frame itself fracture into a significantly contested debate (Hallin 1983:9–16, 1986a and Hanisko 1981). This happened occasionally during coverage of the Salvadoran War, especially late in the war after U.S. Congressional Representative Joe Moakley and his Democratic allies stepped up their challenge to the Bush Administration's Salvadoran aid policy. Unfortunately, even then the debate remained narrowly fixed upon questions of political strategy. The purpose, history, and depth of U.S. military intervention were never closely examined in the mainstream press. Whether political elites were in consensus or disagreement, the concept of fairness provided them relatively unfettered access to the news pages.

Stringers tend to conceive of the twin principles somewhat differently than staff. Shawn, for example, feels the principle of fairness allows room for judgment, as long as "fair" standards are consistently applied. He cited his coverage of the January, 1991 FMLN execution of the U.S. military advisors: "In this case, I thought that the FMLN deserved to take some shots. You think in terms of fairness. What if the army had done this?" Whereas, most staff correspondents defined fairness in passive terms—a means of allowing sources to tell their the story without censure—Shawn looks at the issue in terms of critical authorship, as a means of evaluating conflicting perspectives according to consistent criteria.

Although different definitions of the term were given by SPECA journalists, fairness is a general principle upon which most of the American media, both mainstream and alternative, agree. In fact, the leading press watchdog organization on the left, Fairness and Accuracy in Reporting (FAIR), is defined by the term. Of course, as FAIR's serial publication *Extra!* makes clear, alternative and mainstream media differ greatly on the correct application of those standards, each accusing the other of reporting in an unfair, inaccurate, and unbalanced manner. It is the application, however, rather than the rules themselves, which are being contested in this typically "American" debate. In styling their critiques in the language of fairness, balance, and objectivity itself, mainstream and alternative organizations alike demonstrate a shared allegiance to the positivistic principles of U.S. journalism, making it their shared, albeit contested culture.

Objective Texts

The following *Associated Press* report represents a typical application of the principles of "balance" and "fairness" (*Miami Herald* February 28, 1991:11):

SALVADORAN CAPITAL CALM AFTER COMBAT
Deadly clash was attack on leader's home, government says
San Salvador — (AP) — The government reported calm in the capital of El Salvador Wednesday following overnight battles between leftist rebels and loyalist forces that left one civilian dead and ten others injured.

The government said the guerrilla incursion into the upper-class suburb of Escalon was part of an unsuccessful attack on the official residence of President Alfredo Christiani. A communiqué said several 81mm mortars were fired at the Presidential compound, but none struck their target.

Insurgents interviewed during the fighting said the battles were in response to government military operations in northern and eastern parts of the country that are under rebel control.

At least one air force helicopter crewman fired machine-gun

rounds at rebel positions during the fighting. Combat was heavy at times during the two hours before midnight, with sustained exchanges of assault-rifle fire and intermittent explosions of grenades.

Several light tanks and armored personnel carriers backed by an estimated 300 infantry troops patrolled Escalon on Wednesday morning.

The twenty or so rebels who had infiltrated the neighborhood from bases on the San Salvador volcano west of the capital appeared to have withdrawn by dawn. There were no exchanges of fire after daylight.

The government, in a communiqué, called the incursion "a totally terrorist action and a flagrant violation of human rights." It accused the guerrillas of "shielding themselves with the civilian population in order to sow pain and destruction."

The communiqué also said the incursion was part of a guerrilla plan to hinder nationwide legislative and municipal elections scheduled for March 10.

Several sabotaged utility posts were down along Escalon's streets. The walls surrounding some luxurious houses had been inscribed with guerrilla graffiti, including, "If it's war they want, war they'll get."

The AP author has constructed a balanced rhetorical battle. Rather than mirroring the actual battle between FMLN and army troops, however, the dialogic war is fought between "the government" and FMLN "insurgents." In accordance with the principle of fairness, the reporter reproduces FMLN and government positions without explicit editorial comment or "distortion." To demonstrate her sense of fairness, the author "sources" most of the article. In fact, six of the report's nine paragraphs are attributed to sources. Four paragraphs are sourced to the government, two to the guerrillas (if one counts graffiti). The other three are straightforward presentations of fact. The author makes it clear that none of the quoted views or facts represent her own opinions or analyses.

Katherine mentioned one of the problems in applying the twin ethics fairness and balance:

> One of the problems with objectivity, or even fairness, is that you aren't always judging equal elements. I have no illusions about the difficulty it represents to pretend to be fair across the board because you aren't always dealing with the same kinds of people. Someone is lying to you and somebody may not be and everyone has their own version of the truth.

Katherine's concerns apply rather well to the report in question. The piece provides readers with little indication of which "version of the truth," the guerrillas' or the government's, is more accurate. Those most distant from the conflict are left to sort it out on their own.

Unfortunately, there is too little context provided for readers to draw any meaningful conclusions. How many people know what an 81mm mortar is? Why is it significant that an air force helicopter was firing machine-gun rounds? Three hundred troops patrolled Escalon the next morning. Is that a lot? Are the guerrillas really attempting to "hinder" the elections? If so, why? What does it all mean? The report is more like a long headline than an explanatory text. It is a lengthy restatement of the fact that Salvadoran government and rebels have had a gun battle in the city, and that each side blames the other.

I am reminded of an impromptu skit performed by Cary. In the baritone drone of a network news anchor, Cary parodied his own radio reports: "A fierce battle was reported today between the government and the guerrillas. The government don't like the guerrillas, and the guerrillas don't like the government. Meanwhile, in the Persian gulf.... "

Indeed, the balance format can be quite sophomoric and obtuse. Jelisa, who feels fortunate to write for a Latin American news service rather than a U.S. organ, complained that the "simple give this side and that side thing" of U.S. journalism often makes her "dizzy." I would guess most news consumers are similarly confused by much of what they read, see, and hear. Objective journalism is superficial journalism. The demands of balance and fairness, the emphasis on elite sources, and the fetishization of fact lead to a simplistic, and at times, cryptic discourse. In the AP report excerpted above, we learn almost nothing about the war, its causes, it implications, it effects on the civilian population, nor "our" relationship to it. Such analyses are mostly segregated onto the editorial pages, taking the analytical initiative away from field reporters and giving it to office-bound editors thousands of miles away. Balanced and fair journalism is, as Bob notes, a sort of "neuter journalism."

The Argument Underneath

Despite their cryptic tendencies, there are still authorial arguments to be found in balanced and fair reports. In order to make facts and quotations comprehensible, reporters do make certain, albeit greatly limited, judgments. The reporter and editor of the above AP story, for example, make an implicit claim that the FMLN action is important by reporting it in the first place. Note that the "government military operations in northern and eastern parts of the country" to which the "insurgents" referred, were never themselves actually reported. Conversely, guerrilla activities, such as this one, were measured with a fairly constant gaze. In U.S. news, the "leftists are always attacking, fighting, or rebelling," writes Anderson, while "the legitimate government is continually under a state of siege" (1988:243).

Balanced quotes and facts are also arranged in logical, argumentative fashion. By juxtaposing government claims with FMLN "graffiti" and acts of sabotage, the author makes a subtle, perhaps even unwitting criticism of the rebels. The relatively voiceless guerrillas are framed as vandals and terrorists.[2]

Sam was one of the few U.S. journalists in my study who recognized, or at least admitted, the inevitable process of argumentation that goes into every news report. "You don't say that you're convinced," explained Sam, "You put evidence in that convinces the reader.... You sort of build a case for your vision." In other words, the facts do not "speak for themselves," but instead for a point of view, whether that of a reporter, editor, press, government, marketing system or coalition thereof.

Bart's more conventional conception of news writing differs dramatically from Sam's:

> The only real honest journalism is one that lets what's happening tell itself. Basically, you describe what's happening and let people tell their sides of the story. You try to get a number of sides in and then it will kind of shake-out. Then you won't have this thing where you have to say, "This is the truth," in the first act. The truth will become evident in some kind of subliminal way almost.

Like Bart, most U.S. reporters claim to represent the facts with little authorial intervention. They argue that readers, not the journalist, should act as judge and jury in determining which "side" is telling the truth. The trial metaphor is often used. "Each side gets direct examination and cross examination," explained Othello, "I find that model in my own head helpful. I've never seen it in a book or anything, but it seems to make a certain sort of sense."

A British stringer disagreed with Othello's trial model:

> In a court case you listen to the evidence, but when you write a story you've already assimilated all the evidence and you are using it. It is not a question of presenting it and letting the reader sort it out. You sort it out first.

This is anathema to the belief structure of U.S. journalism, however, in which professionalism "means avoiding as much as possible the overt intrusion of the reporter's personal values into a news story and minimizing explicit interpretation" (Sigal 1986:15).

The standard news narrative provides a ready-made formula for producing news that appears objective, from both the author's and consumers' shared perspectives. The objective narrative format has now become nearly synonymous with the principle of objectivity itself. Reports exhibiting the particular phrasing, format, and tenor of "balance and fairness" are considered, by definition, objective.

News as Dramatic Narrative

Like other narrative forms, news stories involve setting, plot development, dialogue, and a set of central characters. The clearest examples are television news reports. In televised journalism, heavy emphasis is placed upon visual setting, boldly-drawn characters, dramatic plot and, quite often, a moral (see chapter 11). However, even the most skeletal and formulaic wire service reports, such as the above AP story, exhibit this basic dramaturgical structure. The guerrillas attack, the government responds, and the story ends with an ominous warning: "If it's war they want, war they'll get." When Shawn and others told me about the fighting immediately afterwards (I slept through it), each emphasized and/or ended their tales with that same vignette. They hoped the rebel warning was foreshadowing an even more dramatic sequel.

A good story demands more than dramatic plot, however, it also requires identifiable characters. Rather than collective groups or concepts, news stories are usually constructed around the beliefs and actions of individuals, specifically, political elites (Kertzer 1988:6–7). "The press," explains Sigal, "typically reduces politics to a clash of personalities" (1986:13). "The individual," he goes on to explain, usually "stands for a social aggregate" (1986:13). In news of late-war El Salvador, President Christiani represented the Salvadoran government, Villalobos and other guerrilla leaders represented the FMLN, while the U.S. President and Ambassador represented the United States. Groups and collective categories without titular leaders, such as "the people" of El Salvador, are generally either missing from the news or represented by these same elites.

There was no shortage of dramatic personalities during the Salvadoran war: Archbishop Romero, Major D'Aubuisson, Ronald Reagan, Juaquin Villalobos, and Napoleon Duarte to name a few. These men made the news. Their involvement in an issue or event would elevate it from mere happenstance to news. It was Reagan's insistence, for example, that the U.S. "show the world that we want no hostile, communist colonies here in the Americas" that brought the press to Central America in such great numbers in the first place (Reagan in Gettleman 1986:14). "Reagan's witching tales about little bands of Soviet and Cuban terrorists" (Alegria 1986:38) provided the prerequisite "hook" for the Central American story.

Events and issues often fail to rate for lack of important character-participants. Right before the 1991 National Assembly elections, I asked Marla about her visit to a recent ARENA rally. She replied:

> We thought Major Bob [D'Aubuisson] was going to be there. The people who were there, Calderon Sol and Ochoa Perez, were just as hard-line, but they don't have the same charismatic relationship to the crowd. Without him there, you can't call up your editor on the phone and say, 'Hey, I have this feature. Remember that guy, Major Bob D'Aubuisson?' Then you can sell

that story. These other people were saying pretty much the same things as D'Aubuisson does, but without him, it made the trip become just background as opposed to featured news.

Editors expect to see the recognizable figures in the news. Sam laments, "Editors tend to think in terms of personality profiles." Reporters meet the editorial mandate by constructing appropriate characters from the stock of personalities (usually sources) surrounding them. "As a feature writer," explained Bob, "you find someone that exemplifies what you are trying to show." Ideas become embodied in the actions of news person-alities (Gitlin 1980:146–79).

As in fiction, news characters serve as literary vehicles for essential con-cepts. Sometimes, character representations must be modified to fit dom-inant frames. Soon after winning the 1989 elections, for example, Christiani changed from "the standard bearer of the far-right Republican National Alliance" (the *New York Times Index* 1989:465) to a "moder-ate," so designated after a carefully orchestrated campaign by the State Department to present him to the press as such through a series of Presidential meetings (*New York Times* April 8,1989:6) and media-satu-rated diplomatic exchanges (*New York Times* 1989: June 2:3; June 2:7; June 14:1; June 14:3, June 18,IV:2). For U.S. support of the Salvadoran government to appear consistent and morally correct, Christiani had to be transformed into a U.S.-style moderate, at least on (news)paper. It was not until after his reign ended that journalists began mentioning Christiani's extreme right political views and actions once again (see the *Los Angeles Times*, April 3, 1994:A2). "Marxist" Villalobos and "ultra-rightist" D'Aubuisson went through similar transitions. News caricatures changed rather dramatically over time to meet the developing needs of frame-management, always drawn in the "broader and blunter strokes" (Malcolm 1990:122) of fictional characters, never explored in their human complexity.

As Todd Gitlin points out, the U.S. news narrative is descended from the quintessential American art form, the western.[3] U.S. news reporting of El Salvador was often a reduction of the war's complexities to the lit-eral and figurative gun play of primary news characters. The definitions changed from time to time, who was good and who was bad, but the fun-damentally "American" narrative of "good guys and bad guys" remained. "Many come with their ideas already clear," said Jorge of his North American colleagues, "who is good and who is bad.... It is like they are watching a movie: good guys and bad guys."

Janet Malcolm described "the difficulty of knowing the truth about anything" in her provocative study *The Journalist and the Murderer,* how a reporter "could spend years" covering an issue "and end up with no certain answer to the question of what 'really' happened" (134).

Objective news reports, however, must appear to demonstrate what "really happened." Ironically, this is where the dramatic narrative is most useful. In drama and other fictions, especially American fiction, people and issues are reduced to their simplest forms. Things can be known with great certainty, from beginning to end. The dramatic (or perhaps melodramatic) narrative provides a convenient formula for reducing complex issues into 800 word news reports and, more importantly, lends the appearance of objective properties (Anderson 1988b:245–48). Two dimensional representations of character, morality and fact are much more likely to appear objective than those that successfully capture the "complex, ambiguous, unpredictable, and particular" persons, events, and truths found in 'real life'" (Malcolm 1990:122). The latter create skepticism as a matter of course. Representations mirroring the complexities, contradictions, and ambiguities of "real life" place readers in a critical mode, forcing them to reflect upon the author's subjective placement, and their own as well. Complexity invites thought, moral ambiguity, and doubt. Conversely, dramatic narrative provides neatly packaged truths in the guise of known events and balanced debates, the certainty of simplification. As a result, journalists have adopted the fictional narrative and made it their own.

Elsa, a Salvadoran SPECA journalist, provides a compelling sociological explanation for the melodramatic nature of U.S. journalism:

> Life in the U.S. is very fast. They are accustomed to very simple questions in the news. They do not have time to examine issues that are not of the immediate moment.

People in the U.S. have become accustomed to simple, dramatic, and superficial communication—millions of images thrown at the audience in a stream of easily digestible units or "sound bites." The melodramatic news narrative is well matched to these contingencies, just as fast food, freeways, and other daily accoutrements facilitate the increasingly compacted, ever-more-stressful work-life of the average American. Unfortunately, issues that are more difficult to "tell" in the melodramatic mode—economy, environment, and culture—receive much less coverage as a result.

This is not to say journalists should abandon narrative structure. Story telling is a fundamental form of human communication. Instead, reporters should become more aware of the narrative structures and subjectivities they have inherited, rather than falsely denying their existence. Unfortunately, objectivity—an ethic created in part to overcome the tendentious reporting of the last century—has become a doctrinaire obstacle to informed and enlightening newswriting, limiting rather than facilitating the journalists ability to tell the most important stories, and to tell them well.

Nationalism, Capitalism, and the Central American News Agenda

Asked what factors most heavily effect the international news agenda, George replied:

> News is an extension of anything you would like to go up to your family and say, "Hey, guess what happened."…stories usually select themselves.

News is "whatever interests the Kansas City milkman," added the affable staffer. Oddly enough, George has never actually been to Kansas City. Another reporter, when asked "who or what sets the U.S. news agenda?" gave credit to "some guy in New York."

Almost every other SPECA reporter, however, North American or otherwise, gave credit to the White House. The journalists demonstrated an unusual degree of agreement on that point. Typical responses were as follows:

Janice: "The U.S. administration sets the news agenda."

Shawn: "The agenda is set in Washington. That is what people are interested in; well, what editors are interested in, not *people*."

Justin: "The press follows Washington's lead. They follow the smell of shit."

Harold: "The agenda is set in Washington. But, no reporter likes the fact that the agenda is set in Washington…. The coverage [of El Salvador] is changing because the situation has changed, at least in Washington."

Rosa: "The story started to die as soon as Bush said that Central America was no longer an important area of operations. Plus, since we now have democracy here…ha ha ha."

Fred: "Washington dictates what happens in the foreign press."

Iver: "U.S. aid is an extremely important part of it. Christiani is in D.C. as we speak."

Francine: "If you look at Central America since the Reagan administration, it is gone. It is not on the map. Reagan had an obsession with Central America and Nicaragua especially. If you remove that, it is just Central America, which they [editors] don't really care about."

The graph on the following page illustrates the news agenda of the *New York Times*, a fairly accurate indicator of the U.S. news agenda as a whole.[4]

The *New York Times* agenda partially follows the level of violence during the war. 1980–1982 was by far the most brutal period. Yet, the level of violence has not been nearly as punctuated as the news agenda would indicate. The 1970s, for example, was an extremely violent period, yet received almost no coverage. Furthermore, *battle* casualties were rather constant throughout the war. Although the news frame prematurely

Number of Reports and Editorials in the *New York Times*, 1978–1992

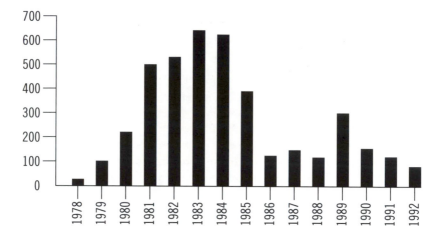

turned to peace in 1990 and 1991, the level of battlefield violence in those years remained as high, or higher, than in many previous years.

News agenda shifts were more closely correlated with developments in U.S. foreign policy. Coverage was highest in the period between Reagan's first public declarations about El Salvador in 1981 and the election of Napoleon Duarte in 1984. In fact, more reports were written in that four year period, than all others combined. Coverage fell off dramatically thereafter when Reagan and Bush stopped calling attention to the situation (Lent 1983:42, McAnany 1983:210). Aid kept flowing and the U.S. war policy continued apace after 1984, but the official voice of the government had turned away from the region and, as a result, so did the press.

The November, 1989 FMLN offensive caused a momentary increase in coverage, as it appeared that El Salvador was once again in danger of "falling," but the overall decline in coverage continued. By the time peace arrived, coverage was nearly down to pre-war levels. "For editors to cover this," complained Bart in 1992, "they're going to have to pick up their guns and start fighting again." If history is an accurate index, however, it will take even more than renewed fighting; it will take another presidential "obsession" to bring the press back to Central America.

War and death, as compelling as they are to the international press, are simply not enough. It has to be the right kind of war. El Salvador's neighbor to the north, Guatemala, has been embroiled in a war for over thirty years, yet has received very scant coverage. I asked the SPECA reporters to explain why this is so. Bart's explanation mirrored that of nearly every other SPECA journalist:

Guatemala probably is the most glaring example of lack of coverage in the region. In the early Eighties they had a blood bath worse than the one here.... Lack of U.S. aid is a big part of the explanation. When you've got a country like El Salvador—which is the biggest recipient of U.S. aid in the Western Hemisphere—for logical reasons, editors feel like their readers are going to be more interested.

"The U.S. is not involved in Guatemala," Katherine explained in similar vein, "they have given them very little aid. It is not a major policy issue." While the U.S. government has a history of intervention in Guatemala, including a CIA-supported coup in 1954, it severely cut financial assistance in the 1980s and, at times, has completely curtailed it (Immerman 1982, Schlesinger and Kinzer 1982).

Of course, when reporters say "the U.S." they mean the *government* of the United States of America. They are not referring to the involvement of U.S. citizens or corporations. In fact, U.S. corporations are a fundamental part of Guatemala's economic infrastructure. By 1978, U.S. companies were investing more money in Guatemala than in any other Central American republic: a total of $221 million that year (Torres-Rivas 1983:32). That same year, El Salvador ranked last in the region, receiving $111 million worth of U.S. investment.

In other words, news coverage of the two countries has been inversely related to the level of U.S. corporate involvement. This is because news is primarily understood in political and juridical frames. Power is conceived almost exclusively in political terms, while corporate activities and labor issues are almost completely ignored. As a result, the political struggles that dominate news coverage are represented outside their material contexts of power—political intrigue vs. political economy. A U.S. reporter driving through Guatemala stops at a Texaco gas station, buys a Coke, smokes a Camel, and then drives down to the McDonald's for dinner, passing the free trade zones where Guatemalan workers turn out boatloads of "American" products.[5] But, from the journalist's perspective, "the U.S. is not involved in Guatemala."

This distinction was made clear to me early in 1991, as reporters where rushing to Nicaragua to cover political rallies and strikes by Sandinista loyalists against the newly elected Chamorro government. At the same time, as many as 100,000 Honduran workers were striking against Chiquita and other U.S. and European transnationals. It would seem that, of the two, the Honduran strikes would have had a much more direct relevance to U.S. news consumers, because it directly involved U.S. companies. I asked the reporters why they chose to cover the Sandinista event rather than the Honduran strike. Bob explained:

Even labor coverage in the U.S. is something that hardly ever gets covered in a serious way, with much sensitivity. So, labor in the third world? You don't see much stuff about it.... They *would* want to publicize how the

Sandinistas try and destablize a friendly, democratically elected government. Whereas, in Honduras, it is not something they would want to publicize. They would be much more happy with the blackout [on the Honduran strikes] because, there it is local unions that are complaining about being run roughshod by a major U.S. multinational corporation that is violating all kinds of labor agreements, strong arming independent banana producers and growers.... They don't want that kind of news—how U.S. companies act and mistreat the local populations and third world people.... They want people to believe that the U.S. is a good force in the world which stands for democracy.

U.S. companies are allowed to conduct business as usual in Honduras, Guatemala, and even El Salvador without fear of becoming part of the U.S. news agenda. In obedience to the liberal capitalist ideology, which governs corporate media, journalists portray Central Americans in the roles of warriors and statesmen, rather than as workers, entrepreneurs, and/or land owners. In addition to obfuscating the underlying causes of violence, such coverage has a strong "distancing effect" (Brentlinger 1990:4–6), making it difficult for North American readers to identify with the Central American people.

Both sources and subjects are constructed in political terms, as battling wills competing for governmental power. Journalists rarely consider other aspects of human existence, such as the economic or class positions of their subjects. U.S. laborers, for example, rarely receive coverage, except during strikes—the "offensive" actions of labor. Most of that coverage is drawn from the perspective of consumers inconvenienced by actions of organized labor, rather than the perspectives of workers who have been "inconvenienced" by corporate actions. News readers are spoken to as consumers, distanced from the subjectified workers and alienated from their own working personas. The audience is conceived of, and represented in, nonproductive capacities: consumers, parents, voters, etc. The news has us think almost solely in terms of imagined communities (the state) and subordinate institutions (family), rather than in terms of the corporate structures in which we spend the majority of our time.[6] Although they wield the greatest influence over people's daily lives and communal life-chances, corporate institutions and activities are mostly ignored in the news. This oversight is to be expected, of course, because news institutions have themselves been consumed and consolidated by a small clique of large corporations, another subject on which the news media's "self-censorship" is nearly "absolute" (Bagdikian 1990:ix).

The political and juridical biases of U.S. journalism are also reflected in the journalists' extreme interest in national elections. Presidential elections (1982, 1984, and 1989) comprised three of the four most heavily covered stories during the Salvadoran war (Herman and Brodhead 1984:93–152, Spence 1983, 1984). Elections are the primary symbol of liberty in capitalist democracies. They remind us that, in liberal capitalist culture, there is an element of political choice. Conversely, labor unrest reminds us that in the economic sphere of these same cultures, and especially within Third World dependencies, there is relatively little choice for the majority.[7] It is to be expected that corporate media would emphasize those areas of social life where people are ostensibly able to exercise control over their individual and communal destinies, as is seemingly the case during democratic elections, while ignoring those contexts in which most people have very little real influence (the factory floor, data entry terminal, board room, etc.).

In addition to operating under the meta-narrative of liberal capitalism, press institutions exhibit several other ethnocentric tendencies. The "Western diplomat" attribution, for example, is predicated upon an ethnocentric claim to western rationality. The official western sources are posited as cool, authoritative, and rational voices in a wilderness of primitive conflict. Furthermore, the use of the "Western diplomat" appellation represents a misunderstanding of Latin American cultures, societies that are as "western" as the United States, and in some ways more so. Yet, U.S. news is filled with comments of "Western diplomats" as distinguished from the quotes of Latin American officials, as if the two categories are mutually exclusive.

The most obvious manifestation of ethnocentric bias, however, is the emphasis journalists place on events and issues involving U.S. citizens. This was particularly obvious in the news coverage of the 1991 FMLN execution of two U.S. advisors. As mentioned previously, 41% of U.S. network television news coverage was devoted to the advisors' deaths in 1991, a highly inordinate level of attention paid to two deaths which, aside from the victims' national affiliations, were fairly unexceptional.

However, ethnocentric bias is neither endemic to U.S. journalism, nor new (Taussig 1987:21–22). Throughout the war, Canadian coverage tended to emphasize the activities of Canadian nationals, such as the detention of six McGill University students in August, 1991 (*Globe and Mail* August 29, 1991:14). Spanish newspapers also exhibited an exaggerated focus on their citizens' involvement in the war, including the death of a Spanish doctor in January, 1991 (*El Pais* January 15, 1991:14). Ethnocentrism as a news value is as perhaps as universal as ethnocentrism itself.

What is new and interesting about the coverage of the Salvadoran war and other "low intensity conflicts," however, is the way in which military strategists have taken advantage of the press' ethnocentric tendencies. Learning from their failures in Vietnam, Pentagon strategists have moved away from the use of American ground troops in situations where they are at great risk of prolonged engagement and high death tolls. Their use of surrogate armies, including the Nicaraguan Contras and Salvadoran military, has increased considerably, as has their application of mechanical surrogates ("smart weapons") and saturation bombing techniques, both of which were witnessed and celebrated during the Panama Invasion and Persian Gulf War. Both of these surrogate strategies serve to limit the number of U.S. deaths, thus pulling attention away from war's human effects and dulling public criticism.

Now, the international press is leaving El Salvador at a rapid rate. Many journalists argue this is at it should be. They feel that as a small republic, El Salvador deserves no greater coverage than any other nation its size. As Ted pointed out, "There are American cities with bigger populations than the whole country of El Salvador." Most reporters, while embittered by the sudden lack of institutional interest, have rationalized their withdrawal in similar fashion. Of course, they were not making the same argument earlier in the war when Reagan turned the region into a top story. The agenda comes and goes, as do the reporters who must follow it, and it is not the fickle tastes of the "Kansas City milkman" or even the reporters themselves who most strongly determine its outcome. The convergent interests of the U.S. government, transnational corporations, and the ideological structure upon which they are predicated, largely determined the agenda of U.S. news coverage in Central America.

The Shifting Agenda Syndrome

The U.S. press tends to focus its resources upon one issue at a time. Once governmental and/or editorial interest runs its course days or weeks later, the theme is exhausted and the main agenda shifts once again. The fall of the Berlin Wall, the Panama invasion, the Russian coup—an endless bombardment of dramatic moments wrested from the underlying continuities from which they emerge, images that dazzle the news consumer as they bloom and wither in passing (McAnany 1983). J. Laurence Day calls this the "now playing" system of foreign news reporting (1987:308–309).

"Except for Israel," explains Othello, "there is no continuous foreign story in the U.S. press." Indeed, Central America may be one of the most radically discontinuous. It neither occupies the news netherworld of regions like the South Pacific, nor serves as a repeated highlight like Russia or the Middle East. Central America is used as needed.

Calixto, a Latin American journalist, sees the shifting agenda syndrome as the greatest fault of the U.S. press:

> When Central America is no longer an object of interest in U.S. politics, they are all going to close their offices. They have already stopped spending the millions of dollars to maintain TV crews and pay all of their drivers.

Calixto complained that U.S. media spent eight years in Nicaragua writing "dramatic stories," but have now abandoned the country. "There is much more hunger there than a year before," he protested, "Why don't they write about that?" He continued:

If you look in the Mexican papers these days, you will see a lot of coverage of the Persian Gulf War, whether bad or good. Yet, they never stop reporting Central America and other parts of the world as well. This is a primary difference between the U.S. press and most others.

The problem is compounded by the fact that U.S. newspapers present so little international news, less than half, on average, of their Western European counterparts (Hartman 1982). Similarly, the U.S. news networks in 1994 were presenting barely half the amount of international news broadcast just ten years ago.[8] Global reality is being presented to the U.S. news consumer in highly segmented, limited, and concentrated bursts.

The shifting agenda syndrome not only effects the readers ability to comprehend the world, but also inhibits the foreign correspondents' professional development. As they rush around the world from hot spot to hot spot, reporters gain little competency in the cultures they visit and scant knowledge in the topics they cover (Cline 1981, Massing 1989).

"Caught Up in a Total Whirlwind"

Katherine derides her readers for making unrealistic demands upon news institutions:

> People who read newspapers have to be less gullible. They have to realize that a newspaper is nothing more than an honest attempt…. The idea of the free press is not only that you have a press trying to be objective and fair, but that you have a readership that is capable of intelligent reading.

However, critical readings are discouraged by press institutions themselves. Media conglomerates facilitate the production of an acritical readership by continuing to promote themselves as objective and independent. They claim to provide "All You Need To Know" (KNX Los Angeles) and "All The News That's Fit to Print" (the *New York Times*), a far cry from "nothing more than an honest attempt." The objective claims of the industry put great pressure on journalists, as they are asked to achieve unobtainable standards and meet illusory goals.

Jerry detailed the unrealistic expectations and "enormous limitations" reporters face every day:

> You write this stuff knowing about all of your own inadequacies, and about the problems that you are under, the pressures of time and what have you, knowing that people are going to be lying to you all the time while you are searching desperately to find the truth amongst all of that. There are enormous limitations to what you have written. And, having to write on deadline, and then you get back home and people say, "Oh yeah, I read that," and of course when you have read a newspaper you expect it to be right. They expect that when you wrote that article you were perfectly clear

about everything…. You are writing in an extremely simplified way and cutting out all of the extraneous detail, which has a much greater effect on the story itself, really. And they miss that. When you get back people assume that you are this sort of clear thinking, all-seeing individual who has been to some understandable part of the world and written a story that makes sense. Of course, none of that could be further from the truth. Of course, that is essentially what you try to do, but they miss the fact that you are caught up in a total whirlwind.

The "whirlwind" Jerry describes leaves little time for reflection. "While the conflict still rages," explained Juaquin, "it is important just to document everything. We will stop to think once the war is over." Few journalists, however, can afford to "stop to think" for long. Steeped in deadlines and editors' demands, the exigencies of journalism demand complete and continuous attention to detail.

As Terilyn noted, "Journalists are supposed to create an aura of objectivity." The standard news narrative and concomitant practices allow journalists to create that "aura" without excess energy devoted to heuristic considerations. Terylin explained how she was learning to write objectively:

Jerry is helpful. He says that, "if you are going to write this, you need to talk to a person in the government" [for balance]. He doesn't need to point it out anymore.

The narrative form of objective journalism has become synonymous with its philosophical goal. Once internalized, balance, fairness, and the other narrative conventions are no longer conceived of as methodological tools for creating objective texts, but are instead considered objective forms in and of themselves. The interpretive interventions of reporters, sources, and editors are made to seem quite minimal when news is written according to the accepted conventions. Conformity feels like freedom. Like culture itself, the fairly rigid symbolic structures of objective journalism are most effective in their patterning silence, unnoticed and unchallenged until seriously violated, deconstructed, or compared with hitherto unimagined alternatives. For the time being, positivism persists.

PEACE COMES TO TELEVISION

The parachute pack returned to El Salvador for a brief but intense spate of coverage in January and February of 1992. Three events were highlighted: completion of the peace negotiations on New Years Day, 1992, official signing ceremony in Chapultapec Park, Mexico City, on January 16, and final cease-fire on February 1. The following is an examination of CBS' New Years Day broadcast. The complete text is as follows:

EL SALVADOR PEACE AGREEMENT

Visual 1: Connie Chung and graphic of Salvadoran flag. (ten seconds)

Chung: "In El Salvador, both sides in a long civil war have accepted a U.N.-sponsored peace plan aimed at ending a struggle that has taken 75,000 lives. Doug Tunnell has the story."

Visual 2: Government/military and FMLN negotiators rise from table and shake hands. (sixteen seconds)

Tunnell: "Government officials and rebel leaders from El Salvador shook hands and wished each other a happy New Year in a ceremony marking the first diplomatic landmark of 1992, an agreement both sides say will mark the end of the civil war in El Salvador."

Visual 3: Bernard Aronson (eight seconds)

Tunnell: "Assistant Secretary of State Bernard Aronson helped broker the agreement."

Aronson: "For the Salvadoran People it's the best New Years Day present they could have."

Visual 4: Salvadorans setting off fireworks (three seconds)

Tunnell: "Some Salvadorans celebrated the agreement with fireworks and flags early today...."

Visual 5: Another shot of Salvadorans setting off fireworks (two seconds)

Visual 6: Salvadorans waving flags and banners (six seconds)

Tunnell: ...even though many technical details of the agreement have yet to be worked out."

Visual 7: Soldier shooting from foxhole (two seconds)

Tunnell: "After twelve years of combat there is to be a cease fire...."

Visual 8: Soldiers running across street (five seconds)

Tunnell: ...beginning in February and lasting for a minimum of nine months...."

Visual 9: Another shot of soldiers running across street (five seconds)

Tunnell: ...while the government and the rebels work out the details and implement them."

Visual 10: Wounded and bloody Salvadoran man, wearing jeans and a t-shirt, laying on the ground (three seconds)

Tunnell: "But after so many years and so many victims...."

Visual 11: Salvadoran woman crying (four seconds)

Tunnell: ...analysts warn keeping the promise of peace will not be easy."

Visual 12: Mark Rosenberg, Florida International University (nine seconds)

Rosenberg: "There is a lot of animosity after ten ah, twelve, thirteen years of people killing each other that isn't going to end overnight with the signing of a single document."

Visual 13: bloody corpse (three seconds)

Tunnell: "Clandestine death squads...."

Visual 14: UCA Jesuit priests and cook—murdered in November, 1989—laid out on lawn (seven seconds)

Tunnell: ...like the one that murdered six Jesuit priests in 1989 remain active and largely beyond the reach of El Salvador's government."

Visual 15: Burning four wheel drive vehicle (four seconds)

Tunnell: "Some of them may have already registered unhappiness with the new peace agreement."

Visual 16: Salvadoran men trying to douse flames of burning vehicle (three seconds)

Tunnell: "In downtown San Salvador today a bomb marked the beginning of the New Year."

Visual 17: Long shot of burning vehicle (five seconds)

Tunnell: "A car owned by a foreign news agency correspondent was set ablaze."

Visual 18: Another shot of Salvadoran men trying to douse flames of burning vehicle (five seconds)

Tunnell: "Doug Tunnell, CBS news, Miami."

Visual 19: Chung.

Chung: (segue to story about Perez de Cuellar): The Salvador peace agreement was a crowning achievement for U.N. Secretary General Javier Perez de Cuellar, who says he left office feeling light as a feather....

The CBS report involved two sources: U.S. Assistant Secretary of State, Bernard Aronson, and Mark Rosenberg of Florida International University. Aronson is introduced as someone who "helped broker the agreement" even though the Bush Administration had obstructed the negotiation process throughout. Just months before, the U.S. accused U.N. mediator Alvaro de Soto of favoring the FMLN (*New York Times*, February 1, 1991:A3). The U.S. government also withheld evidence in the UCA massacre investigation and provided billions of dollars, planning, and other support to the Salvadoran government. Nevertheless, they are portrayed as a neutral party in the CBS report, a peace "broker." Via the voice of Bernard Aronson, the U.S. government is given free channel to speak, but is never spoken about.

As for the other source in the CBS report, the views of an accomplished scholar are edited down to an obvious, banal sound bite that required neither authority nor knowledge (Rosenberg and Shepard 1983). The voice and reason of the report are entirely North American. Aronson and Rosenberg provide comment from New York and Miami, respectively. Meanwhile, Tunnell reported the story from Miami, a site with no direct relevance to the subject matter of the report.[1]

Whereas, the North American sources give voice and frame to the CBS report, the Salvadoran people are fashioned as mute and bloody subjects—victims without voice. The population is constructed as a passive, neutral, and homogeneous mass caught in the middle of ideological cross fire (an NBC report aired the next day explicitly referred to them as "pawns").

The bloody images—battle scenes, wounded civilians, a crying woman—flash by at blinding speed, filmed in "a jerky 'documentary' camera style" (Anderson 1988b:254). The average time allotted to each shot is 5.1 seconds, 4.3 without the "talking head" segments. The eye has little time to focus on each bloody image in television's "now...this" (Postman 1985:99–113) discourse. We are invited to peek into terror, but never allowed sustained and intimate examination of its larger context and meaning.

Calixto, a SPECA international, complained that U.S. television news turns violence into a "show":

> U.S. television journalism, from what I have seen, is terrible. They have millions of dollars, yet their coverage is still really bad. It is bad because there is a lot of pressure to make the news into a show.

In the TV news "show," verbal text is little more than filler; a useful way to link together action sequences. Like Hollywood adventure films, the television news spectacle exhibits blood and death in quick, disjointed, and aesthetically acceptable arrangements. Safely situated behind gun and camera, the viewer occupies the position of killer and voyeur, properly distanced from the subject-victims' pain. By reducing the world to spectacle, the visual media that once promised to "bring us closer to the world," have instead removed us further from it (Anderson 1988:251–52, Brentlinger 1990:4–5, Jones 1981).

Riding atop the disturbingly seductive blood sport of the CBS report is a verbal text riddled with errors. For example, "clandestine death squads" did not kill the Jesuits. The Jesuits' killers were the soldiers put on trial and convicted in September of 1991, and the military high command who issued the order, as cited by the U.N. Truth Commission. CBS should have known better, having presented reports of the trial just three months earlier (CBS Evening News September 26 and 29, 1991). As was true of the New Years Day broadcast, however, no correspondents or producers were directly involved in CBS UCA trial coverage. The first day of that trial, I was approached by the CBS office manager. The young Salvadoran needed help in preparing questions for post-trial interviews. She was frantic. As an office manager, she had never been called upon to conduct interviews before and, to make matters worse, was not completely fluent in English.

To calm her down, I borrowed Shawn's words. "Don't worry, a monkey could do it," I told her. She gave me a quizzical glance and replied: "That's what they said." According to the young woman, the CBS foreign desk manager in New York had used the same phrase when issuing the order for the young Salvadoran to cover the trial. The office manager was amazed that all these gringos, including her CBS superiors, did not take television news more seriously. Together we prepared several basic questions. She did the interviews, and the report went on the air (she did a fine job). Unfortunately, Tunnell apparently forgot to watch it. Instead, he placed the Jesuit killers "beyond the reach of El Salvador's government," when in fact they were an integral part of the Salvadoran government.

Remaining consistent with the dominant frame, but once again deviating from the truth, Tunnell suggests that, "Some of them [clandestine death squads] may have" bombed a foreign journalist's car, an act which, according to Tunnell, may have represented "unhappiness with the new peace agreement." The members of SPECA knew better, however. They understood that the bombing was probably committed by the head of the Salvadoran National Police, whose girlfriend had been having an affair with the foreign journalist. Therefore, it was not a death squad "largely beyond the reach of El Salvador's government," and it probably had little or nothing to do with the peace accords. SPECA knew better. The remote control parachuter (Tunnell) did not.

For Tunnell and his viewers, a new story was created—a new reality manufactured with bits and pieces and images of both truth and fiction. The burning car provided violent and dramatic evidence for the CBS news frame and supplied the sort of cautionary climax war correspondents prefer (note the similarities to the conclusion of the AP report in chapter 10) (Anderson 1988b:245).

The logistical complexity of reporting for television, along with the networks' extreme emphasis on production values, force television journalists to package their stories in simplified and predetermined frames that often have little to do with actual events. Clarice, a television correspondent, explains:

> Sometimes I have to do the stand-up out in the field before even starting the story. Before I did TV I thought that was crazy, making the conclusions before talking to anyone. But, that is the nature of TV.

Therefore, TV journalism is not really "reporting" in the conventional sense of the term. Television correspondents rarely have the luxury of conducting investigations or reaching conclusions based on acquired evidence. They often know what they will say before the plane even sets down, or in the case of CBS' New Years day report, before the correspondent arrives at his Miami studio.

U.S. news magazines and, to a lesser extent, newspapers framed the Salvadoran cease-fire in much the same manner as the television networks. The U.S. government was presented as a force for peace and democracy, Salvadoran citizens were mostly reduced to mute and neutral victims, while the Salvadoran government was posited as a moderate buffer between violent extremes of left and right.[2] These stories provided a fitting narrative wrap to the war. Peace was made to vindicate U.S. diplomacy while the depth, intensity, and complexity of the U.S.' low intensity war strategy continued to be ignored. As throughout the war, U.S. authorities were allowed to project their fears and rationalizations onto the screen, calling them Salvador (Vietnam, Panama, Iraq...). While television news claims to present a "mirror on the world," it is more often a mirror of power—reflecting its savagery in the brutalized subject.

Difference

and

Domination

ALONZO'S DREAM

"We only become what we are by the radical and deep-seated refusal of that which others have made of us."

—Sartre, in Frantz Fanon's *The Wretched of the Earth*

"I am afraid of what we are becoming."

—Alonzo

Alonzo was one of thirty-four Salvadoran journalists in SPECA. He and his compatriots comprised about 42% of the international press corps during the latter part of the war. During our first interview in June, 1990, Alonzo expressed concern for his sanity and his moral consciousness. "The normal ways of journalists are not normal," said Alonzo, "You have to accept any kind of thinking—leftists, rightists, whatever. It is hard to maintain good morals. Eventually, you become neurotic." Alonzo discussed the corps' behavior, how they stand around at assassination sites with corpses lying bloody at their feet, talking about a party the night before or even "making jokes." For Alonzo, this seemingly callous behavior is a way to cope with the violence:

This is a way to survive. You have been here since you were born and you have been working here for five years. If in all this time you were crying all the time, you would be dead already. You would die. This way of acting is a way to fight that. It is a way to escape.

Alonzo's escape attempt has been unsuccessful. "It has killed me, something in my mind," explained Alonzo, "I can't sleep. I can't talk with people that don't think like me." Alonzo has partially cut himself off from Salvadoran society. His identity and practice are as much "international journalist" as they are Salvadoran. SPECA is his community and his primary source of identity. It is what Alonzo is "becoming," and what he is afraid of. The following is one of Alonzo's dreams.

"I am Afraid of What We Are Becoming"

A wave of police sirens pierces through the chilled night rain as steam rises from warm pavement around Alonzo's feet, a perfectly apocalyptic scene. The earnest young reporter is intent upon exposing the Salvadoran military's participation in the illegal, yet widespread, prostitution trade. Salvadorans and journalists alike believe that many of the most popular brothels are owned by high ranking military officials. They are means of intelligence gathering, profit taking, and of course, control. Tonight, however, Alonzo is not covering the high-rent district frequented by the officers, but is instead entering one of the crowded, noisy, and dirty barrios where grunts visit cheap prostitutes, the ones who work for just enough to eat, drink, and kill the pain.

The neophyte correspondent walks down one of the most dangerous streets of San Salvador, excited, afraid, and slightly disoriented. The scene is both culturally and geographically distant from the comfortable and well-protected neighborhood where Alonzo was raised. In places like this—much of El Salvador—the lies, contradictions, and brutal truths of the military state lie at the surface. The worn excuses of counter-insurgency and *patria* (fatherland) melt away as the soldiers do their best to make enemies of their own people. Terror is a daily discipline.

An orphaned child approaches Alonzo, decorated in clown-face after a day spent directing traffic and amusing drivers for spare change. The boy's make-up runs in the rain, giving him the face of an old man.

As a professional journalist, Alonzo wants to expose these truths to the North American reader. As a Salvadoran, he would like to shove their face in it. He hopes his employer, a prestigious U.S. newspaper, will accept his article for publication, but knows there is little chance of that happening. Alonzo and his Salvadoran colleagues, some of the most highly trained journalists in Central America, rarely get to do more than grunt-work for their U.S. correspondent patrons.

Alonzo's thoughts jerk back to the moment as a column of troops advances toward him. He freezes with fear as they pass, trying not to stare at their expressionless faces hidden behind an oily mix of green and black face paint. Their plastic rain ponchos glow with a satin sheen, reflecting the feeble yellow lights hanging in the windows of the wood and tin shacks lining the street. To complete the absurd pageant, each soldier is wearing an umbrella-hat, a clownish, unmilitary, and feminine complement to the otherwise martial ensemble. The moment is surreal, terrifying, and oddly beautiful.

Drawing in a calming breath of relief, Alonzo watches the line of troops begin to pass him by. He looks across the moving column and sees an attractive woman standing just out of reach in an implausibly clean white dress. She stares back. The strobe effect of the passing combatants makes her seem more of a ghost, or fantasy, than flesh. Yet, she is more familiar than the faceless warriors separating them.

Instantly moved from fascination to fear, Alonzo witnesses the sort of horror he had come here to report. The woman's purse snags on a soldier's gun as the entire contingent turns and fires upon her, an automatic and collective response. Their commanding officer stands over her bleeding torso with a video camera in one hand, a machine gun in the other. The soldiers shoot the young woman in the abdomen. She falls to her knees, looking across to Alonzo with a hurt, wounded expression as the next set of shots blow through her skull. Alonzo turns to run as the soldiers realign and march off into the darkness. He falls to the pavement, crying, helpless.

Next, Alonzo awakens in his warm and "safe" bed, dying of thirst. Alonzo is left with a lingering sense of terror, relief, guilt, confusion, sadness, anger, impotence—a nearly endless set of competing and contradictory emotions. Alonzo, a liminal initiate into the world of foreign press, worries about the long term effects of sublimating those emotions. He describes this "way of thinking":

> We go with the view of the working press, not the view of a man with feelings. There are people with their families and relatives and all that there, and feelings, strong feelings. But, we go and look at the body, to look at it from different angles, and we ask the people, 'How did this happen? Who was the killer? What do you think about this?.... We don't have any more feelings.

Alonzo repeats the final sentence: "We don't have any more feelings."

Yet, as he made clear in telling me his dream, Alonzo's feelings are still there; they are just not allowed to penetrate the practice. Alonzo's dream, therefore, is everything the news is not. It is a forbidden text, one with felt emotion and a sense of truth, not just facts and quotes. Alonzo's dream, as with the other expressions of hope and fear I encountered in the corps, represents the stored-up frustration of a journalist whose ideas and experiences are not, and cannot be, represented in the news texts he creates (or is kept from creating). As collections of experience, the journalists' dreams embody levels of authenticity and truth rarely found in the news itself. Emotion, if not humanity itself, is the first element to be filtered out in the disciplinary process.

Alonzo, who no longer finds comfort in the collective lie, says aloud what most other SPECA journalists will not: "I am afraid of what we are becoming." While that statement holds multiple meanings, the most honest, universal, and important message is contained in the first three words: "I am afraid…"

THE SALVADORANS
OF SPECA

salvadorans of speca the salvadorans salvadorans of speca the salvadorans

"Really, we are asking journalists to perform a task which is almost impossible, and almost heroic. Unfortunately, intellectual labor does not pay.... This is the sad story of the consuming mercantilism of our society; talent, dedication, and public service are politically, socially, and economically devalued and defenseless."

—Ignacio Ellacuria, in *El Periodismo en una Sociedad en Crisis*

Upon entering the second floor of the Camino, I was almost always immediately drawn into a joking exchange with the Salvadoran television crews as they gambled and/or chatted in the narrow hallway. Among them I had garnered several nicknames, including "Professor" and "*El Dueno de Coco*" (master of the coconut). A man I called "Mayor" would stroke his head upon my arrival, a joking reference to my baldness. Many of the locals' jokes were aimed at their foreign colleagues, whom they would play as somewhat stiff, yet foolish characters (the same way they characterized me).

Public officials were also lampooned by SPECA Salvadorans. One afternoon a group of local reporters gathered in the Reuters office to heckle President Christiani's televised address to the United Nations. As the president concluded his speech, a reporter walked up to the screen and declared the talk *puro paja* (rubbish), as if speaking directly to Christiani. Another mimed the act of masturbation. The president never had a tougher audience.

This was a highly entertaining, yet perplexing piece of political theater. Somehow I had to square the dissent I was observing in these group sessions (and had heard in solo interviews), with the Salvadorans' seemingly "conservative" voting record in SPECA meetings. An examination of the local journalists' life histories, motivations, and working contexts resolved this paradox.

"Involved and in the Middle"

As explained in chapter 2, Salvadoran reporters often cast the deciding votes in SPECA meetings. Most supported the cautious positions of their *A Team* employers, which greatly angered the stringers, some of whom branded their Salvadoran colleagues as "conservatives." A few stringers even claimed that these "conservative" Salvadorans secretly sided with the military. The statements of a few Salvadorans would seem to support those charges. "Every army has some form of press control," said one. "They are in the middle of a war. They have every right." That sentiment was rarely articulated so explicitly, however. While most of the Salvadoran journalists were resigned to military control, very few actually supported it.

Several stringers claimed that the locals' SPECA voting record was symbolic of their upper class backgrounds and affiliations. This claim is also misleading. It is true that most Salvadorans in SPECA have been raised in relatively privileged, upper class families. That is, privileged by Salvadoran standards. Most come from El Salvador's "rickety middle class" (Alegria 1986:28), an underpopulated sector comprised of Salvadoran professionals and small business owners, most of whom are college educated. Many of the Salvadorans who occupy this precarious position live in material conditions that would be considered working class, at best, in the U.S. They are sandwiched between the powerful rich and the impoverished majority. Therefore, although they belong to an upper class cohort, most SPECA Salvadorans are not from what is commonly referred to as the "oligarchy."

The stringers' assertion of conservatism, however, is completely unfounded. An examination of the Salvadoran journalists' life histories makes this evident. Several SPECA reporters filled positions in the Salvadoran government during failed reform attempts in the early 1980s. Each of these resigned or was fired when the reforms were defeated. Several worked in the local alternative press, including Catholic church radio and other media institutions closed down near the start of the war. Others worked in the mainstream media, but were forced out or resigned due to political differences with their right wing employers.

Several SPECA Salvadorans have even been forced into exile during various periods of the war. Most had experienced some form of intimidation from the death squads, military, and/or government. To argue that these people are in collusion with the military, government and/or oligarchy is patently absurd. As is true for the corps as a whole, there are few true conservatives among the SPECA Salvadorans. Conversely, there are many self-defined leftists.

If anything, what the Salvadoran journalists had learned from over a decade of war was the futility of resisting the military. They found the stringers' aggressive attitude toward the salvoconducto system understandable, yet naive, and from their vulnerable position, potentially dangerous. When a Salvadoran reporter stood up at a SPECA meeting and yelled: "The armed forces is king here. We have to live with that!" he was not voicing support for the military, as the stringers' believed, but simply acting out the Salvadorans' well founded fear of army retribution. The Salvadorans of SPECA knew they would be left behind after the foreigners completed their relatively short stints in El Salvador, paying the price for the association's defiance. "The military has greater respect for the foreigners," explained Alonzo, "They have less respect for the Salvadoran journalists. Before killing a gringo, they think 100 times. Before killing a Salvadoran, they think twice or not at all." As in the famous case of press aid Dith Pran, dramatized in "The Killing Fields," locals often pay the highest price for international press freedom.

Louisa, who has worked in the press for well over a decade, describes her past experiences:

> Back in the early 80s, I had trouble with both the Death Squads and the National Guard; first with the National Guard. The problem is that they read my work and announced that I was a guerrilla. They took me in to the National Guard headquarters and interrogated me at Section 2, the section for intelligence gathering.

Subsequently, Louisa received death threats, but nevertheless refused to leave the country.

Many of the threats have been matched by action. Over half of the journalists killed in the last fifteen years were Salvadoran. In one incident, two Salvadoran journalists were ambushed after arguing with a couple of soldiers over access to a conflicted zone. Thinking that they had won the argument, they were sent on ahead and shot. One died, the other was badly wounded. He lost the use of his hand. For a photographer, this is doubly tragic. An artist as well, he had to learn how to work with one hand. For the rest of SPECA, this one-handed photographer is a constant reminder of the military's antipathy for their work. Having recovered, returned, and retrained, he is a constant inspiration for them as well.

The Salvadorans' sense of insecurity is compounded by their tenuous relationship with employers. This was another reason they voted with the *A Team*. It would have been professional suicide to contradict their bosses in the politically charged SPECA meetings. There is no safety net for the Salvadorans should they loose their jobs. For them, press work in El Salvador is not merely one episode in a career, it *is* their career, their life.

The difference between the foreign journalists' experience and that of their Salvadoran colleagues was made clear one day as I was interviewing Mateo, a young man working for an international wire agency. At first, I was a bit put off by Mateo. I had just interviewed his boss, a very kind and giving informant. Mateo was not so forthright. He seemed to be a bit defensive, no matter what the topic. Fortunately, he eventually loosened up, perhaps sensing that I was becoming disinterested in what little he initially had to say. Just as Mateo was beginning to open up, an earthquake hit. It lasted for at least fifteen seconds and had us all a little worried and shaken. The tremblor shook loose many of Mateo's remaining inhibitions as well. Immediately after we sat back down to conclude the interview, he told me about his brother's death:

> If someone important is killed, someone they care about in the United States, it gets reported *afuera* [literally "outside"; in the international press]. If a simple person dies, no one cares. Take my brother, who was in the army. He died in combat, Sunday of last week.

Mateo discussed the meaning of his brother's death, explicitly comparing his feelings with the "cold" statistical descriptions found in international news. "I do not blame the guerrillas for killing him," he finished, "It is a war." For Mateo, the war was much more than an object of study, a job, or "fun."

Many Salvadorans see their foreign colleagues as lacking understanding and sensitivity. "Perhaps because we have lived through ten years of war," explains Pedro, a Salvadoran photographer, "we tend to see it in a much more profound way.... Some reporters do not understand it very well, because they are foreigners, because they are a little insensitive." Pedro added, "El Salvador is an experience for them, not a place in which they have invested their more profound feelings."

Whereas, foreign work is often a *Means of Escape* (Caputo 1991) for First World reporters, it is a means of involvement for local journalists. Ricki explains:

> It is here that we were born. It is here that we were raised, and it will be here that we die.... Many foreigners think that they know more than us about the war, but it is a form of knowledge based on theory. It is not the same as having lived it. There are moments that we arrive to a place, and we realize that the people lying there dead are a part of us. The difference is significant.

Pedro's assessment was similar:

> We have much greater fear because we have families here. I have children. I have a spouse. This is also a difference between us and the foreign reporters, who have fewer compromises.

The SPECA Salvadorans are, in Henri's words, "the most effected, the most involved and in the middle of all this."

Although Salvadoran journalists see news events and issues from

Salvadoran perspectives, news work is still an act of discovery for them. Basha told of her first extended visit to a rural area of San Salvador. She had not ventured into the more remote regions of the country until she began working with the corps during the final few years of the war. After arriving in a small village in the conflicted zones, she offered a child a Pepsi. He reached out to take it from Basha, then quickly withdrew his hand, shocked by the icy sensation of the cold bottle. The child had never experienced refrigerated food. Basha "had no idea" that people lived like that in her country.

As Basha's story indicates, it is facile to claim Salvadoran journalists are, by virtue of their national and ethnic origin, intimately tuned to the interests of the Salvadoran majority. Culture is made up of more than phenomenological experience, however. Culture is a shared stock of symbols, a means of communication, and a fundamental source of identification. People may interpret reality in different, even contradictory ways, and they may have had greatly different life experiences, but if they draw upon a shared set of symbolic references, it can be said that at some level they share a common culture. This is the level at which the Salvadoran journalists relate to their compatriots. They have a shared language, history, destiny, and geographic territory. "A great deal of what is in my head," explained Emilio, "is in the minds of other Salvadorans."

Elicia feels the difference between national and foreign reporters is not just one of perspective, but also a matter "passion:"

> There are differences in terms of optics—that is to say, the means by which they see the problem…the foreign journalists, particularly the gringos, make decisions according to the liberal school of U.S. journalism. They have a manner which is calmer. They work with much less passion.

Elicia's view is shared by many Salvadorans, both within and outside the corps. Salvadorans often use *frio* (cold) to describe gringos. Similarly, the SPECA Salvadorans tend to see North American journalism as frio. Several argued journalism should be more profound, analytical, and at the same time "*mas humano*" (more human or "humane"). Their primary goal, according to Pedro, is "to put a sense of humanity into the technique and to examine reality in a more profound manner." While the U.S. journalists argue for professional, balanced, and fair journalism, terms lacking the emotive dimension (frio, if you will), the Salvadorans see no reason to excise passion from their search for truth.

Journalism in El Salvador

I asked Emilio what readers should know in order to better understand the news coverage of El Salvador. Without hesitation he responded, "You first have to teach people how to read." The issue of literacy dominated the Salvadoran responses, yet was not once mentioned by the foreign members of SPECA. This is just one of many indicators that Salvadoran and foreign journalists work within very different social and psychological contexts. Foreign correspondents have First World audiences in mind as they write. Conversely, Salvadoran reporters imagine their audience as Third World, or more specifically, Salvadoran, the only audience they really know.

The working consciousness of the Salvadorans was largely formed within the structures of the local press. Radio has had the strongest influence. In a country with a high level of illiteracy, little disposable income, and relatively poor transportation, radio has continued to be the dominant means of mass communication. Many SPECA Salvadorans spoke of listening to the radio as children, fascinated by the news and news people. "From the time I was a little child I was interested in the news," Rogelio remarked, "My mother talks about how I would listen to the radio late into the night."

Although weaned on local media, SPECA Salvadorans despise the press system that dominates their country. A combination of ownership by the oligarchy, low salaries, coercion, and bribe-taking has led to a national press that is "servile to the interests of money," to quote a Salvadoran scholar. In El Salvador, they call news bribes *menta* (mint), because they "sweeten" the work of the reporter.[1] "Most journalists in the local press are like prostitutes," explained Ernesto, a SPECA Salvadoran.

The oligarchy and associated interests have nearly complete power to determine the shape of local news coverage. Just as the system of power and governance in El Salvador is more direct, brutal, and perhaps, honest than those of First World democracies, the Salvadoran system of communication is also more simple, direct, and openly fraudulent. Whereas, working in the U.S. press involves subtle gradations of discipline—a system of corrections, censures and rewards—the local Salvadoran journalist is faced with overpowering repression, a system that demands complete obedience.

One day I interviewed a very courageous young reporter in a back room of a local press office. He described his publisher's draconian tactics, how an editor had recently fired a friend for writing about a police attack upon himself. The fired friend fled the country and applied for asylum in the United States. His plea was not granted. Fortunately, as the presence of the SPECA Salvadorans demonstrates, not all dissenting local journalists have fared as poorly. Many have found work in the foreign press. Alternative media institutions have hired others.

The Salvadorans working in the international press continue to maintain contact with journalists working in local, mainly alternative, media institutions. Journalists from *Diario Latino* and alternative radio stations spent a great deal of time with their compatriots on the second floor. The foreign press Salvadorans and their local counterparts form a network of mutual aid and information. Some of the Salvadorans even work double duty, reporting for both local alternative and international press. While this is extremely taxing, there are certain rewards. "There is not much satisfaction working only for foreign audiences," explained Rogelio.

The local university journalism programs have had a large effect on the work of the Salvadorans of SPECA. Most of them have completed advanced degrees or are currently working on their theses. The majority of the SPECA Salvadorans' theses involve critical condemnations of local media coverage, including analyses of corruption, propagandistic use of photographs, and social responsibility. Rather than preparing their students to accept menta and censorship, the two largest programs (the National University and the UCA) emphasize ethical principles, research methodology, and theory. They form a countervailing force against the corruption of local publishers and press institutions.

The Salvadoran journalism instructors I interviewed also tend to be highly critical of the U.S. press, and objective journalism in particular. Despite years of work for U.S. employers, their ex-students in SPECA remain equally disenchanted with the North Americans' positivistic principles.

Objectivity is for *Gringos*

The Salvadorans are not strong believers in objective journalism. When queried on the issue, several responded with the joke, "Objectivity is relative." Louisa's view was typical:

> I do not believe in journalistic objectivity. For me, objectivity cannot exist, because we are human beings, with feelings, thoughts, and the capacity to analyze. We are not simply transcribers of what one or the other says. We have a right and duty to analyze what is said.... Once you make a selection of any sort, it is not objective. The only people for whom objectivity is important are the gringos.

The Salvadorans found the objective pretenses of their North American colleagues to be, at best, a naive and alien affectation. When I asked Victor about objectivity, he simply replied, "All of that is a myth."

"What is most important," argued Norma, "is that we remain truthful." For Norma, the primary goal of journalism is to present an honest and truthful interpretation of the world. "But," she added, "even this depends upon the company one works for. There is a lot of propaganda out there, so it is always difficult." Therefore, although the Salvadorans argue for committed and honest journalism, they find it difficult to "remain truthful" in the bureaucratic milieu within which they work. Pedro lamented:

> With the politics of work, there is always a *patron* (sponsor/boss).... They do

not encourage it, but we look for other aspects of El Salvador which are important parts of the culture.

Salvadorans were under great pressure to adopt the concepts and codes of objective journalism. "My job," argued one, "is to report the news as objectively as possible." Then, he shut off the tape recorder, leaned forward, and gave a passionate speech concerning the need for committed and honest journalism, along with a scathing critique of objective journalism. The censored Salvadoran knew he was supposed to be an objective journalist, but remained fundamentally opposed to the foreign concept.

Much of the pressure comes from U.S. journalists who want to "professionalize" the locals. Two U.S. journalists who work with Alonzo were trying to "professionalize" him in this way. They wanted him to attend journalism school in the United States, so that he might learn in a more "professional atmosphere." This was a great insult to Alonzo, who was just finishing an advanced degree program at a Salvadoran university. He had received several more years of formal education than one of the North Americans arguing the point, and just as much as the other. Conversely, Janice—who was highly critical of U.S. journalism and journalists—argued that Alonzo's enrollment in a North American journalism program would be "a bad idea." She felt the Americans were being elitist and patronistic towards Alonzo.

Many Salvadorans find it difficult to adopt, or at least mimic, the objective narrative. Louisa often has "a problem with the editors. They say, 'You are too subjective, make it more objective.'" As an outsider, Louisa recognizes her editors' objectivity for what it is: a subjective, alien, and arrogant perspective staking an exclusive claim to truth. Louisa and her compatriots would prefer to work differently, to be more analytical and passionate in their reporting.

Identity and Contradiction

Despite their philosophical and political disagreements with the North Americans, SPECA Salvadorans felt they had learned much from them. They were particularly impressed with their international colleagues' technological resources, technical abilities, and organizational skills. Louisa, who was extremely critical of the "gringo mentality," nevertheless admitted:

> The North Americans have an impressive technique, apart from their mentality.... They never stop being gringos, but they have helped Salvadoran journalism to develop.

Louisa offered the example of U.S. video technique and technology. Victor, a Salvadoran journalist whose views differ greatly from those of his U.S. colleagues, nevertheless praised SPECA as "a journalism school for local journalists."

Although thankful for the international press' technical training and resources, many Salvadorans feel their talents were, and continue to be, misapplied. They feel underutilized and poorly rewarded. The tasks assigned to most SPECA Salvadorans include: support work, scheduling, file-keeping, arranging source contacts, office management, photography, and/or video work. Only a third of the local corps write news stories on a consistent basis. While alternative wire agencies and/or Latin American media often employ Salvadoran journalists as news authors, most major international institutions place them in secondary roles, as aids or temporary replacements for foreign journalists. The locals are expected to produce news material and facilitate the reporting of foreign correspondents, but are rarely taken seriously in terms of creative input. Although the Salvadoran journalists (and drivers and secretaries) had been in El Salvador their entire lives, the foreign journalists tended to discount their points of view.

Elicia described herself as "the eyes and feelings" of her foreign correspondent-employer. She keeps a news archive, runs the office, attends news events, and maintains contacts with primary sources "both left, right, and of course, in the center." About the only thing Elicia is not responsible for is "going to the battlefield." Elicia complained:

> In some cases, the U.S. press doesn't value the work of the locals. I don't like the fact that many photographers and camera people don't have any security. They have worked for them through the entire war, yet have absolutely no security.... They have a lack of respect for the locals, for their rights and dignity.

In bitter resignation to his station, Pedro likewise lamented, "Security is for foreigners."

It should also be noted, however, that few Salvadoran journalists are bilingual. This also limits their chances for advancement in the international press. However, even the few bilingual Salvadoran reporters generally found themselves without adequate compensation or job security. Indeed, most SPECA Salvadorans are rather poorly paid. "You cannot make much money working for the foreign press," complained a veteran Salvadoran photographer. He made less than half the salary of his young and inexperienced U.S. coworker. "The locals are exploited," agreed Warren, "Henri is treated very poorly by [the agency].... I would not work here for $800 a month. Well, at least I would like them to think that I wouldn't." Yet, even $800 per month is higher salary than most SPECA Salvadorans earn.

As a result of their position in the SPECA hierarchy, Salvadorans look at the entire foreign press—particularly the dominant U.S. contingent—

in much the same way stringers view staffers. Francisco's description of U.S. journalists illustrates:

> The relation they have established with us is a little bit like that of the bigger brother or, that is, the richer brother.... A North American journalist who comes to El Salvador has a big salary, great working conditions. In a situation involving conflict, they will be helped by The Embassy. There have been moments when foreign journalists receive privileges in press conferences and reports locals do not.

The Salvadorans' resentment formed an underlying theme of several SPECA meetings. At one meeting a U.S. journalist proposed that SPECA commission a plaque to commemorate journalists killed during the war.[2] The proposal read "Salvadoran *Foreign* Press Corps Association" rather than "Salvadoran Press Corps Association (SPECA)," the correct name of the organization. The proposed wording implied that all members of SPECA were foreigners, whereas the correct title acknowledges the presence of Salvadorans in the international corps. Naturally, this mistake angered the locals, who saw it as a symbol of their colleagues' depreciative attitude towards them. "They are going to be putting this thing into stone," Alonzo complained, "It should show that Salvadorans have worked in SPECA as well." The mistake was not intentional and the wording was corrected immediately, but not before the Salvadorans felt that yet once again their work had gone unnoticed.

The confusion concerning the plaque inscription represented another tension as well, the SPECA Salvadorans' dual identities. As Alonzo's dream makes clear, the Salvadoran journalist is a bit of both, *Salvadoran* and *journalist*. The dream also illustrates the inevitable contradictions between those two halves of the Salvadoran journalist's persona. At the very moment he is to uncover the dark truths of oppression, Alonzo finds himself paralyzed, unable to help his compatriot-victim. She is in arm's reach, but separated by a gulf of fear and discipline.

Like Alonzo, many Salvadorans are afraid and uncertain of what they are "becoming." The Salvadorans feel confusion and fear, anxieties produced in the tension between their obligations as Salvadorans and limitations as journalists. After we returned from witnessing a corpse, I asked Sergio to describe his thoughts and feelings about what we had just observed:

> One corpse is not going to change the war. One looks at it in a rather cold way, in an intellectual manner. As opposed to the rest of the population, you have seen every one of the corpses, a great quantity of corpses. After a while, it becomes just one more. Nevertheless, it hurts you as a Salvadoran because the dead person is your compatriot.

The journalists have gained intimate contact with some of the worst effects of war, and at the same time, a sense of anesthetized distance, having experienced the same scenes too often. The professional routines and practices of journalism differentiate the SPECA Salvadorans from "the rest of the population." Meanwhile, practice and proximity link them with "other" foreign journalists. In other words, the Salvadoran journalists are neither completely Salvadoran nor, by the foreigners' standards, professional journalists. This leads to confusion, anger, fear, and above all, anxiety. Speaking of a Salvadoran journalist and friend, Paul stated: "She does not know if she is a Salvadoran, a journalist, or what." The Salvadorans spend much of their time in that liminal space, the boundary region of "or what." It is not a pleasant place.

The Colima Bridge Incident

These contradictions between the SPECA Salvadorans dual identities and practices were manifested in a number of ways. The clearest example during the period of my research, and perhaps the entire war, was that of the Colima Bridge incident. On April 16, 1991, several days after the death of Antonio Cardenal in Chalatenango, and two days following the corps' failed attempt to access the Chalatenango hinterlands (detailed in chapter 2), the pack made another attempt to reach the conflicted zones. They were hoping to witness the delivery of Cardenal's body to his Nicaraguan relatives. Several local alternative press reporters joined the SPECA pack on their second attempt to access the conflicted zones. Unfortunately, the pack was once again rebuffed by their military overseers. Perhaps as punishment for our earlier transgressions, the army stopped the entire pack at the Colima Bridge, a point halfway between San Salvador and Chalatenango. Soldiers placed tires and chains in front of the press vehicles and a stand-off ensued. As usual, the SPECA reporters, both foreign and Salvadoran, sat back and waited, hoping for the best but conditioned to expect the worst.

Things got worse. The local alternative press contingent was not so patient, nor as willing to accede to the military's demands. In an unprecedented act of defiance, they started to remove the tire blockade. This infuriated the soldiers, who began shooting into the air. The reporters ran back to their vehicles. Fortunately, no one was injured.

COPREFA quickly disseminated a report about the incident. By law, every media institution in El Salvador was obligated to run the COPREFA piece. It played frequently on both television and radio. The COPREFA text claimed that "the military, in accord with the established regulations, impeded the journalists, who traveled without the corresponding authorization to enter the conflicted zones." They explained that the reporters were traveling to Chalatenango to cover the "propaganda" of the "FMLN terrorists." "The journalists provoked the military officials in a violent manner," according to the COPREFA report, "The military has collaborated openly with the journalists so that they can conduct their reporting activities under the protection of the military. The journalists defame their profession by acting in this manner."

COPREFA videotaped the incident. The footage includes journalists removing the blockade, honking their car horns, and shouting at the military. The same scenes were repeated several times over in the report, making the journalists appear violent and aggressive. The prensa enemiga was acting-up again; this time on national TV.

Officially, the government was not requiring salvoconducto passes at the time of the Colima Bridge incident. The journalists were traveling "without the corresponding authorization" because none had been legally required or offered since the elections. "We hold our breath each time access is allowed," explained Othello, "Of course, this time it all ended with a bang." The cost was much greater for the local press. Two local TV reporters were suspended from their positions at Channel 12, the only Salvadoran news broadcast that remains fairly independent from the military.

Members of the foreign press were split on the issue. The *A Team* reporters, represented by Bart, where infuriated by the actions of the locals. The stringers were somewhat ambivalent. The SPECA locals, a few of whom participated in the resistance, were mostly behind their compatriots. For perhaps the first time during the war, the major division in the corps was not a matter of *A Team/B Team* rivalry. It was more a schism of local versus foreign blocs.

The Colima Bridge confrontation was the main topic of a very charged SPECA meeting. Bart argued:

> We don't win anything by clashing with the military. We are not a revolutionary group. When we try to run through retens we give them propaganda materials.

Later, he added:

> Calixto and I disagree over the best method of dealing with the problem. We must not sound threatening. It is not a question of right and wrong, but who has the resources to present their case to the Salvadoran people.

Only one Salvadoran publicly backed Bart, however, an employee who dutifully mouthed Bart's pet phrase "We are not a union."

Several SPECA Salvadorans were angered by Bart's attitude. "We cannot tell the journalists in the local press what to do," Pedro argued, "They are individuals and this is a historic moment for them." Pedro spoke in favor of the locals' act of civil disobedience. Shawn agreed. He called for SPECA action, proposing a resolution condemning the military officials responsible for the blockade. Only half in jest, others suggested they cite each member of the military high command.

Paul agreed with Shawn's proposal. As usual, Cal took a middle position. He condemned the locals' aggressive actions, but agreed that the intransigence of the military was ultimately to blame.

Speaking to the undecided, Victor stated "this was done in a moment of hot blood, but we cannot simply abandon them." No definite action was taken, but limited support for the fired journalists was finally put into resolution form. Near the end of the meeting, however, the current SPECA president announced his resignation and an upcoming vote for new leadership was planned.

Only twenty-nine journalists were present at this meeting. It was hoped that at least forty could attend the next in order to vote in the new leadership. SPECA was starting to become much smaller and the *A Team*, such that it was, had nearly disappeared as a political force within SPECA. Of course, *A Team* reporters and parachuters continued to cover the big stories, but they were no longer an integral part of SPECA itself. As a result, SPECA Salvadorans were becoming bolder and proportionately more important within the association. However, the association was becoming much less relevant as international news attention waned. The Colima Bridge incident marked the end of an era for the SPECA Salvadorans. A period of steady employment and fear was slowly giving way to an equally confusing era of peacetime optimism and job insecurity.

Jonna's Garden

The Salvadorans in SPECA are extremely nervous about their future. While some still occupy tenuous positions with international news organizations, many others have lost their jobs and membership in the corps. Ernesto describes the anxiety of the remaining few:

> Already, the foreign interest in El Salvador is disappearing. I think my company will cut jobs this year or next. The most logical thing would be for the locals to take the North Americans' positions, but in my case it will not happen.... They might say, "Thanks for your work, now go home." I do not want to return to the local press.

Almost every SPECA Salvadoran expressed similar fears. As a result, some were becoming nostalgic about the "good times" of war and the secure employment it brought.

I asked all reporters how they felt about future job prospects. The most memorable answer came from Abner. Months after our initial interview, the middle-aged reporter approached me at the Camino. "Remember that question you asked about the future? Well, it is here," said Abner, "I am unemployed as of yesterday."

Yet, the outlook for SPECA Salvadorans is not entirely bad. One of the most hopeful developments is the Union of Salvadoran Journalists and Communications Professionals (*Sindicato de Periodistas y Similares en El*

Salvador: SINPESS), a group of reporters working for both international and local alternative media (Rodriguez 1991). Montel explains the purpose of SINPESS:

> We are forming a space for alternative news. We want more attention paid to issues like ecology, for example. This involves the health of everyone, even Christiani. The local papers will not cover the issue of the environment because it will damage tobacco companies and others who support those papers.

SINPESS is a response to the establishment politics of the Salvadoran Press Association (APES). According to Montel, "APES is just a way to make more money. They are not really journalists. They all get paid off." SINPESS represents a hope for an alternative to the heavily controlled and corrupt national press system.

In addition to SINPESS, a few alternative, global press institutions provide some hope for sustained future employment for SPECA Salvadorans. These agencies include the Central American News Service (ACAN), Salvadoran Press Agency (SALPRESS), and the Inter Press Service (IPS). IPS, headquartered in Italy, relies heavily upon locals and knowledgeable regional journalists. It was designed as an alternative to the dominant international news services—AP, Reuters, UPI, and AFP. The IPS news net is just as wide, and arguably, much deeper than those of its competitors. Regional news magazines, *Pensamiento Propio* and *Panorama*, also provide hope for sustained employment. Latin American television services, including *Televisa* and *Univision*, likewise continue to provide employment while North American and European media withdraw from the region.

Sergio and other SINPESS proponents see the withdrawal of the foreign press as a chance for liberation and exploration of peace. "We have worked so long in war, and have invested much in the war," stated Sergio, "Fortunately, we have the opportunity to work in peace.... Now I get to experience other facets of my country, the culture, the environment, and all the rest."

Unfortunately, the local alternative media is just now regrouping from over a decade of violent repression, trying to regain the relatively small share of the Salvadoran audience they held before the war began. Meanwhile, in postwar El Salvador new forces of national, regional, and international capital are making their work even more difficult. The same is true for Salvadoran universities which supply much of the talent, expertise, and spirit for media reform. The National University is a bombed-out skeleton of its former self, while the UCA is trying to recover from the massacre of 1989. I asked a professor at the UCA how well the university was recovering. "With difficulty," he replied, "The university has not recuperated its old role as an animator of peace."

The political opposition and alternative press are competing on an extremely uneven playing field in postwar El Salvador. ARENA and the oligarchy it represents still own almost the entire means of mass communication and are empowered by the latest techniques and technologies. Meanwhile, the opposition is forced to compete for the populations' attentions with outmoded equipment and capabilities. Radio Venceremos, an organization that has managed to maintain a radio program throughout the war, must now compete with the advanced broadcast technologies of the right wing press (Lopez Vigil 1991). The Salvadoran right promises a "progressive" (*progresista*) future, a term whose meaning is greatly different in El Salvador than in the U.S. For many Salvadorans, ARENA's U.S.-styled and designed *propaganda* (literally "advertising") seems proof positive they portend a future of consumer progress and magic, a world like the ones in the movies, like the one in *Los Estados* (Alegria 1986:30). Meanwhile, the left only promises freedom and justice. The right dangles images of sex, consumption, and modernity in front of the population's eyes, while the left merely promises years of struggle against the "progressive" forces of modernity, the United States and U.S.-style development. The narrative myths of development and consumer capitalism have taken fire, a new religion made manifest in the living screen, just out of reach, but much more real than the dying Gods of revolution.

Both the left and right are empowered by the population's widespread dissatisfaction. Unfortunately, power has the ability to not only produce, but to define, manipulate, and rechannel discontent. As always, the opposition marches one step behind, trying to make up the deficit with truth. Unfortunately, the *Pedagogy of the Oppressed* (Freire 1970) has proven to be a much weaker weapon than the techniques of oppression. As Ellacuria pessimistically opined, Salvadoran journalists are saddled with "a task which is almost impossible, and almost heroic" (APES 1990:77).

However, neither our written nor lived narratives are fixed in fate. Therefore, I choose to end with an anecdote of hope. The event was an interview with Jonna, a SPECA journalist whose father had been a major figure in the Salvadoran resistance. I asked Jonna what he planned to do after the war. I expected something big, another quote taken from and adding to the grand narrative of revolution and apocalypse, war and redemption. Jonna paused to look out the window, his thoughtful gaze resting on a bed of flowers rising out of a small patch of soil behind his home. "I would like to do some gardening."

There is something typically Salvadoran, yet wonderfully universal about that sentiment.

ALTERNATIVES

True compassion is more than flinging a coin to a beggar; it understands that an edifice which produces beggars needs restructuring.

—Martin Luther King, Jr., *Where Do We Go From Here?*

The purpose of this chapter is to suggest global press alternatives. I will look at current news options as well as journalists' ideas for future changes in the international press. The SPECA "internationals"—Canadian, Australian, Asian, European, and Latin American journalists who comprise 18% of the corps—were particularly helpful in this regard. Their work provided a rich comparative sample of alternative styles and structures.

The first section, introduced through the words of Calixto, deals with alternative institutions. The second concerns gender censorship and feminist alternatives. The third, drawing special reference to Maria's coverage of El Salvador, is about individual practice and professional ethics.

Mulitperspectival, Polyvocal, and Global News Alternatives

Calixto, a Latin American journalist, works for an alternative international news service. Like many of the internationals, Calixto often drew comparisons between his reporting and that of U.S. correspondents. He called his U.S. counterparts "somewhat ethnocentric." They have a particularly hard time "escaping the political realities and concepts of their own country," he said.

Calixto made light of "the fundamental principle of the North American press," objective journalism:

> I have seen that they will not let sources pay when they take them to breakfast. They will not let them pay the check because they fear this will corrupt their sense of objectivity. To me, this seems somewhat stupid. I do not care who pays the bill. It is a principle [objectivity] that I do not respect.... To me, total objectivity is a lie.

"The most important thing is that you are honest," said Calixto, "that you play with your cards on the table." He feels the principles of objective journalism force the U.S. press to act in a "dishonest" manner. Calixto was particularly critical of his North American colleagues' use of the "Western Diplomat" attribution, stating, "They lose credibility that way."

Calixto is very interested in democratizing global communication. "A North American in Bolivia sends a cable in English to New York," he complained, "where it is translated and returns to Latin American newspapers because they subscribe to AP, UPI, and/or Reuters for their news." This forces Latin Americans to see their situations "through North American eyes," argues Calixto. It is his intention, and that of his organization, to reverse that trend. Calixto sees his organization as an alternative to the U.S. and European transnationals that currently dominate the international news communication system.

An editorial in the Salvadoran journal *Dialogo*, provides an overview of the "cultural imperialism" critique to which Calixto and many media scholars subscribe (1991:6):

> In matters of communication, we depend on the North American transnationals. The news, press, radio, television, film, etc., are all subordinate in terms of form and content to that which the powerful centers of North American communication decide to transmit.[1]

The anonymous authors of the *Dialogo* article define North American media influence as "cultural intervention." They believe that U.S. media fortify and reproduce "cultural schemes of oppression, war, and loss of national identity."[2] Calixto is trying to offer an alternative to first world domination of global media.

In addition to Calixto, other SPECA internationals are also working to democratize the international news system. Pati is part of an organization that brings together Third World journalists and First World editors to "find a better way to get locals involved directly in the mainstream Western press." Pati's group is affiliated with an alternative news network that provides reports on a sliding scale basis to small, cash-strapped news institutions. At this point, the network only distributes six reports a week but, as Pati states with guarded optimism, "That is six more than before."

Daniel is involved in a similar pursuit. He is hoping to take advantage of new technologies—fax, personal computers, and online services—to create an alternative international news service. He is particularly interested in improving coverage of the third world. Daniel wants the new network to have a "human" orientation, "Not just what happens, but how people experience it."

In the preceding chapter I discussed several alternative news services for whom SPECA reporters work.[3] The most important of these are the Inter Press Service (IPS) and the Salvadoran Press Agency (SALPRESS). Both of these differ greatly from the major world services. AP and UPI work mainly with the U.S. market in mind. Reuters, as a British service, produces news primarily for U.S. and British audiences. AFP is concerned mainly with the French market, and so on. Although each of these services distribute reports worldwide, they tend to target their products towards their most affluent and concentrated markets. In contrast, IPS is a relatively decentered network. IPS services are designed for a plurality of small and alternative news institutions (Galtung and Vincent 1992:27–28, 145–68). Likewise, IPS employs a much more diverse range of reporters. Local and regional journalists produce a great deal of IPS' total news output.

SALPRESS—a regional network based in El Salvador, but spread throughout Mexico and Central America—is also rooted in the ethic of self-reporting. It was formed to counter the narrow perspectives represented by mainstream news syndicates. A SALPRESS reporter explained:

> Our emphasis is not only on official sources, but all social organizations. We will cover the Committee for National Debate (CPDN), for example. Sometimes, we are the only reporters there. SALPRESS gives more coverage to a variety of sectors.

Alternative agencies like SALPRESS and IPS make a conscious effort to reach beyond the inter-elite quarrels presented in the duplicative reporting of the objective giants, AP and Reuters.

Unfortunately, SALPRESS, IPS, and other alternative services have had great difficulty breaking into the major markets. U.S. news organs, for example, locked in incestuous competition, rarely stray from the major wires and syndicates. They steadfastly refuse to take advantage of the growing number of international press options, even though these alternative services are far less expensive than the major syndicates.[4] The U.S. press' distrust of foreign media can only be described as xenophobic. The *New York Times'* election period coverage of March, 1991, for example, was written solely by U.S. journalists (mainly staff parachuters, with one contribution from a stringer). Meanwhile, election period reports in *El Pais*, Spain's major newspaper, were derived from Agence France Press, Reuters, EFE (Spanish), Deutsche Presse Agentur (DPA) and staff. The Mexican daily, *Excelsior*, used Salvadoran election period reports from

Reuters, AFP, EFE, ANSA, SALPRESS, DPA, UPI, AP, IPS, and staff. While *Excelsior* and *El Pais* each have distinct political tendencies, as does the *New York Times*, their representations of the world are much more diverse. Their coverage, by default or design, is fairly "multiperspectival."

Another problem with international news is just that: it remains inter-*national* in a world whose major trends and influences are increasingly global. Much of the world's news coverage is still arranged according to national boundaries and constructed in terms of national interests. Readerships are arranged and spoken to as nation-state collectives, rather than as part of a global (or local) community.[5] Most "foreign" news in the U.S. media, for example, is really *national* news, produced by and for American reporters and institutions. We are reporting the world to ourselves. There is little active communication with those whom we are ostensibly "covering."[6] Angelica, who works for an alternative global service, complains:

> Our coverage of Latin America is more profound than that of U.S. companies. It is only logical. The U.S. networks' public is American. They are interested in news that involves Americans and nothing more. Our public is interested in all the news happening in Latin America because they are more involved in the news.

SPECA reporters joke that you can get the U.S. to do anything in Central America except read about it. Before blaming the situation on readers, however, it is important to note how limited the U.S. press presentation of the world is.

Part of the reason for the narrowness and superficiality of U.S. news is that foreign correspondents, as generalists, are often under prepared. They lack the training, tools, and time to stray beyond coverage of the staple events: natural disasters, combat, and political intrigue. With this problem in mind, Adriana suggested an alternative two-tiered approach to the current homogeneous and duplicative system. "Why not *thematic* reporters," offered Adriana, "law, human rights, environment, economy.... The specialists would see things in a more global way." As for the types of events which are less amenable to special-feature coverage, Adriana suggests, "Let the wires do the straight breaking news."

These traveling specialists—parachuters with a purpose—would bring greater knowledge, depth, and diversity to international news. The news "net" would be spread more widely and reach much deeper. Of course, Adriana's plan would also increase the parachute pool, a tendency I have criticized throughout (perhaps having adopted the biases of my SPECA subjects). However, the current system is already heavily dependent upon parachuters. Most of the current lot, however, are neither grounded in the localized issues they are sent to cover, nor conversant in specialized fields of knowledge (Rosenblum 1979:44). Conversely, the specialist-parachuters in Adriana's plan would land with advanced levels of training and information suited to the issues they are sent to cover. Rather than having to rely completely upon the claims of sources and experts, the specialist-parachuters would be qualified to evaluate the various positions they encounter and provide greater historical and social context to ongoing news trends and issues. Granted, a sense of familiarity with geographic context and "place" would certainly be lost in Adriana's scheme. For that, I suggest the addition of a third tier: local reporters. Resident reporters, such as the SPECA Salvadorans, would provide a greater sense of local perspective and definition to global news coverage.

To summarize the modified "Adriana" plan: permanently based wire reporters would cover breaking news; specialist-parachuters would cover thematic issues such as economics, human rights, ecology, and international politics; and finally, resident reporters would provide local definition. Each sector's intrinsic advantages would be more fully exploited in this plan.

Global alternatives are sorely needed. A better system of communication is necessary if we are to gain an adequate understanding of our place and potential within "the world house" (King 1967:167–91). It is unlikely humanity will solve the daunting political and ecological problems it now faces without a new way to communicate across borders, both actual and imagined.

Gender Censorship and Feminist Alternatives

There were only a few women in the corps when the war began. Now more than a third of the Salvador corps is female.[7] The numbers do not necessarily translate into power or textual transformation, however. "The fact that there are a lot of women working here makes it better," said Pati, "but it still is not good. The media here has been dominated by men for a long time and there is a perception that women shouldn't be covering war."

"[A]n underlying prejudice is revealed from time to time:" agrees Jorge Lewinski, "a woman may be treated as a voyeur, or a sightseer who has no right to be where she is, or she may be considered to be incompetent and unreliable" (1978:29). Rosa spoke of similar attitudes among her editors: "They would ask, 'You seem like a nice girl. What are you doing down there?' It was just sort of sad."

Most of the women in SPECA have experienced gender discrimination. "I have suffered," said Shari, "because of my political views and the fact that I am a woman." At war's end, Shari's company hired "three young white males" at the same time they were canceling her long-standing contract.

Maria also feels that women "face incredible discrimination in the profession," and notes that, despite gains made at lower levels, "[T]he chief editor or upper manager is always a man."[8]

In addition to problems with editors and institutions, SPECA women had to deal with sexist views and behaviors from within the corps itself. As illustrated in chapter 8, women are often peripheral in the press corps ritual performances, members of the audience rather than full participants. SPECA women were resentful of this marginalization. "There are very different standards," complained Marla, "of how women can act."

According to most female respondents, editors actively discourage reporters from covering issues and events they consider "women's" stories. Marla argues that "stories about women and the long term *social* effects of the war tend to be ghettoized to a different part of the paper." Marla gave the example of a story she wrote about prostitution:

> People wanted to trivialize the story, in a way. It would appear in papers under headings like "Letter from El Salvador." It would appear as something quaint when, in fact, I think issues of the social costs of the war and how this group of prostitutes was affected by a decade of civil war is a hard news story as well.

Similarly, Pati noted that almost all the opposition and union leaders in El Salvador are male, even though 70% of the workforce is comprised of women. "I think that is a story," she argued, "but, try to sell that to my editor, ha ha ha. He wouldn't be interested." Pati continued:

> There is an incredible amount of wife battering in this country— abandonment, women selling lottery tickets with four or five little kids on the street. It strikes me because I am a woman. Because the press is dominated by men these issues are not covered. If the issue has not been covered before, it makes it harder for you to write a story about it. It's not news if AP and the *New York Times* are not covering it.

Pati's interests as a woman and a reporter were overwhelmed and censored by institutional inertia, the men surrounding her, and the androcentric news values of the press system (Creedon 1989:164–246).

Teri noted similar problems with her editors. Her bosses complain when she attempts to "seek out women as sources":

> I am amazed how defensive men are. It makes me laugh on one hand, but on the other it makes me see how grave the situation is, if we are ever hoping to get any balance in reflecting our reality. Most papers do not reflect how society is. When you admit you seek another point of view and make a conscious attempt to find a woman, they get very indignant and say you are skewing the news…. But, they think it is truth if it is said by Joe Blow.

Indeed, the news is already skewed. The news narrative and agenda is extremely male oriented. As such, it appears objective and rational to the men who manage it. The particular is framed as universal, the androcentric promoted as neutral (Schaef 1981). Therefore, women's truths deviate by definition. In acting in the manner described by Teri, Pati, Marla, and others, the editor-gatekeepers act to both repress, remodel, and reinterpret this potentially subversive discourse (Mills 1988:2).

As a result, many journalists have attempted to develop, or at least conceive of, feminist alternatives. It is important to imagine what such alternatives might look like. Marla's answer:

> It sounds cliché, but if there were more women in the press, matters of the social affects and costs of war might be explored more fully.... There would be more women as sources.

Like most of the women in SPECA, Janice agreed with Marla's assessment.[9] She explained the difference:

> Men and women are constructed differently socially and culturally. Women are more interested in things like ecology. Tests show that there are human feces in all the food, that all the food is contaminated here. That is a really important story in a country about to be invaded by cholera. A woman might be more interested in doing that then a man who wants to get out and do a war story and be a real boy and cover the *real* stuff.

Although the alternative press has been more open to feminist reporting on domestic issues, they "seem to be no less willing" to deal with gender issues in international contexts (Roach 1993:185–86). Marla protested this oversight and double standard:

> There has not been any critical analysis I have seen of the lack of autonomy of the women's movement within the social movements here. I know countless women here who are very embittered about their treatment. Those stories don't appear in the alternative press, basically because they want to say, "Rah rah, someone is sticking up to the army here," which, yeah, I can see. But there is severe tension between women's groups and others, and there are a lot of women within male dominated organizations who feel they are being dealt with in a very unprofessional, sexist way. Reporters are afraid to broach those issues.

Journalists are "afraid to broach those issues" partly because of a broad, androcentric consensus among the press, the politicians, and powers both right and left that "women's issues" are secondary. Therefore, feminist news alternatives must be developed, not only for the sake of a more complete record and better news representation, but because said "women's issues" tend to be those that most profoundly effect us all.

Maria

Maria's tastes and practices are unique. She has an insatiable curiosity about Salvadoran society and is constantly striving to experience new facets of the culture, both for work and as a matter of personal curiosity.

I asked Maria to tell me about her favorite stories from the preceding year. "They were definitely not about war," she said, laughing, "They were *cosas humanos* (human things)—cultural issues. I wrote about the symphony, for example." Maria reported the struggle of Salvadoran musicians, artists, and performers to create a meaningful cultural space for art amid the violence and poverty. Maria was constantly searching out unique angles to important issues.

Maria's educational background is distinct as well. She studied art, and is both a painter and an architect. Like most of the journalists in her home country, she did not obtain a degree in journalism. In fact, few SPECA internationals received formal journalistic training before beginning their reporting careers. Beatriz, for example, earned her university degree in Anthropology. Other internationals were trained as lawyers and teachers. There was even an agronomist among them.

Maria spoke often of the need to translate the realities of El Salvador to First World audiences. She was particularly concerned about helping the European readership understand the Salvadoran war, differentiating low intensity conflict from the "the great battles" they are more familiar with. Like many Anthropologists, Maria is concerned with the problem of "writing effectively against terror" (Taussig 1987b:241).[10]

Like most SPECA journalists, however, Maria is frustrated by her agency's lack of interest in Latin America. "Journalists are human beings, right?" asked Maria. "We must meet the demands of our editors and this puts a mark on the type of work we are able to do and our attitude towards reality." Nevertheless, Maria feels there are considerable differences between journalists of her home country and those of the United States. Once again, the philosophy of objectivity is the major distinguishing factor. "Objectivity simply does not exist," argued Maria. "It is a very abstract concept. What exists is a profession, like any other, within which one can operate with honesty." Maria describes what she means by "honesty:"

> Honesty is a personal concept. I mean to say that when one writes about something, that you do it with a conscience. Who can say whether what you write and think would be the most correct? Here the situation is delicate. There is conflict, and so it is very difficult to verify any piece of information. You can never really know what is truly the reality. Therefore, you have to talk to as many different sectors as possible, but then, you have to think several more times before writing. You do not have to censor yourself, but rather be very reflexive concerning what you finally write. The information you write can be used for destructive purposes. You might have the best intentions, but you must be extremely careful because the information can be used in another way. Eventually, you will become another source.

As this quote demonstrates, Maria was concerned with the politics and pedagogy of the press.

I am reminded of my first encounter with Troy, who represents a very different, U.S. perspective. "What is your research about?" asked the amiable American when I first met him. "The culture of SPECA," I replied, "including the methods reporters use to make news." Of course, I meant to say, "the methods journalists use to *report* news," realizing what a turn-off the prior construction would be to an objective journalist. Troy corrected me immediately. "We don't *make* the news," he reproached, using the patient tone of a teacher correcting an earnest, yet slow, child, "We *report* the news." Maria worked under no such pretense, however. She was aware that in reporting, the journalist is inevitably constructing or "making" news as well.[11] "Many speak of finding *the truth*, or presenting *the reality*," said Maria, "but there are many realities and there are many truths."

As in Calixto's case, Maria believes honesty should be the fundamental ethic of journalism. Maria places the ethic of honest journalism between two types of communication she considers fundamentally dishonest: objective journalism and propaganda. The greatest falsehood of objectivity is its disingenuous claim to unbiased and unmitigated truths. Objective journalists deny their subjectivities, rather than acknowledge and critically challenge them. They reduce complexities, rather than explain them. They evade contradiction, rather than letting the reader in on the inevitable doubts and difficulties encountered in any act of discovery. "The reader should know that the reporter never has all of the information or all the truth," said Maria. "The reporter must always offer an element of doubt." The principles of objective journalism compel reporters to forge a false sense of certainty, an overly simplified and concretized view of reality which chokes curiosity and inhibits critical thought.

Propaganda, on the other hand, is more self-consciously dishonest. Authors of propaganda purposely disseminate false positions and facts in order to support what they consider "higher" truths.

Objective and propagandistic reporters deny, and thus abuse their power of authorship. The goals of honest reporting are distinct. The honest journalist engages readers in a creative dialogue, rather than dominating them via the paths of reduction or false construction. Several internationals spoke of news reporting in this vein, as a "contract" between journalist and audience. All three forms—objective, propagandistic, and honest journalism—involve an authorial agenda. Only the third, however, lets readers in on that process.

Existential Journalism

"Do not bear false witness."
—anonymous

Maria's perspective is similar to what John Merrill calls *Existential*

Journalism (1977). Merrill criticizes modern journalism for having become bureaucratic, banal, and formulaic. He "strikes out" at "'corporate' journalism, this depersonalized, conformist type of journalism." In particular, Merrill laments the viral spread of "robopathy" (1977:17):

> We seem overly concerned about the system and the media retaining freedom from government or from other outside forces, but we are little concerned about the individual journalist who has become hardly more than a robot or conformist functionary of the journalistic enterprise for which he works.

The existential journalist is one who "rebels against being buried in this type of modern corporate journalism" (1977:19). The existential journalist is first and foremost an honest journalist.

In SPECA, the most knowledgeable critics of U.S. journalism are the "in-betweens," European stringers who write for both European and U.S. media. The in-betweens agree with Merrill's assessment of contemporary reporting. One repeatedly complained that U.S. news writing style is "too formulaic." Another argued that U.S. news is "overly sourced and flat":

> There is more of an assumption in Europe that the reporter can make judgments. You don't need a diplomat's quote for everything. You can be more opinionated. There is more room for creative writing.

Another in-between explained:

> My theory is much more of an investment oriented concept of journalism. I believe you should go out and listen to people and build up as big a picture as you can. I think this is encouraged by most European systems of journalism. However, the U.S. system demands a quote.... The result of that is a very bitty sort of "he said this, they said that." So what? Was it true?

This "bitty sort" of writing is extremely frustrating for the in-between stringers, reporters who have also tasted the relative freedom of writing for media outside the objective discipline.

Of course, as Maria's case makes clear, bureaucratic disciplines are not exclusive to the U.S. press, but exist to some degree everywhere. A SPECA reporter raised and trained in Cuba, for example, complained of severe limitations in that nation's state-controlled news. He is a strong critic of Salvadoran and North American media as well. By virtue of his past experience, he has come to see that it is not merely capitalism, fascism, or communism which are to blame, but the bureaucratic structures that underlie each and intersect all three.

Therefore, alternative structures must be developed if the aforementioned ethics of independence, commitment, creativity, and honesty are to prosper. Based on my observations of SPECA, I found six structural conditions to be particularly conducive to this sort of reporting.

First, the most creative and independent journalists generally work for smaller institutions. Such organizations have neither the will nor resources to effectively discipline their reporters. In terms of fostering freedom and creativity, *Small is Beautiful* (Schumacher 1973).

Second, the most independent, self-satisfied, and existential SPECA journalists write within pluralistic media systems, those which provide the ideological space for journalists to present their work in a more profound, communicative, and self-reflexive manner. As Emilio, a SPECA Salvadoran argued, "There needs to be an opposition press, a leftist press, a union press, and others. Democracy is characterized by the free play of ideas."

Third, narrative forms must be sufficiently fluid to allow for experimentation and a diversity of styles. Objective journalism is cryptic and ideologically-delimited, a "bitty sort" of journalism. The postmodern condition cannot be adequately represented through traditional forms alone.

Fourth, the best articles published during the Salvadoran war were written by journalists free from the obligations of daily reporting and breaking news. Herr explains (1968:212):

> [N]o matter how much I love the sound of it, there's no way that I can think of myself as a war correspondent without stopping to acknowledge the degree to which it's pure affectation. I never had to run back to any bureau office to file.... I never had to race out to the Danang airfield to get my film on the eight-o'clock scatback to Saigon; there wasn't any bureau, there wasn't any film, my ties to New York were as slight as my assignment was vague. I wasn't really an oddity in the press corps, but I was a peculiarity, an extremely privileged one.

Thanks to that "privilege," Herr was free to write some of the most memorable pieces of journalism produced during the Vietnam war (Jameson 1984:84, Cumings 1992:7). Carlin and Millman were also privileged, as were a handful of other institutionally unencumbered reporters whose writings continue to gain highest praise among the corps.[12]

Fifth, the finest reporting in SPECA was conducted by journalists trained in fields other than journalism. Maria, the artist, brings a sensibility and knowledge to her work, which elevates it beyond standard battle fare. Othello, a theologian, has connections to the religious community of El Salvador which greatly enliven his social reporting. Millman, an economist, made startling discoveries about the Salvadoran military through interviews with their accountants and study of financial records, which conventional war correspondents missed.

Sixth, the best reporters belong to cooperative networks of writers and intellectuals. The stringers have each other. Their support and camaraderie is a contravening force against the discipline of corporate media clients, often distinguishing their work from that of the *A Team*. A lucky few, like Adriana, belong to media cooperatives. These more "organic" institutions provide networks of mutual support and creative interchange.

I recognize the quixotic improbability underlying any attempt to radically change the structure and culture of corporate news media. Unfortunately, the limited measures normally advocated—improving journalistic training, methods, etc.—will continue to fall well short of the current need.[13] As the eagerly awaited "information super highway" continues the tradition of highways past—accelerating the destruction and reformation of our natural, social and cultural environments—we will be asked to limit our choices to "which channel?" "which brand?" and "which candidate?" As I have hopefully made clear in this chapter and elsewhere in the book, many SPECA journalists have refused to limit themselves to the small questions, even while forced to limit their practices to small answers. Therein lies the potential for change. The alternatives already exist, albeit in nascent and marginal forms. We must grab them and engage ourselves in the task of developing more creative, informative and humane forms of communication.

LEAVING
THE CAMINO

"And I am sure that I never read any memorable news in a newspaper. If we read of one man robbed, or murdered, or killed by accident…we never need read another. One is enough. If you are acquainted with the principle, what do you care for a myriad of instances and applications?"

—Henry David Thoreau

As the Salvador corps dissolves and its members move on to other wars, I wonder, did U.S. news readers learn anything about El Salvador during the last twelve years? Can they distinguish the Salvadoran war from other conflicts? Or is Thoreau right in his assertion that news is little more than a redundant panoply of "accidents?"

War is not an accident. Unfortunately, it is reported as if it were. Social causes and human meanings of violence are rarely explored. Instead, the reader is treated to a balanced, dispassionate, and banal play of quotes culled from leaders whose purpose is anything but the careful explication of events. The result is a kaleidoscope of vague and unsettling images of the world.

Inevitably, there will be major gaps in the news representation of any issue or event. There is no such thing as "the complete story." However, the gaps in the coverage of El Salvador are conspicuous. Missing from the news is the barefoot, dirty, skinny, little girl who sells the *Diario de Hoy* outside the Camino Real Hotel—lucky she has a job, because across the street is a pack of kids whose only recourse is to steal and beg for food. The young *miserables* share whatever scraps they can scrounge outside the "The

Happy World," a small amusement park where children of upper class families laugh and scream, gorging themselves on ice cream and milk shakes. All of this was within sight of the Camino Real press bureaus, but rarely within sight of the news reader.

Less than a block away was a surf shop. They sold T-shirts emblazoned with the name of Major Bob (D'Aubuisson), a hero to many upper class youth, and disturbingly, a popular figure for many in the working classes as well. Hidden behind the street and surf shop is a huge *barranca* (ravine) where hundreds are crowded into tin shacks and hovels, forced to drink and bathe in sewer water runoff. It runs along Calle Sisimiles all the way up to the Volcan de San Salvador. U.S. military advisors dubbed the verdant sewer "Ho Chi Min Trail," because of the protection its steep banks afforded the FMLN whenever they entered the city from hideouts further up the Volcano.

Beyond the barranca is Colonia Centro America, a middle-class neighborhood where I lived. As I took my morning walk to the Camino every day, I saw little kids from the barranca standing outside the security fence of a small kindergarten, staring through iron bars at the energetic tots inside. The privileged children played on, already inured to the jaundiced stares of their future maids and gardeners.

All of this, the extreme social injustice and fear that defines Salvadoran culture, is missing from the news. Without it, none of the surface violence makes sense. The war was represented as a clash of ideologies, rather than a symptom of much more profound social ills. Now the war is gone, but the injustice survives and multiplies.

Ricki, a SPECA Salvadoran, expressed fear that the foreign audience, particularly U.S. news consumers, never really understood the costs and causes of the war:

> They should know that the war is not over. There is still the same amount of poverty and injustice…. Here they are fighting for land and justice, but it is difficult for people to understand. They think that we are a warlike people, but we are not…. The gringos have participated and have invested so much in the injustice. They should understand that.

Melisand was left with a similar feeling of bitterness after her work for U.S. news media ended. "The U.S. press is only interested in where U.S. dollars are going," she stated, "Now, poverty is all that is left, and they do not give a shit."

As I have explained, however, many of them truly do "give a shit." "I'm not neutral," proclaimed Paul, spitting out the last word with contempt. "I don't see how anybody could be. But if they are, I wonder, what are those assholes doing here?" Those "assholes" were merely doing their job. Some went along willingly, adopting whatever frames would help them advance. Others rebelled in big and little ways, sometimes with effect, usually with little to show except frustration and anger. Most were somewhere in between, neither fully compliant nor truly dissident.

Individual reporters are not the problem, however, any more than bank tellers were to blame for the Savings and Loans crisis in the U.S. Tom Koch puts it nicely (1990:180):

> In this whole process reporters are like bank tellers on a busy day. For the latter, all the money flows through their hands and very little stays in the way of a weekly paycheck. They learn the ways of the bank, the pattern of behavior expected of officials, and the forms by which the medium of money is exchanged. If they do well and accept the constraints of their environment, a few might in the course of time move up to account officer and, maybe to vice president of a branch. Power flows through the newsperson's hands in precisely the same way.

In other words, it matters not whether the teller or scribe "give a shit" (to borrow Melisand's uncharitable prose). To care is to butt your head against an unfeeling bureaucracy and reporting conventions whose very purpose is to produce dehumanized knowledge. The objective journalists are told to sublimate their concern until for some it finally disappears altogether. Objective journalism produces disinterest, or at least a play-acted pretense thereof. "I don't give a shit about what happens to this place," repeats Harold *ad nauseam*.

The objective stance is best described by Bourdieu in his *Outline of a Theory of Practice* (1977:96):

> Objectivism constitutes the social world as a spectacle presented to an observer who takes up a "point of view" on the action, who stands back so as to observe it and, transferring into the object the principles of his relation to the object, conceives of it as a totality intended for cognition alone, in which all interactions are reduced to symbolic exchanges. This point of view is the one afforded by high positions in the social structure, from which the social world appears as a representation (in the sense of idealist philosophy but also as used in painting or the theatre) and practices are no more than "executions," stage parts, performances of scores, or the implementing of plans.

Objective relations are a "reduced," dehumanized way of interacting with and knowing the world. Objective journalists are to display neither passion nor opinion. They are themselves "reduced" as they take up an objective "point of view," remaking the world into surface "spectacle."

Their humanity negated, journalists seek the healing salve of ritual, play-acting the roles of Orwell and Hemingway in the safe, backstage regions of the corps. Yet, it is not merely a case of false consciousness nor shallow self-deception on their part. In keeping alive the myths of war correspondence, journalists retain and renew their desire to break rank with discipline, to tell their stories and make news that matters. Unfortunately, at present we are wasting paper on redundant versions of an institutionalized story that neither illuminates nor ameliorates—news as official quote and cliché.

Octavio, a Salvadoran soldier I once met, described the human stakes of international news coverage more clearly than I could ever hope to. I talked with the young combatant while his girlfriend, a stationery store clerk, made copies of several news reports I had cut out of the *Diario Latino*. Octavio looked through my stack of articles with great interest, most of which detailed human rights abuses by the military. After examining the grisly photos and accusations, Octavio smiled and began telling his own story.

Octavio fell asleep on guard duty one night while posted at the back door of a supply warehouse. His best friend was guarding the front door. FMLN compas slipped in to the compound, slit his friend's throat, and stole several loads of supplies. They spared Octavio's life, however, letting him sleep through the incident. When he awoke, his friend was dead and the FMLN were gone. Octavio was genuinely grateful to the guerrillas for having spared his life. Like most Salvadoran soldiers, Octavio was a conscript. He did not ask for the war, nor want to be part of it.

After he finished telling the story, Octavio asked, "What do the people of the U.S. think about the war?" "Most know very little about it," I answered. Octavio was shocked. "How could that be?" he asked. The tired young soldier looked down at the ground and thought for a few moments. He looked back up at me and concluded, "It is like a mother not knowing her own child."

We have spawned war. Our government, which claims to speak for us, and "our" corporations—whose actions go almost entirely unchecked—utilize our collective social power for purposes to which few of us would consciously provide consent. Meanwhile, news continues to devolve into entertainment, neither more nor less enlightening than the melodramas it increasingly imitates. The promise of five hundred channels portends more of the same, only bigger, brighter, even more banal, ever more fragmented.

Our culture produces many things: goods, power, knowledge, profit. Most importantly, it produces us—passive participants and active consumers of a culture of growth and glut. The world has become our spectacle, our playground, our resource, our waste product, our servant, our victim, ourselves. Either we know and don't care, or care and don't know. Either way, I guess that is how it happens, Octavio.

EPILOGUE

As I was writing this, Carmelo (his real name was Heleno Castro) was shot and killed. On October 30, he and another man got into a heated exchange following a minor collision of their two cars. Carmelo's killer was a wealthy landowner. Carmelo was the head of the FMLN land commission at the time of his death. Human rights organizations, North American academics, and journalists alike have written-off Carmelo's murder as "nonpolitical."

I mention this for three reasons.

First, as in the killing detailed at the beginning of this book, Carmelo's death was mostly ignored by the news media. His murder did not fit their narrow definition of newsworthiness, for many of the same reasons.

Second, Carmelo's death, and his life, have had a significant influence on my work, and colors much of what is written here.

Finally, Carmelo's murder, and those of many other FMLN ex-combatants, indicate the war did not end on January 1, 1992, but continues to this day.

APPENDIX: THE JOURNALISTS

The Salvadoran Press Corps Association (SPECA)

A Team (21%)[1]
Bart
Clarice
Francine
Frederick
George
Harold
Katherine
Maude
Michael
Nell
Percy
Sam
Sheena
Terrence
Troy

B Team (13%)
Bob
Cary
Jerry
Marla
Othello
Ronald
Shawn
Terilyn
Tracy

Others (16%)
Angelica
Beatriz
Calixto
Frances
Janice
Margarita
Maria
Mercedes
Pati
Patricia
Teri

Photo (10%)
Adrian
Joe
Michele
Paul
Shari
Stephanie
William

Salvadorans (40%)
Abner
Alonzo
Basha
Carlos

Efran
Elba
Elicia
Elsa
Emilio
Estefan
Ferdinand
Henri
Jauquin
Jorge
Lisa
Louisa
Marta
Mateo
Miguel
Montel
Norma
Paco
Pedro
Rachel
Ricardo
Rogelio
Rosa Blanca
Sergio
Thomas
Victor

International Journalists Interviewed in Mexico and Central America

Ashley
Benjamin
Bernardo
Casandra
Clarice
David
Edgar

Enrique
Everett
Felicia
Fred
Iver
Jaimie
Justin

Katie
Lana
Lenny
Luigi
Mathew
Melisand
Ted

NOTES

The following are bibliographic references. The sources of direct quotes, excepting epigrams, are cited within the text itself.

Introduction: Reporting *Salvador*

1. SPECA is normally abbreviated as "S.P.C.A." According to press corps lore, the name and acronym were decided upon in a drinking session during the early part of the war. As a joke, journalists borrowed the acronym from the Society for the Prevention of Cruelty to Animals (SPCA). I have added a written "e" to increase textual flow and match the verbalized form.

2. Roach 1993:17–21, describes the current form and function of the "military-industrial-communication complex."

3. In order to provide nominal anonymity to my research subjects, I will use pseudonyms, will limit my use of their published work, and will not provide citations thereof. Although very few of my subjects requested anonymity, I feel obligated to offer its limited protection to all.

4. See Weschler 1990 and Day 1987, for overviews of Latin American news coverage in U.S. news media, and reasons for the considerable lack thereof.

5. See Cumings 1992:19–20, concerning the role of "subversive" reading in the contemporary cultural economy.

6. This is especially true of television news (Cumings 1992:21).

7. A few minutes after watching the nightly television news, fifty-one percent of those polled in a University of California at Berkeley study could not remember a single news story (Barrett 1973:7, Diamond 1975:66–77). Similarly, a recent poll commissioned by the *Los Angeles Times* discovered that "The American public" had "failed to absorb even basic facts of many recent news stories" (*Los Angeles Times*, May 19:A19).

8. See Marcus and Fischer 1986:138, concerning the Anthropological method of "defamiliarization by cross-cultural juxtaposition."

Chapter 1: War Games

1. The solidarity movement is composed of political and religious organizations in the United States and elsewhere whose aim is to provide support to various grass roots human rights, labor, and political organizations in Central America. After the electoral defeat of the Sandinista government in Nicaragua on February 25, 1990, the size and commitment of the international solidarity movement decreased significantly due to frustration, disillusionment, exhaustion, declining interest, and lack of funding.

2. In accord with an editorial in the local newspaper *Diario Latino* entitled, "The *Diario Latino* is not part of the opposition," I will refer to the small segment of the Salvadoran press that is not explicitly right wing and supportive of the

military, as the Salvadoran "alternative" press.

3. This tendency has increased due to the enforced use of journalistic "pools" during the recent wars in Panama and Iraq. When "pooled," correspondents are forced to remain sequestered at safe, remote locations while select individuals gather the news from sites carefully managed by military press officers. If the system works as intended the journalists share or "pool" the information with each other (Fialka 1991). Thus, journalists covering "Operation Desert Storm" joked: "When there's news in the gulf, we're in the pool."

Chapter 2: Terror and Control

1. The ascendance of TV news has further shortened the life span of a breaking story. Most events must be covered within 24 hours of their occurrence, or they are no longer newsworthy.

2. There were two stories involving regional censorship in 1982. Both mentioned El Salvador. There were ten stories involving the battlefield deaths of journalists and other problems for reporters in El Salvador in the 1981 index. Those reports were written during the tenure of Ray Bonner, however, who was later fired for his critical reporting.

3. See Sol 1984:64, Coad 1981, Vernau 1989:95–102. El Salvador is certainly not unique in this respect. According to the Committee to Protect Journalists, a record number of journalists, sixty-one, were killed throughout the world in 1991.

4. See Gonzales 1977, Alegria 1986:29, Vernau 1989:95–102, for earlier cases involving the local press and arson, none of which were provided as historical background in U.S. reporting of the *Diario Latino* attack.

5. Most U.S. reporters are self-described liberals or moderates (Gaziano 1987:7). Most SPECA journalists from the U.S. are self-described liberals.

6. Similarly, during the Vietnam War, the US allied South Vietnamese regime referred to the international press as "the enemy within" (Knightley 1975:425).

7. These and other elements of the Salvadoran military were borrowed directly from European Fascists (Krauss 1991:63–64).

8. I have used Millman's real name since he was not a subject of my ethnographic study and does not currently work in El Salvador.

Chapter 4: A Team, B Team

1. The *New York Times*' reporters had been refraining from using the adjective "Marxist" in reference to the guerrillas for over a year before they reported this supposed "striking departure," an indication they had begun shifting frames earlier, in conjunction with the larger government-media movement away from cold war rhetoric.

2. John Brentlinger found the same sort of social "distancing" among the Nicaraguan corps (1990:4)

3. Of these groups, stringers had the least affinity for solidarity groups, especially the Committee in Solidarity with the People of El Salvador (CISPES), which they criticized in very strong terms.

4. As Bruce Cumings notes (1992:14–16), "liberalism presents itself as the modal politics of capitalism." U.S. liberals, moderates, and conservatives alike are "liberals" in this sense. I am differentiating "liberal" and "moderate" here, however, using the North American vernacular.

5. Many journalists make a distinction between "stringers" and "freelancers," the latter group being comprised of a select and relatively well paid set of journalists who write high profile feature pieces, mainly for magazines. Although a few of my subjects in Guatemala and Mexico fit that description, only one SPECA journalist could accurately be described as a "freelancer" according to this restrictive definition.

Chapter 5: Discipline and Publish

1. Ironically, Embassy officials were angered whenever U.S. journalists failed to label information from rebel radio with explicit labels and disclaimers (Drucker 1984:47).

2. See Maslow and Arana 1981, concerning media obedience to specious CIA claims concerning Cuban and Nicaraguan arms supplies to the FMLN.

3. See *Extra!* January/February 1990:8, concerning a typical case of Embassy propaganda.

4. Breaking with tradition, the Associated Press Managing Editors Association scheduled a vote in 1994 on the adoption of a more specific code of ethics.

5. Hallin 1983:16–17. Freedom House was a major source of information for the press during all Salvadoran elections, including those of 1991. They maintained a Camino Real office amidst the press bureaus throughout the March, 1991 elections. Few of the journalists knew much about them, other than the fact that they were an extremely accessible source of information.

6. See also Accuracy in Media's "Report" 1982, 11(4), written from the perspective of those who initiated and led the anti-Bonner campaign.

7. The CBS *Sixty Minutes* report, "Massacre at El Mozote," was produced by David Gelber.

Chapter 6: The Source War

1. See Lutz and Collins 1993, concerning *National Geographic* and issues of representation.

2. See *La Jornada* October 13, 1991:13, for a detailed report of the Encounter.

3. See Kerns 1983, Taylor 1963, concerning the Black Carib or Garifuna.

Chapter 7: Practice

1. See Fishman 1980:28–30, for a description of the "beat."

2. Gans lists a set of myths or "enduring values" which pattern most U.S. news reporting. I would add the fundamental tenets of "growth" and "con-

sumerism" to his otherwise exhaustive list (1979:42–69).

3. The control aspect of psuedo-events was demonstrated clearly in 1982 when the Reagan Administration put a gag rule in effect for all "photo opportunities" with foreign dignitaries, refusing access to any photographers or network camera operators who asked questions during the image-making sessions (Bates 1989:114).

4. Blame cannot be placed solely upon journalists and reporting conventions, however. Many of the SPECA journalists complained that academic writings are often too narrow, esoteric, and poorly written to be of value in their work.

Chapter 8: Recreational Rituals

1. Niels Braroe (1975:5) encountered a similar inter-ethnic double standard in his observations of the behavior of white men with Native American women in a small Canadian town.

2. Please note, I was neither a participant, nor observer of this activity, and thus have a somewhat limited perspective. For an interesting analysis of sexuality as a factor in ethnographic field research, see Newton (1993).

3. During my last visit I told several journalists that I was going to write about their "recreational" drug usage. They laughed. "Recreational, hell!" said one, "What about _____?" They went on to list occasions when they and their colleagues had been high while covering the news. Despite this testimonial, however, I never once saw a journalist working while high (slightly intoxicated from alcohol, sure) and believe the incidents they were recalling to be relatively rare, thus memorable for them.

4. One of the most interesting and exhaustive surveys of the multiple roles of myth and ritual is William Doty's *Mythography: The Study of Myths and Rituals* (1986).

5. Robert Edgerton calls such cultures "sick societies" (1992).

Chapter 9: War Photography

1. See Hall 1974, for a description of the *Magnum Photos* agency.

2. I chose to analyze the magazine photographs of 1985, because it was the mid point of the war.

3. See Forche 1983, an excellent photo documentary of the Salvadoran war.

4. Embassy officials and many *A Team* journalists maintained this view throughout the war (Drucker 1984:45–46).

Chapter 10: The Narrative Structure and Agenda of Objective Journalism

1. See Anderson 1988:239–41, concerning photography and the equalization frame.

2. See Hallin 1983:8, concerning similar juxtapositions of image and text.

3. Stated in conversation. Similarly, Edward Said has shown how news reports of Islam in the United States "reveal as much about the West and the United

States as they do, in a far less concrete and interesting way, about Islam" (1981:4).

4. Hallin 1983:17, for an illustration of changes in the volume of U.S. network news coverage of El Salvador in relation to presidential press strategies.
5. See Frundt 1982, concerning the involvement of U.S. corporations in Guatemala.
6. See Anderson 1991, regarding the development and dissemination of the nation-state concept.
7. See Brentlinger 1990:11–13, concerning ethnocentric conceptions of democracy in U.S. news coverage.
8. Rosenstiel, Thomas. 1994. "Role of TV in Shaping Foreign Policy Under Increasing Scrutiny." *Los Angeles Times* July 25:A14–15.

Chapter 11: Peace Comes to Television

1. CBS News, which once staffed twenty international offices, is now down to just four foreign bureaus. As a result, a much greater percentage of their stories are reported from the U.S., as was the case in this report.
2. A notable exception was Juan Vasquez' January 31, 1992, CBS report, a summary of the war and analysis of the peace process. Vasquez' story included peasant, rebel, and church sources. Even more remarkable is Vasquez' description of the war's political economic context. Vasquez describes the low pay and difficult working conditions of the Salvadoran majority, implying that these injustices were partly to blame for the war. Vasquez' report was strikingly different from the other television news reports of the Salvadoran peace process.

Chapter 13: The Salvadorans of SPECA

1. In Guatemala they call journalistic bribes "fafa," a derivation of the English term "half and half" (Carpio 1979:77).
2. The plaque is now hanging on the wall in the basement chamber of the National Cathedral. It lists the names of eighteen journalists who died or disappeared during the war, and acknowledges the deaths of other journalists, those from "both sides who because of their ideas were victims of this war." The individual names of the second group of journalists are not listed on the plaque. I was at the meeting where SPECA completed the grisly task of determining which of the fallen could be considered "professional journalists," and which were instead committed to one of the "two sides."

Chapter 14: Alternatives

1. See also Alegria 1986, Beltran and Fox 1980, Dorfman and Mattelart 1975, Galtung and Ruge 1965, Galtung and Vincent 1992, Horton 1978, Mankekar 1978, Schiller 1993.
2. John Tomlinson provides a useful critique of the *Cultural Imperialism* thesis (1991). Among other points, he demonstrates the way in which critics of cul-

tural intervention have tended to legitimate state domination (as in the *Dialogo* editorialists' promotion of "national identity") in their attempt to combat international (more accurately understood as "global") forms of hegemony.

3. See Roach 1993:33–34,243–48, for a further listing of alternative media organizations.

4. IPS reports are accessible via the Institute for Global Communications (IGC) computer networks (including Peacenet), the Internet, and selected foreign newspapers.

5. See Bagdikian 1972:47–56, 1990: 17, 219, regarding the causes and consequences of the rapid decline of local newspapers in the United States.

6. See Ginsburg 1992, concerning efforts by indigenous peoples to create their own media alternatives.

7. See Schultz-Brooks 1984, for a description of gains made by women in the U.S. press and Carty and Carty 1987, for information concerning the status of women in Latin American media.

8. See also Craft 1989 and *Media Report to Women*, especially 1992 20(4):4–5 (radio and TV); 1991 19(3):4–5 (newspapers); 1991–92 19–20(4–6):7 (news magazines).

9. See *Media Report to Women* 1992, 20(4):2–3, regarding gender differences in the reporting of abortion rights.

10. One of the most successful is Linda Green's "Fear as a Way of Life," 1994.

11. The productive aspect of "making" news is emphasized in several important sociological studies, as demonstrated in their "making" and "manufacturing" titles: *Making News* (Tuchman 1978), *Manufacturing the News* (Fishman 1980), *Deciding What's News* (Gans 1980) and *Manufacturing Consent* (Herman and Chomsky 1988).

12. John Carlin's "Just Little Brown Men" appeared in *The Independent*, December 29, 1988. Joel Millman's "A Force Unto Itself" was published in the *New York Times Magazine* December 10, 1990.

13. See Kessler 1984, Watson, Jr. 1979, Glessing 1970 concerning the alternative press tradition in the United States.

Appendix

1. The *A Team* contingent is deceptively large in this listing. During the period of my fieldwork, the staff correspondents' coverage of El Salvador was sporadic. Only five staff correspondents spent all or most of their time living in El Salvador.

REFERENCES

Albers, Patricia C., and James, William R. 1990. "Private and Public images: A Study of Photographic Contrasts in Postcard Pictures of Great Basin Indians, 1898–1919." *Visual Anthropology* 3:343–366.

Alegria, Claribel. 1986. "Clash of Cultures." *Index on Censorship* 15 (8):28–36.

Althusser, Louis. 1971. *Lenin, Philosophy, and other Essays*. New York: Monthly Review Press.

Anderson, Benedict. 1991. *Imagined Communities: Reflections on the Origin and Spread of Nationalism*. New York: Verso.

Anderson, Robin. 1988a. "The Ideological Significance of News Photography: The Case of El Salvador." *Ideologies and Literature* 3 (2):227–65.

———. 1988b. "Visions of Instability: U.S. Television's Law and Order News of El Salvador" *Media Culture and Society* 10 (2):239–65.

———. 1990. "The Press and El Salvador." *Lies of Our Times* 1 (1):4–5.

Anderson, Thomas. 1981. *Matanza: El Salvador's Communist Revolt of 1932*. Lincoln: University of Nebraska Press.

Anson, Robert Sam. 1989. *War News: A Young Reporter in Indochina*. New York: Simon and Schuster.

APES. 1990. *El Periodismo en una Sociedad en Crisis*. San Salvador, El Salvador: Publicorp.

Bagdikian, Ben H. 1972. *The Effete Conspiracy: and Other Crimes By the Press*. New York: Harper and Row.

———. 1990. *The Media Monopoly*. Boston: Beacon.

Barnes, Kathleen. 1990. *Trial by Fire: A Woman Correspondent's Journey to the Frontline*. New York: Thunder's Mouth Press.

Barre, Marie-Chantal. 1989. "La presencia indigena en los procesos sociopoliticos contemporaneos de Centroamerica." *Nueva Antropologia* 10 (35): 9–28.

Barrett, Marvin, ed. 1973. *The Politics of Broadcasting*. New York: Crowell.

Bates, Stephen. 1989. *If No News Send Rumors: Anecdotes of American Journalism*. New York: Henry Holt and Company.

Beltran, Luis Ramiro, and Elizabeth Fox de Cardona. 1980. *Comunicacion Dominada: Estados Unidos en los Medios de America Latina*. Mexico: Editorial Nueva Imagen.

Bonner, Raymond. 1984. *Weakness and Deceit: U.S. Policy and El Salvador*. New York: Times Books.

Boorstin, Daniel. 1962. *The Image*. New York: Atheneum.

Bourdieu, Pierre. 1977. *Outline of a Theory of Practice*. Cambridge: Cambridge University Press.

Bourdieu, Pierre. 1984. *Distinction: A Social Critique of the Judgement of Taste*. Cambridge: Harvard University Press.

Braroe, Niels Winther. 1975. *Indian and White: Self-Image and Interaction in a Canadian Plains Community*. Stanford, CA: Stanford University Press.

Brentlinger. 1990. "Nicaragua and the Politics of Representation Part Two." *Confluencia* 6 (1):3–18.

Caputo, Philip. 1991. *Means of Escape*. New York: Harper Collins.

Carpio Nicolle, Mario. 1979. *El Negocio de la Prensa*. Guatemala City: Universidad de San Carlos.

Carty, James W. Jr., and Marjorie T. Carty. 1987. "Notes on Latin American Women in the Media: A Mid-1980's Sample of Voices and Groups." *Studies in Latin American Popular Culture* 6:311–42.

Chagnon, Napoleon. 1968. *Yanomamo: The Fierce People*. New York: Holt, Rinehart and Winston.

Chapin, Mac. 1990. *La Poblacion Indigena De El Salvador*. San Salvador: Ministerio De Educacion.

Chomsky, Noam. 1985. *Turning the Tide: United States Intervention in Central America and the Struggle for Peace*. Boston: South End Press.

Christians, Clifford G. 1986. "Reporting and the Oppressed." In *Responsible Journalism*, ed. Deni Elliott, 109–30. New York: Sage.

Clifford, James, ed. 1986. *Writing Culture*. Berkeley: University of California Press.

Cline, Carolyn Garrett. 1981. *Our Neglected Neighbors: How the U.S. Elite Media Covered Latin America in 1977*. Ph.D. dissertation, Indiana university.

Coad, Malcolm. 1981. "How El Salvador Treats the Press" *Index on Censorship* 10 (3):54–58.

Cockburn, Alexander. 1989. "Beat the Devil." *The Nation* April 3, 1989:438–39.

Cooper, Marc. 1986. "El Salvador: War of Words" *Index on Censorship* 15 (8):32–33.

Craft, Christine. 1986. *Christine Craft: An Anchorwoman's Story*. Santa Barbara: Capra Press.

Creedon, Pamela, ed. 1989. *Women in Mass Communication: Challenging Gender Values*. Newbury Park: Sage.

Cumings, Bruce. 1992. *War and Television*. New York: Verso.

Curran, James, and Colin Sparks. 1991. "Press and Popular Culture." *Media Culture and Society* 13 (2):215–37.

Dalton, Roque. 1987. *Poemas Clandestinas*. San Jose, Costa Rica: EDUCA.

Danner, Mark. 1993. "The Truth of El Mozote." *The New Yorker* Dec. 6:50–133.

Day, J. Laurence. 1987. "United States News Coverage of Latin America: A Short Historical Perspective." *Studies in Latin American Popular Culture*. 6:301–309.

Dennis, Everette E., and William L. Rivers. 1974. *Other Voices: The New Journalism in America*. San Francisco: Canfield Press.

Diamond, Edwin. 1975. *The Tin Kazoo: Politics, Television, and the News*. Cambridge, Massachusetts: MIT Press.

Didion, Joan. 1983. *Salvador*. New York: Pocket Books.

Diskin, Martin, ed. 1983. *Trouble in our Backyard*. New York: Pantheon Books.

Dorfman, Ariel, and Armand Mattelart. 1975. *How to Read Donald Duck: Imperialist Ideology in the Disney Comic*. New York: International General Editions.

Doty, William. 1986. *Mythography: The Study of Myths and Rituals*. Tuscaloosa: The University of Alabama Press.

Drucker, Linda. 1984. "Radio Venceremos: Static Over a Guerrilla Source." *Columbia Journalism Review* March/April: 44–47.

Edgerton, Robert B. 1992. *Sick Societies: Challenging the Myth of Primitive Harmony*.New York: Free Press.

Edwards, Elizabeth. 1990. "Photographic 'Types': The Pursuit of Method." *Visual Anthropology*, Volume 3:235–58.

Emerson, Gloria. 1984. "Susan Meiselas at War." *Esquire*. December: 165–74.

Fanon, Frantz. 1963. *The Wretched of the Earth*. New York: Grove Press.

Fialka, John J. 1991. *Hotel Warriors: Covering the Gulf War*. Baltimore: John Hopkins University Press.

Fishman, Mark. 1980. *Manufacturing the News*. Austin: University of Texas Press.

Fiske, John. 1987. *Television Culture*. New York and London: Routledge.

Fiske, John. 1989. *Reading the Popular*. London: Unwin Hyman.

Forche, Carolyn. 1983. *El Salvador: The Work of Thirty Photographers*. New York: W. W. Norton.

Foucault, Michel. 1984. *The Foucault Reader*, ed. Paul Rabinow. New York: Pantheon.

Fried, Mark. 1987. "Medea's Children." *NACLA Report on the Americas*. 21(2): 7–8.

Freire, Pauolo. 1970. *Pedagogy of the Oppressed*. NY: Continuum.

Freund, Gisele. 1980. *Photography and Society*. Boston: David R. Godine.

Frundt, Henry J. 1982. *Refreshing Pauses: Coca Cola and Human Rights in Guatemala*. New York: Praeger.

Galtung, Johan, and Mari Holmboe Ruge. 1965. "The Structure of Foreign News." *Journal of Peace Research* 2:64–91.

Galtung, Johan, and Richard C. Vincent. 1992. *Global Glasnost: Toward a New World Information and Communication Order?* Cresskill, NJ: Hampton.

Gans, Herbert J. 1980. *Deciding What's News*. New York: Vintage Books.

Gaziano, Cecilie. 1987. "News People's Ideology and the Credibility Debate." *Newspaper Research Journal* 9 (1): 1–18.

Geertz, Clifford. 1973. *The Interpretation of Cultures*. New York: Basic Books.

Gettleman, M., P. Lacefield, L. Menashe, and D. Mermelstein, eds. 1986. *El Salvador: Central America in the New Cold War*. New York: Grove Press.

Ginsburg, Faye. 1992. "Indigenous Media: Faustian Contract or Global Village." In *Rereading Cultural Anthropology*, ed. George Marcus, 356–376. Durham: Duke University Press.

Gitlin, Todd. 1980. *The Whole World is Watching: Mass Media in the Making and the Unmaking of the New Left*. Berkeley: University of California Press.

———. 1983. *Inside Prime Time*. New York: Pantheon.

———. 1989. "Postmodernism: Roots and Politics." In *Cultural Politics in Contemporary America*, eds. Ian Angus and Sut Jhally, 347–360. New York and London: Routledge.

Glessing, Robert J. 1970. *The Underground Press in America*. Bloomington, IN: Indiana University Press.

Goffman, Erving. 1974. *Frame Analysis: An Essay on the Organization of Experience*. New York: Harper and Row.

Goldstein, Tom. 1985. *The News At Any Cost*. New York: Simon and Schuster.

Gonzales, Jose Napoleon. 1977. "El Salvador: A Silenced Voice." *Index on Censorship* 6 (6): 20–23.

Goodenough, Ward G. 1957. "Cultural Anthropology and Linguistics." In *Report of the Seventh Annual Round Table Meeting on Linguistics and Language Study*, ed. Paul Garvin, *Georgetown University Monograph Series on Language and Linguistics* 9:167–73.

Gramsci, Antonio. 1971. *Selections from the Prison Notebooks*, eds. Q. Hoare and G. Nowell Smith. London: Lawrence and Wishart.

Green, Linda. 1994. "Fear as a Way of Life." *Cultural Anthropology* 9 (2):227–56.

Hall, James Baker. 1974. "The Last Happy Band of Brothers." *Esquire* April: 117.

Hallin, Daniel C. 1983. "The Media Go to War: From Vietnam to Central America." *NACLA Report on the Americas* 17 (4):2–26.

———. 1986a. *The "Uncensored War": The Media and Vietnam*. Berkeley: University of California Press.

———. 1986b. "We Keep America On Top of the World." In *Watching Television*, ed. Todd Gitlin. New York: Pantheon Books.

Hanisko, Sandralee Mary. 1981. *Foreign Affairs Perspective Toward Revolution in El Salvador: The Unfolding of U.S. Officials' Rhetorical Experiences*. Ph.D. dissertation, University of Nebraska, Lincoln.

Harris, J.D. 1979. *War Reporter*. New York: Manor Books.

Hartman, Carl. 1982. "There's a Lot of *There* out There." *The Quill* 70(11): 14–21.

Henry, Jules. 1963. *Culture Against Man*. New York: Vintage.

Herman, Edward S. 1990. "Responsibility at the Top: East and West." In *Lies of our Times*. November: 5–6.

Herman, Edward S., and Frank Brodhead. 1984. *Demonstration Elections: U.S.-Staged Elections in the Dominican Republic, Vietnam, and El Salvador*. Boston: South End Press.

Herman, Edward S., and Noam Chomsky. 1988. *Manufacturing Consent: The Political Economy of the Mass Media*. New York: Pantheon.

Herr, Michael. 1968. *Dispatches*. New York: Avon.

Hertsgaard, Mark. 1988. *On Bended Knee: The Press and the Reagan Presidency*. New York: Schocken Books.

Horton, Philip C. 1978. *The Third World and Press Freedom*. New York: Praeger.

Hoyt, Mike. 1993. "The Mozote Massacre." *Columbia Journalism Review* January/February: 31–34.

Huff, Melrose E. 1994. "El Salvador's Persistent Press." *Toward Freedom* 43 (4):13–14.

Husarska, Anna. 1992. "News from Hell." *The New Yorker* October 5:89.

Immerman, Richard H. 1982. *The CIA in Guatemala: The Foreign Policy of Intervention*. Austin, TX: University of Texas Press.

Iyengar, Shanto, and Donald R. Kinder. 1987. *News That Matters: Television and American Opinion*. Chicago: University of Chicago Press.

Jameson, Fredric. 1984. "Postmodernism, or the Cultural Logic of Late Capitalism." *New Left Review*. July/August 146:53–93.

Johnson, Michael L. 1971. *The New Journalism: The Underground Press, the Artists of Nonfiction, and Changes in the Established Media*. Lawrence, Kansas: University of Kansas Press.

Jones, Rufus. 1981. "TV 'Covers' the War." *NACLA Report on the Americas* 16 (6):38–45.

Jung, Harold. 1986. "Social Forces and Ideologies in the Making of Contemporary El Salvador." In *El Salvador: Central America in the New Cold War*, eds. M. Gettleman, P. Lacefield, L. Menashe, and D. Mermelstein. New York: Grove Press.

Kerns, Virginia. 1983. *Women and the Ancestors: Black Carib Kinship and Ritual*. Urbana, IL: University of Illinois Press.

Kertzer, David I. 1988. *Ritual, Politics, and Power*. New Haven: Yale University Press.

Kessler, Lauren. 1984. *The Dissident Press: Alternative Journalism in American History*. Beverly Hills: Sage.

King, Martin Luther, Jr.. 1967. *Where Do We Go From Here: Chaos or Community?* Boston: Beacon Press.

Knightley, Phillip. 1975. *The First Casualty*. New York: Harcourt Brace Jovanich.

Koch, Tom. 1990. *The News As Myth: Fact and Context in Journalism*. New York: Greenwood.

Kozloff, Max. 1987. *The Privileged Eye: Essays on Photography*. Albuquerque: University of New Mexico Press.

Krauss, Clifford. 1991. *Inside Central America: Its People, Politics, and History*. New York: Simon and Schuster.

Krouse, Susan Applegate. 1990. "Photographing the Vanishing Race." *Visual Anthropology* 3: 213–33.

Langton, M.. 1991. "Photo Coverage of the Third World in Four Prestigious U.S. Newspapers." *Newspaper Research Journal*. Fall: 98–107.

Leiss, William, Stephen Kline, and Sut Jhally. 1985. *Social Communication in Advertising: Persons, Products and Images of Well-Being*. New York and London: Routledge.

Lent, John A. 1983. "United States Foreign Coverage and the Case of Central America." *Revista/Review Interamericana* 13 (1–4):40–8.

Levi-Strauss, Claude. 1967. *Structural Anthropology*. Garden City, New York: Anchor.

Lewinski, Jorge. 1978. *A History of War Photography from 1848 to Present Day*. W. H. Allen: London.

Lichter, S. Robert, Stanley Rothman, and Linda S. Lichter. 1986. *The Media Elite*. New York: Adler and Adler.

Lopez Vigil, Jose Ignacio. 1991. *Las mil y una Historia de Radio Venceremos*. San Salvador, El Salvador: UCA Editores.

Lord, Arthur. 1984. "The Most Comfortable War? The Scariest? The Safest?" *TV Guide*. September 29:12–14.

Lutz, Catherine, and Jane L. Collins. 1993. *Reading National Geographic*, Chicago: University of Chicago Press.

McAnany, Emile G. 1983. "Television and Crisis: Ten Years of Network News Coverage of Central America, 1972–1981." *Media, Culture, and Society* 5 (2):199–212.

McClintock, Michael. 1985. *The American Connection: Volume 1, State Terror and Popular Resistance in El Salvador.* London: Zed Books.

McConahay, Mary Jo. 1986. "Living Under El Salvador's Air War." In *El Salvador: Central America in the New Cold War.* eds. M. Gettleman, P. Lacefield, L. Menashe, and D. Mermelstein, 235–39. New York: Grove Press.

McCoy, Tom. 1992. "The New York Times Coverage of El Salvador." *Newspaper Research Journal* 13 (3):67–84.

McKerrow, Richard. 1991. "Atrocities and Elections: Grim Cycle in Salvador." *Lies of Our Times* April: 14–15.

McLellan, David. 1986. *Ideology: Concepts in Social Thought.* Minneapolis: University of Minnesota Press.

Malcolm, Janet. 1990. *The Journalist and the Murderer.* New York: Knopf.

Malinowski, Bronislaw. 1922. *Argonauts of the Western Pacific.* New York: Dutton.

Mankekar, D. R.. 1978. *One Way Free Flow: Neo-colonialism via News Media.* Delhi: Indian Book Company.

Marcus, George, and Michael Fischer. 1986. *Anthropology as Cultural Critique: An Experimental Moment in the Human Sciences.* Chicago: The University of Chicago Press.

Maslow, Jonathan Evan, and Ana Arana. 1981. "Operation El Salvador" *Columbia Journalism Review* May/June: 52–58.

Massing, Michael. 1982. "Central America: A Tale of Three Countries." *Columbia Journalism Review.* July/August: 47–52.

———. 1989. "When More Means Less." *Columbia Journalism Review* July/August: 42–44.

Menchu, Rigoberta. 1984. *I, Rigoberta Menchu,* ed. Elisabeth Burgos-Debray. New York: Verso.

Merrill, John C.. 1977. *Existential Journalism.* New York: Hastings House.

Mills, C. Wright. 1959. *Sociological Imagination.* Oxford: Oxford University Press.

Mills, Kay. 1988. *A Place in the News: From the Women's Pages to the Front Pages.* New York: Dodd, Mead, and Company.

Montgomery, Tommy Sue. 1982. *Revolution in El Salvador: Origins and Evolution.* Boulder, Colorado: Westview Press.

Morley, D. 1980. *The Nationwide Audience: Structure and Decoding.* London: British Film Institute.

Morris, Joe Alex. 1957. *Deadline Every Minute: The Story of the United Press.* Garden City, New York: Doubleday.

Morris, Meaghan. 1988. "Banality in Cultural Studies." Discourse X.2:3–29.

Mott, Frank Luther. 1952. *The News in America.* Cambridge: Harvard University Press.

Murphy, Robert. 1990. "The Dialectics of Deeds and Words: or Anti-the-Antis. and the Anti-Antis." *Cultural Anthropology* 5 (3):331–37.

Newton, Esther. 1993. "My Best Informant's Dress: The Erotic Equation in Fieldwork." *Cultural Anthropology* 8 (1):3–23.

North, Liisa. 1985. *Bitter Grounds: Roots of Revolt in El Salvador.* Westport, CN: Lawrence Hill.

Olaciregui, Demetrio. 1981. "The Silencers" *Columbia Journalism Review* May/June: 56–7.

Parenti, Michael. 1986. *Inventing Reality: The Politics of the Mass Media.* New York: St. Martin's Press.

Parkman, Patricia. 1988. *Nonviolent Insurrection in El Salvador: The Fall of Maximiliano Hernandez Martinez.* Tucson, AZ: University of Arizona Press.

Pedelty, Mark. 1993. "News Photography and Indigenous Peoples: An 'Encounter' in Guatemala." *Visual Anthropology* 6(3):285–301.

Pinto, Jorge. 1981. "In Salvador, Nooseprint." The *New York Times* May 6:31.

Popkin, Margaret. 1991. "Human Rights in the Duarte Years." In *A Decade of War: El*

Salvador Confronts the Future, eds. Anjali Sundaram and George Gelber. New York: Monthly Review Press.

Postman, Neil. 1985. *Amusing Ourselves to Death: Public Discourse in the Age of Show Business.* New York: Viking.

Powdermaker, Hortense. 1950. *Hollywood The Dream Factory: An Anthropologist Looks at the Movie-Makers.* Boston: Little, Brown and Company.

Pyes, Craig. 1983. "Salvadoran Patriots: The Deadly Patriots." *Albuquerque Journal* December 18–22, 1983.

———. 1986. "ARENA's Bid for Power." In *El Salvador: Central America in the New Cold War,* eds. M. Gettleman, P. Lacefield, L. Menashe, and D. Mermelstein, 165–73. New York: Grove Press.

Rachlin, Allen. 1988. *News as Hegemonic Reality: American Political Culture and the Framing of News Accounts.* New York: Praeger.

Radway, Janice. 1984. *Reading the Romance: Women, Patriarchy, and Popular Literature* Chapel Hill: The University of North Carolina Press.

Roach, Colleen, ed. 1993. *Communication and Culture in War and Peace.* Newbury Park: Sage.

Rodriguez, Francisco. 1991. "La Democratization de los Medios de Comunicacion social." *Dialogo* 1 (1):15–26.

Rosenberg, Mark, and Philip L. Shephard. 1983. *Two Approaches to an Understanding of U.S.—Honduran Relations.* Occasional Papers Series. Dialogues: No. 14. Miami, FL: Los Angeles and Caribbean Center, Florida International University.

Rosenblum, Mort. 1979. *Coups and Earthquakes: Reporting the World to America.* New York: Harper and Row.

Rota, Josep, and Gilda S. Rota. 1987. "A Content Analysis of international News Published by the Leading Newspapers in Mexico City" *Studies in Latin American Popular Culture.* 6: 165–81.

Said, Edward. 1981. *Covering Islam: How the Media and the Experts Determine How We See the Rest of the World.* New York: Pantheon.

Sapir, Edward. 1949. *Selected Writings of Edward Sapir in Culture, Language, and Personality,* ed. David G. Mandelbaum. Berkeley: University of California.

Saunders, Allan Wayne. 1991. *Media and Hegemony: The United States and the Central American War.* Ph.D. dissertation, University of Guelph. Canada.

Scarry, Elaine. 1985. *The Body in Pain: The Making and Unmaking of the World.* Oxford: Oxford University Press.

———. 1993. "Watching and Authorizing the Gulf War." In *Media Spectacles,* eds. M. Garber, Jann Matlock, and R. Walkowitz. New York and London: Routledge.

Schaef, Anne Wilson. 1981. *Women's Reality: An Emerging Female System in a White Male Society.* New York: Harper and Row.

Scheper-Hughes, Nancy, and Margaret Lock. 1987. "The Mindful Body: A Prolegomenon to Future Work in Medical Anthropology. "*Medical Anthropology Quarterly* 1 (1):6–41.

Schiller, Herbert I. 1989. *Culture, Inc.: The Corporate Takeover of Public Expression.* Oxford: Oxford University Press.

———. 1993. "Not Yet the Postimperialist Era." In *Communication and Culture in War and Peace.,* ed. Colleen Roach, 97–116. Newbury Park: Sage.

Schlesinger, Stephen, and Stephen Kinzer. 1982. *Bitter Fruit: The Untold Story of the American Coup in Guatemala.* Garden City, New York: Double Day.

Schudson, Michael. 1978. *Discovering the News: A Social History of American Newspapers.* New York: Basic Books.

Schultz-Brooks, Terri. 1984. "Getting There: Women in the Newsroom." *Columbia Journalism Review* March/April: 25–31.

Schumacher, E. F. 1973. *Small is Beautiful: Economics as if People Mattered.* New York: Harper and Row.

Sigal, Leon V. 1986. "Sources Make The News." In *Reading the News*, eds. Robert Karl Manoff and Michael Schudson, 9–37. New York: Pantheon.

Simon, Jean-Marie. 1987. *Guatemala: Eternal Spring, Eternal Tyranny*. New York: W. W. Norton and Company.

Smith, Anthony. 1980. "Is Objectivity Obsolete" *Columbia Journalism Review* May/June: 61–65.

Soderland, Walter C. 1985. "Reporting on El Salvador and Nicaragua in Leading Canadian and American Newspapers." *Canadian Journal of Communication* 11 (4):252–68.

Soderland, Walter C., and Carmen Schmidt. 1985. "El Salvador's Civil War as Seen in the North and the South American Press." *Journalism Quarterly* 63 (2):268–75.

Sol, Ricardo. 1984. *El Salvador Medio Masivos y Comunicacion Popular*. San Jose, Costa Rica: Editorial Porvenir.

Sontag, Susan. 1977. *On Photography*. New York: Doubleday.

Spence, Jack. 1983. "Media Coverage of El Salvador's Election." *Socialist Review* 13 (2):29–57.

Spence, Jack. 1984. "Second Time Around: How to Cover an Election" *Columbia Journalism Review* March/April: 41–43.

Sturdevant, Saundra Pollock, and Brenda Stoltzfus. 1992. *Let the Good Times Roll: Prostitution and the U.S. Military in Asia*. New York: The New York Press.

Sumser, J. 1987. "Labels Used to Define the Central American Situation." *Journalism Quarterly* 64 (4):850–53.

Sundaram, Anjali. 1991. "Taking Center Stage: The Reagan Era." In *A Decade of War: El Salvador Confronts the Future*, eds. Anjali Sudaram and George Gelber, 128–63. New York: Monthly Review Press.

Taussig, Michael. 1987. *Shamanism, Colonialism, and the Wild Man: A Study in Terror and Healing*. Chicago: The University of Chicago Press.

Taylor, Douglas Macrae. 1963. *The Black Carib of British Honduras*. Publications in Anthropology, Number 17. New York: The Viking Fund.

Tetzlaff, David. 1991. "Divide and Conquer: Popular Culture and Social Control in Late Capitalism." *Media Culture and Society* 13 (1):9–33.

Thompson, E. P. 1967. "Time, Work-Discipline, and Industrial Capitalism." In *Past and Present*. 38:56–97.

Thompson, John B. 1990. *Ideology and Modern Culture: Critical Social Theory in the Era of Mass Communications*. Stanford, California: Stanford University Press.

Thompson, Kate. 1992. "Media Complicity." *Lies of Our Times* March: 28.

Tomlinson, John. 1991. *Cultural Imperialism*. Baltimore: John Hopkins University Press.

Torres-Rivas, Edelberto. 1983. "Central America Today: A Study in Regional Dependency." In *Trouble in our Backyard*, ed. Martin Diskin, 1–33. New York: Pantheon.

Tuchman, Gaye. 1978. *Making News*. New York: Free Press.

Tuohy, William. 1987. *Dangerous Company: Inside the World's Hottest Trouble Spots with a Pulitzer Prize-Winning War Correspondent*. New York: William Morrow.

Turk, Seyda. 1986. *Images of Foreign Nations: A Descriptive and Functional Analysis*. Ph.D. dissertation, University of Washington.

Vernau, Judi. 1989. *An Index to An Index on Censorship*. London: Hans Zell.

Watson, Francis M., Jr. 1979. *The Alternative Media: Dismantling Two Centuries of Progress*. Rockford: Rockford College Institute.

Weschler, Lawrence. 1990. "The Media's One and Only Freedom Story." *Columbia Journalism Review* March/April 1990:25–31.

White, David M. 1950. "The 'Gatekeeper': A Case Study in the Selection of News." *Journalism Quarterly* 27: 383–90.

Wolf, Eric. 1959. *Sons of the Shaking Earth*. Chicago: University of Chicago Press.

INDEX